I0415354

The Narcissist's Vocation

and the Economic Debacle

by Greg Horsman

Copyright © 2011 Greg Horsman
All rights reserved.

ISBN: 1456486500
ISBN-13: 9781456486501

Contents

"Nothing exists except atoms and empty space; everything else is opinion."

Democritus

"Three great forces rule the world: stupidity, fear, and greed."

Albert Einstein

"Each age tries to form its own conception of the past. Each age writes the history of the past anew with reference to the conditions uppermost in its own time."

Frederick Jackson Turner

Dedication

To my family

Forward

At the end of the first decade of the 21st century it is beginning to dawn on more and more people that things changed dramatically over the prior three decades. The worldwide financial debacle was a wake up call that these changes are real, and they are significant. The decline in the stock market from the fiasco of asset-backed commercial paper is a consequence of a culture that peddles entitlement, greed and self-centeredness. These characteristics are associated with extreme individualism. The problem is not about the fundamentals of capitalism; it is about culture.

Individualism is a balance between self-reliance, personal responsibility and egotism. The rise of individualism is about people living and acting as individuals rather than as members of a larger group. In addition, the belief that one must do whatever he can to achieve positive self-esteem has become a movement with broad societal effects. Today, the cult of self-esteem has migrated from the schools into the workplace. In the culture of extreme individualism, a sense of entitlement gives people the perceived high ground; at the same time, they experience a declining sense of personal responsibility. Everyone and everything are mere instruments and objects available for pursuit of narcissistic gratification.

The 'narcissist's vocation' comprises the activities of a person with characteristics of a narcissistic personality who manipulates his daily environment and workplace, including financial services offices. This narcissism is fed by extreme individualism. The birth of individualism and its development can be traced through the Renaissance, the Reformation, and the rise of capitalism. It was part of a radical ideological revolution that altered the face of the established church in the West.

In the cult of self-esteem, individuals who avoid self-criticism react to events in various ways. Individuals nurtured on the cult of self-esteem, angry about the economic challenges facing the USA, have a high probability of responding to emotional debates. The individual living the narcissist's vocation, and employed in the financial services industry, genuinely believes he is entitled to a high rate of compensation and will become enraged when challenged. *The Narcissist's Vocation and the Economic Debacle* identifies the need for corporations to be accountable – besides regulations, this requires a change in culture to prevent the next financial crisis.

Introduction

During a visit, a friend commented that he believed he had recently received poor quality advice from a financial adviser with respect to money he had invested. He wanted to invest it in farmland, but the financial advisor steered him into stocks and mutual funds "that would provide a much higher return." Six hundred miles away, a young surgeon, who has been training for ten years, learned that the job he had been promised had disappeared as the old surgeon decided to work for a few more years to rebuild his investment portfolio. With the market failures in 2008, they, along with many others, watched with disbelief as their investments, including homes and retirement funds, lost up to 40% of their value. For others, there was the further shock of losing their jobs. The market crisis has many people asking questions. Many wonder if this is more than just another downturn in the market, but rather a negative aspect of the globalization of markets that expanded rapidly over the past few years. Today, the questions that are uppermost, and that will become increasingly more important, are not so much political as economic.[1]

What is the explanation for the economic meltdown? There are two diametrically opposed explanations to this question. One explanation proposes this is just another market cycle associated with the bursting of the housing bubble. The response from this group is the need for less regulation in order to keep it from occurring again. Another explanation identifies this as a watershed event in the world finance system, calling for major reforms, including more regulation. Prior to 2007, many of us were content to study economic debates at a distance and allow investment advisors to direct our investments unquestioningly. However, the events of 2008 have affected the value of the two most expensive assets of the middle class: their home and their pension. This is a wake up call to the middle class that their standard of living is no longer rising.[2] Driven by the fear of future world-wide financial melt downs, there is a desire to study what exists out there in order to understand the conditions that came together to create the environment (particularly in the Americas), for this to occur.

The size of the economic melt down is driven home by the fact that it vies in severity with the Great Depression of the 1930s. The problems seem obvious, as financial instruments that were opaque and hard to value were linked to mortgages and other products leading to the loss in confidence of the market. The solution also seems obvious, with the necessity to reign in such excesses of risk taking. There appeared to be no rush to reform the financial services industry, as lobbyists paralyzed government action.

What philosophy or mind-set supports maintaining a system of small government and no regulation in the first decade of the 21st century? One philosophy from the last half of the 20th century that supports small government and deregulation is the laissez-faire economics of Ayn Rand. Objectivism, a philosophy developed by Ayn Rand during the Cold

War, blends free markets, reason, and individualism. Rand's philosophy supports globalization, which enables the spread of individualism around the world (discussed in Chapter 1). Rand attracted a group of supporters. During the development of objectivism, her path crossed with two individuals associated with the events of the past three decades. The years when objectivism was being defined, a young Alan Greenspan and Nathaniel Branden belonged to Ayn Rand's inner group. Alan Greenspan, the Chairman of the Board of Governors of the Federal Reserve from 1987 to 2006, held the interest rate near historic lows for over a decade, and after the burst of the Internet bubble, this policy had considerable political support, as the housing market was used as the engine to drive the US economy.[3] Branden, once an ardent Rand supporter, split with the objectivists, moved to California and became part of the self-esteem pop movement that was developing in California in the 1960s. This was not a new topic for Branden; Ayn Rand had identified self-esteem as an important aspect of objectivism.

Nathaniel Branden, in his 1969 publication of *The Psychology of Self-Esteem*, promoted self-esteem as the single most important facet of a person. The belief that one must do whatever he can to achieve positive self-esteem has become a movement with broad societal effects.[4] During the 1980s, school systems lowered educational standards to protect children from failure. This self-esteem movement has had a significant impact on the school system – in order to ensure positive self-esteem, educational standards were lowered, creating a milieu for extreme individualism. The world would be saved from crime, drug abuse and under-achieving through bolstering self-esteem. When there is too much self-esteem, there are problems of self-tolerance, entitlement and narcissism. This person demands automatic and full compliance with his/her expectations.

With the self-esteem movement embedded in the school system, young adults were encouraged to develop image rather than character. The cult of self-esteem that was created in the school system in the 1980s provided a pool of individuals in the 21st century with an exaggerated sense of entitlement in the workplace. The world, viewed from an emotional rather than a rational perspective, allowed personal feelings to override the distinction between right and wrong. "When success is more important than self respect, the culture itself overvalues image and is narcissistic," says Lillian T. Katz.[5] Today, the cult of self-esteem has migrated from the schools to the workplace. Narcissism is an excessive form of self-love that leads to a sense of entitlement and selfish world-view. Narcissists believe that rules do not apply to them and they deserve special treatment. Advocacy and education have an important role to play in countering such a culture.

The media and advertisers created a milieu in which the cult of self-esteem and extreme individualism thrived, creating the cultural hegemony of the West. The Information Age began in 1989 with the fall of the Berlin Wall. The ideals of socialism died, while the ideas of individualism continued to thrive. Individualism is the tendency for a person to act without reference to others, particularly in matters of style, fashion or mode of thought. The rise of individualism is about people living and acting as individuals rather than as members of a larger group. Individualism, which is a positive force behind the development of democracy and free enterprise, continues to evolve. Narcissism is described as extreme individualism. Individualism is now an important aspect of Western culture. The culture of extreme individualism and narcissism appeared that influenced decision-making and accountability. Chapter 2 discusses the nature of individualism and the relationship with the mass media and advertisers.

Extreme individualism leads to narcissism. The characteristics of the narcissist include egotistic and ruthless pursuit of one's gratification, dominance and ambition. He/she feels entitled and expects special treatment. In the extreme, he maintains a tenuous grasp of reality and is given to frustration, anger, and irrationality when he does not get what he wants. In general, reality based television taps into this culture. In extreme individualism, all choices are based on one's personal needs and desires. The self-esteem movement has created a population with an exaggerated sense of entitlement. People follow reality shows that allow them to reshape their identities around the increasingly globalized values of capitalism, values rooted in consumerism, individualism, and narcissism. The media creates cognitive dissonance, the feeling of uncomfortable tension, which comes from holding two conflicting thoughts in the mind at the same time. The cult of individualism makes us particularly prone to cognitive dissonance because our personal identity is very important. We see ourselves as stable self-contained beings. For example, advertising that we may be missing something, or not fitting in, creates anxiety. Increased cognitive dissonance is a source of psychological suffering and the vast amounts of stress we see today. Chapter 3 discusses how cognitive dissonance affects decision-making.

The Narcissist's Vocation and the Economic Debacle explores the interaction between forces, such as globalization, the mass media and the cult of self-esteem in sustaining the present culture of narcissism. For the title, the definition of narcissism is the individual with three or four characteristics of narcissism, without the fixed fantasy, who is adept at manipulating their daily environment. Vocation has the general meaning of daily job or activity. Christian fundamentalism and Islamic fundamentalism both oppose various aspects of modernity, but only provide a small contribution to countering individualism.

The answer to countering individualism lies in the introduction of proper self-esteem into school systems, as well as awareness and advocacy in communities. The rise of the narcissism of extreme individualism, and the corresponding disappearance of accountability, coincided with failures at many levels that led to the market problems that surfaced in 2007. Another aspect of self-centeredness is self-tolerance. Such individuals learn to tolerate their errors and personal flaws and come to accept themselves as okay. They feel justified in asserting themselves and defending their perceived rights. The world owes them. Narcissism and the feeling of entitlement create a group who opposes rational evidence of a debate, leading to polarized positions. In this culture, angry individuals can be recruited to causes without rational debate. In the USA, conservative interests have hijacked anger in the community. However, this tapped anger is not directed at the financial services industry.

The past provides answers that we may consider valid today. In order to comprehend the present culture of narcissism and accompanying self-tolerance, we study the activities of the early church of Western Europe where the seeds were planted that led to the rise of individualism. The early church took on many characteristics of the Roman Empire – centralized bureaucracy, a judicial structure governing ethics and spirituality, the binding authority of priests and bishops, the demand for obedience from church members and its effective enforcement (discussed further in chapter 5). After the fall of the Roman Empire, one of the tools used by the Roman Catholic Church to maintain its power for 1500 years was to label people who disagreed with church dogma as heretics, and systematically persecute them. In order to understand the forces at play, it is helpful to study the growth of the Roman Catholic Church from the 4th century CE to the apogee of power in the Middle Ages, with accumulation of wealth and power as the backdrop for the appearance of individualism. The power of the church was challenged with new ways of thinking ushered in during the 16th and 17th centuries. Individualism appeared with the humanist ideals of the Renaissance (discussed in Chapter 7). The Renaissance introduced new ways of thinking that involved individual rights and freedom that took priority over obligations to the community. The Renaissance helped learning, including humanism, spread through Europe and inspired the spirit of questioning and skepticism that characterized the Reformation.[6]

Chapter 8 discusses early individualism and money. Monopolies were part of the trade route systems that developed. For the 14th and 15th century the Hanseatic League held monopoly in the Baltic region. In the 17th and 18th century the Dutch East Indies Company, the world's first large corporation, held the world monopoly on nutmeg and cloves.

The Age of Enlightenment (discussed in Chapter 11) was the period during the 18th century when science and reason were going to lead to the progressive improvement of people's lives.[7] On a personal level, the Age of Enlightenment held the idea that every individual had the right to determine for him or herself how to live and what to live for; a person's own reason and conscience was the ultimate arbiter of right and wrong. The enlightenment was an intellectual movement. Enlightenment thinkers consciously sought advancement through logic, reason and criticism. These new ideas included distrust of established boundaries and tradition.[8] Initially, philosophers started with challenging ideas such as ethics and morality, but by the late 19th century, they challenged the basis of the church, modernism appeared with a shift from tradition and religion toward individualism and scientific or rational organization. Modernity, which brought freedom from unthinking callous authority of various non-secular traditions, replaced traditional cultural values with rational intuition and reason. With few cultural values driving decision-making, individuals fell back on the rational path provided by modern institutions – a path that encouraged self-serving behaviour that disregarded the well-being of others and society.[9] Individualism (discussed in Chapter 17) was a key component of the thinking of 20th century philosophers, such as Jean-Paul Sartre and Ayn Rand. In the past, individualism undermined the established church, while today, individualism supports the established economic institution, the corporation.

The medieval Catholic Church was an economic entity, a large landowner involved in collecting rents and selling products such as offices. Some of the suppression of rival sects involved concerns about cash flow. The attack on the sale of indulgences had a direct bearing on the economic interests of the Fuggers, a German family who had built up a fortune by trade and banking. They were the richest family in Europe in the 16th century. (It was in Fugger's house in Augsburg that the papal legate Cajetan met with Luther in 1518 to try to silence this critic who was impacting Fugger's investments.) Only with credit, which he had to repay with income from the sale of indulgences by the preacher Tetzel, had Albert of Mainz (1490-1545), one of the Imperial Electors, been able to buy himself worldly and church offices.[10] On many aspects, a modern corporation shares characteristics of the medieval church - in medieval times, the most dominant institution was the church; today, the dominant institution is the corporation. The medieval church suppressed almost any idea that did not support the status quo (largely determined by the church hierarchy), and was condemned as heresy. As the church went into decline, it appeared to be defending many of its rights and dues as a corporation. Today, the corporate strangleholds on information and communication guarantee ongoing support for marketing messages supporting globalization. When the middle class seeks financial advice from the financial services industry, the scripted message is part of the globalization of the financial services industry.

The economic debacle of 2008 is a warning to the middle class that the system has changed. There is a need to understand the effect of the wide-spread appearance of extreme individualism on corporations in general, and the financial services industry, in particular. The middle class needs to become more engaged in ensuring that the changes required in the financial services industry, to prevent a future meltdown, occur. Corporations have usurped power and accountability from governments. Today, a corporation's influence is so pervasive that we can't even see it. With the collapse of the Western Roman Empire, the church was the only central organized force in Western Europe, accumulating power and wealth over the subsequent seven centuries. By the 13th century the papal monarchy reached its zenith. The church's measures to suppress heretics had less to do with spirituality and everything to do with maintaining social and political control. It was impossible to change life, to make progress or advance new ideas coming out of medieval times without changing the church - and changing it fundamentally, shifting power to the individual.[11] With a materialist basis to an expanding market economy during the 19th century, men learned to separate morality and sentiment from self-interest. The leveraging of the market that finally produced the 2008 crisis illustrates the weakness of relying on a system to harness the selfishness of people and direct it to public good, thus freeing itself from the need to depend unrealistically upon the uncertain moral virtues of its participants. Today, fundamental progress in addressing problems depends on changing the culture of the corporation, today's dominant institution.[12]

1

Globalization

lobalization is a significant process of the 21st century that affects the movement of money, goods and ideas in the world. Globalization, as defined by the *Stanford Encyclopedia of Philosophy*, is "a synonym for one or more of the following phenomena: the pursuit of classical liberal (or "free market") policies in the world economy, the growing dominance of Western (or even American) forms of political, economic, and cultural life, the proliferation of new information technologies (the Internet Revolution); as well as the notion humanity stands at the threshold of realizing one single united community in which major sources of social conflict have vanished."[13] Telecommunications, computers and audiovisual media allow instantaneous communication, notwithstanding the vast geographic distances that may be separating jurisdictions. These high-speed technologies allow the cross border flow of commodities with great efficiency. This has led to 'around the world, around the clock' financial markets. Global financial markets challenge the attempts of national governments to regulate their growing power.

Economic fundamentalists declared their victory over Keynesian economic theory as Reagan's and Thatcher's policies took their dogma mainstream. Hayek's pupils continue defending this theology. Many people who became rich and powerful through the unregulated free market system resist any modifications or challenges to it. They develop arguments defending the dogma of economic fundamentalism, much as those who enjoyed power and wealth defended the Medieval Church. This activity laid the groundwork for globalization. There is a communication strategy to advance the corporate agenda behind globalization; the communications are designed to reduce resistance to the process by making it seem both highly beneficent and unstoppable. There is also the psychology of the inevitable. The alleged inability of governments to halt the 'progress' of globalization is widely perceived as beyond human control, which further weakens resistance.[14]

In the Information Age, television and computer screens flooded homes around the world with images of America and messages interpreting world events from an American perspective. Globalization is seen as a threat to communities in both the West and in Third World countries. In Third World countries, communities are exposed to many new ideas from the West due to the dominance of the Western media. In many parts of the world these new ideas challenge tradition, customs, values, ethics and lifestyles of the communities. In this case globalization is seen as erosion of universal moral values with the spread of individualism. Many groups are frustrated by this system. For example, Muslims see themselves as misrepresented in the Western media and associate this as an attack on their way of life and religion.[15]

Globalization is part and parcel of the impersonal forces of modernization. This, in turn, has created considerable anger and resentment against the West in many parts of the world. Globalization was expected to make the world more cosmopolitan, but, in fact, many communities are becoming more and more separated, as defined by community values or prosperity. Globalization is a pervasive process influencing the lives of people everywhere. It is largely driven by technology and economic interest. Economic globalization has helped spread the ethics of individualism and this can represent a significant change in how people think. Those affected become more out-looking, materialistic and individualistic. Muslims warn of the evils of individualism, declaring it can open the door to selfishness. Other Muslims teach that reason is an attempt to set up oneself above God. In 1990, Yusuf al-Qaradawi, a Sunni scholar, described a goal of the "Islamic Movement" in Europe is "to restore Islam to its leadership of society." He is concerned that "expatriates not be swept up by the whirlpool of materialistic trends that prevail in the West." [16] This opposition includes the individualism associated with free choices, such as the promiscuity and feminism seen on cable TV and films.

In the present phase of globalization, countries primarily compete for the world's investment capital. This means capital moves to locations where it will find the best conditions for return. The process of corporate expansion across borders creates rapid change in many communities with subsequent negative consequences. For example, there is little international regulation, an unfortunate fact that could have dire consequences for the safety of people and the environment. Support is provided from its close cousins - deregulation and small government size. The alleged inability of governments to halt the 'progress' of globalization is widely perceived as beyond human control, which further weakens resistance. This sense was apparent in the Third World debt crisis of the 1980s and the Asian financial debacle of 1999. The affected areas experienced considerable financial instability. On one hand the world is being more economically integrated; on the other hand, it is becoming more and more economically polarized.

The guiding principle of globalization is to maximize corporate profits through the promotion of consumerism. The media and advertisers help drive this system. The developed countries account for most of the consumption. Consumption statics report that 12% of the world's population lives in North America and Western Europe and accounts for 60% of private consumption spending, but a third of humanity that lives in South Asia and sub-Saharan Africa accounts for only 3.2%.[17] It has been an era of unprecedented prosperity – as well as staggering poverty and inequality. The system was promoted as being benign under the umbrella of the greatest good for the greatest number. Multinational corporations are responsible for the removal of traditional government accountability to a fixed population from much of politics. This creates a lack of ability of those affected by decisions to protect their legitimate rights and interests. As multinational corporations take control of large sections of the world, the question arises as to whom they are accountable.

Globalization promotes free trade, which ultimately benefits everyone. Because free trade opens access to goods, services, capital, people, information, and technology, it provides countries with their best opportunity for advancement. However, trading systems are not as free as globalization advocates say. Globalization is based on a system of trade that favors wealthy, industrialized countries. These countries control both the rules and the rule-making machinery, and they selectively impose trade barriers when it suits them. The rapid movement of capital out of countries can have devastating economic, political and social consequences for the people in those countries, and has been associated with an increased gap in wealth between developed and Third World countries and an increased gap in wealth between the richest and the poorest in Western countries.

As markets become global, more goods and services are made available at lower cost to a wider group of people. More access leads to rising consumer demand and improved standards of living. While globalization may make less-expensive goods available to a wider consumer base, it is at the expense of the workers themselves. In the higher-wage countries of the West, this leads to job losses due to imports or production shifts abroad. These lost jobs have been replaced by lower paying employment in the service industries. In developing countries, globalization exploits cheap labor and natural resources where laws protecting workers, human rights and the environment are weak or nonexistent. Globalization exposes individuals to different cultures, and this knowledge helps overcome the misconceptions they have harbored. On the other hand, globalization undermines the world's rich diversity of traditional cultures and values by imposing some excesses indentified with Western societies – consumerism, materialism and secularism.

The developing nations have not shared equally in the benefits of globalization. For example, African agricultural exports are not addressed on a level playing field. This creates demands for transparency and calls for greater democratization in the global decision-making process. The International Monetary Fund (IMF), the World Bank, and World Trade Organization (WTO) are three organizations associated with the support of globalization.[18]

The IMF loans to countries are often pegged to a reduction in government spending, which all too often results in reductions in health care dollars. The IMF specifically grants loans in stages based on spending performance targets, putting pressure on governments to comply. Joseph Stiglitz, formerly chief economist of the World Bank describes the operation of the IMF:

> "The IMF likes to go about its business without outsiders asking too many questions. In theory, the fund supports democratic institutions in the nations it assists. In practice, it undermines the democratic process by imposing policies. Officially, of course, the IMF doesn't impose anything. It 'negotiates' the conditions for receiving aid. But all the power in the negotiations is on one side – the IMF's – and the fund rarely allows sufficient time for broad consensus building or even widespread consultations with either parliaments or civil society. Sometimes the IMF dispenses with the pretense of openness altogether and negotiates secret convents." [19]

The World Bank resource role is to provide guarantees to private sector investors in projects in low-income countries, which are intended to generate substantial foreign exchange revenues. Its activities are a source of problems. For example, loans come with guidelines for resettlement, like in the case of Zambian copper mine development. No one thought about the settlers on the land. The corporation defaulted on obligations for the treatment of poor people. Accountability in this case required the company to voluntarily adopt the code of conduct recommended by the World Bank.

The WTO, based in Geneva, was formed after the Second World War. Initially it dealt with rules of trade between two countries, then it developed into a forum where countries can negotiate trade agreements, settle disputes arising from agreements, and help other countries join the negotiations. With globalization, the WTO has taken on the role of trying to lower trade barriers between countries. It is criticized for allowing its agenda to be hijacked by rich countries.

It is said a Third World country will not benefit from globalization unless there is adequate governance infrastructure in place in the country. The *Reference for Business, Encyclopedia for Business, 2*nd *ed.* Identifies globalization as follows:

"In the late 1990s, there was a great deal of debate about how advanced economies and multinational corporations could help developing nations to share in the benefits of globalization. Some experts claim that developing nations need debt relief, an increased flow of direct financial investment and technology, and unrestricted access to markets in advanced countries in order to begin catching up. Others claim that these measures are pointless unless the leaders of the developing nations show a willingness to establish a stable government and invest in the education of their citizens. Before trade and foreign capital can translate into sustainable growth, governments first must deliver political stability, sound economic management, and educated workers... Otherwise, foreign investment would likely lead to government corruption and the exploitation of workers." [20]

Globalization is driven by the desire of corporations to pursue economic liberalization. The consequences of this activity in democratic countries affect the ability of elected leaders to make decisions in the interests of their people and, in other situations, it means supporting dictatorships for the stability that it brings for their interests. There are many gains from globalization for companies around the world as better communication enabled capital to move readily and trade to grow. Economic globalization has helped spread the ethics of individualism.

This individualism drives materialism and cosmopolitanism, in which cultural trends have become a significant aspect worldwide. Technological progress has allowed increased integration of financial markets and rapid movement of information. Because of globalization, the consequences of decision-making in the financial services industry on Wall Street spread quickly to the entire world. The result was the economic debacle of 2008.

2

Individualism

Individualism is a balance between self-reliance and personal responsibility, and egotism. The rise of individualism is about people living and acting as individuals rather than as members of a larger group. Saint-Simonian socialists used the word individualism to describe what they believed was the cause of the disintegration of French society after the 1789 revolution. They criticized the 'laissez-faire' (economic liberalism) approach for its perceived failure to cope with increasing inequality between rich and poor. The word individualism first appeared in the English language when the Owenites of the 1830s used it as a pejorative term with reference to the utopian socialist philosophy of Robert Owen.[21] The word individualism appeared in 1840 English translation of Alexis de Tocqueville's *Democracy in America*. He observed that private interest and personal gain motivated the actions of most Americans which, in turn cultivated a strong sense of individualism. From his observations during his trip across America, de Tocqueville concluded that, as a people, Americans were highly individualistic.[22]

Individualism appeared with the humanist ideals of the Renaissance. The Renaissance introduced new ways of thinking that involved individual rights and freedom that took priority over obligations to the community. The Renaissance helped learning spread through Europe and inspired the spirit of questioning and skepticism that characterized the Reformation. New ideas of the Reformation included Martin Luther's declaration that anyone can read the Bible and can find salvation by faith alone. Newton's theory of gravitation was the final piece of the puzzle that tied together the Copernican theory of the Earth revolving around the sun. This had significant impact on the church. If the Earth is no longer the centre of the universe, then some key teachings of the church must be false. With this event, many philosophers who had previously developed theories in support of the church disappeared. They went their own way in hopes of discovering the truth. This heralded the Age of Enlightenment when science and reason were going to lead to the progressive improvement of people's lives. On a personal level, it was the idea that every individual had the right to determine for him or herself how to live and what to live for; a person's own reason and conscience was the ultimate arbiter of right and wrong. This commitment to human self-determination had a profound effect on the religious life of the West. The Enlightenment thinkers reduced the role of God in the explanation of things and the influence of religion in public life as much as possible. Initially, philosophers started challenging ideas such as ethics and morality, but by the late 19th century, they challenged the basis of the church. They believed people should seek genuine autonomy and live a life without the artificial limits of moral obligation. Nietzsche identified happiness with power so this entailed rejection of romanticism and the Christian religion, which undermined the individual's power.[23]

Individualism is a key component of the thinking of 20th century philosophers, such as Jean-Paul Sartre and Ayn Rand. Individualism forms a significant part of a culture supported by mass media and advertisers and shows no sign of subsiding. Mass media and advertisers have become the cultural hegemony of the West. The Information Age began in 1989 with the fall of the Berlin Wall. Marketing and advertising fed into the cult of individualism. In the 21st century, individualism is pervasive and has become a source of problems. Self-indulgence has replaced self-control. A consequence of the cult of individualism, everyone strives to be different, to be original or to stand out from the crowd. In the extreme, this means feeding their narcissism. Creeping traits of narcissism can affect the way a person responds to his/her country, community, church and/or friends.

Individualism spread with many of the new ideas during the Renaissance. These new ideas were incubating three centuries prior to the Renaissance of the 15th century. Milton Viorst observed, "The seminal notion that the Renaissance introduced to the West was that mankind, not God, is the hub of the social universe." The enlightenment of the 18th century "held that reason is as important as faith, and urged men and women to claim responsibility, free of the clergy, for their own lives. The ideas led, over quarrelsome centuries, to the Reformation, the Enlightenment and the scientific revolution." [24] As there was no Catholic Counter Reformation in America, the Reformation carried on longer in America than Europe, and this accounts for a great deal of the influence that developed the unique American character of individualism.[25]

In the 18th century when Adam Smith laid out the basics of classical economics, religion still played an important part in how one made decisions. His work was popular because it provided an 'ethical' rationale for the capitalist system that explained how, when one acted in their own interest, it actually helped someone they did not even know. Friedrich Hayek admired Adam Smith and built upon the ideas of his teacher Ludwig von Mises. Von Mises, one of the founders of Austrian School economic thought, believed that the complexity of human behavior makes mathematical modeling of an evolving market extremely difficult, and advocates a 'laissez faire' approach to the economy, including smallest role of government involvement, especially in area of money supply.[26] Hayek had a major influence on market liberalization strategies, which included discrediting government economic planning. His polemic against socialism and communism supported the rapidly growing anti-communism that dominated the Cold War. Reagan's and Thatcher's policies took this dogma mainstream to capitalistic individualism. Duncan K. Foley observed that, in the economics of the free enterprise system, "the pursuit of self-interest is guided by objective laws to a socially beneficent outcome" but for all the rest of social life "the pursuit of self-interest is morally problematic and has to be weighed against other ends."[27]

The Cold War represented an intense rivalry between two great power blocks and ideologies: democracy and capitalism in the case of the United States and its allies, and Communism in the case of the Soviet Bloc. From Ayn Rand, western economists found a philosophy they could apply to 'the free market' system during the Cold War. Her descriptions illustrate the underlying self-interest associated with extreme individualism:

> "The moral purpose of a man's life is the achievement of
> his own happiness. This does not mean that he is indif-
> ferent to all men, that human life is of no value to him
> and that he has no reason to help others in an emergency.

But it does mean that he does not subordinate his life to the welfare of others, that he does not sacrifice himself to their needs, that the relief of their suffering is not his primary concern, that any help he gives is an exception, not a rule, an act of generosity, not of moral duty, that it is marginal and incidental—as disasters are marginal and incidental in the course of human existence—and that values, not disasters, are the goal, the first concern and the motive power of his life."[28]

Milton Friedman was influenced by Ayn Rand's ideas. Friedman and his students' free trade recipe that included privatization, deregulation, and drastic cuts to government spending, supported the conditions that nurtured globalization. Globalization is about maximizing production and minimizing cost. It has been accompanied by large concentrations of holdings in industries such as banking and the energy sector. The Oil Industry in the USA exerted a significant influence in the politics on the Middle East, and this coincided with the rise of individualism. This extreme individualism leads to narcissism. The narcissist exaggerates achievements and talents to a point of lying, and demands to be recognized as superior without commensurate achievements.

The belief that one must do whatever he can to achieve positive self-esteem has become a movement with broad societal effects.[29] This self-esteem movement has had a significant impact on the school system – in order to ensure positive self-esteem, educational standards were lowered, creating a milieu for extreme individualism. When there is too much self-esteem, there are problems of self-tolerance, entitlement and narcissism. This person demands automatic and full compliance with his/her expectations.

In the Middle Ages, independent thought was viewed disdainfully. Almost any idea deviating from the status quo, largely determined by the Roman Catholic Church, was condemned as heresy. One convicted of such a grievous offense was often excommunicated or killed, either by means of a proper execution or by a hostile mob. However, with the decline of the Middle Ages, conditions arose for the birth of individualism - the development of which can be traced through the Renaissance, the Reformation, and the rise of capitalism.

Cultural Hegemony

Hegemony is a word that the Greeks used to describe the dominance of one Greek city-state over other city-states. Politically, hegemony is the predominance of one political unit over other units in a political group. Antonio Gramsci (1891-1937), an Italian communist philosopher and thinker, developed the concept of cultural hegemony - whereby the ruling class of a capitalist society coerced the working class to adopt its values in maintaining the State. Gramsci developed the theory to explain why workers in industrialized countries of Europe had not risen up in revolt against the capitalist system as predicted by Marx while in Mussolini's prisons. The theory explains how the ruling (dominant) class maintains its hegemony in civil society. Society is controlled and manipulated as a direct consequence of the practice of a 'false consciousness' and the creation of values and life choices that are to be followed. In 'advanced' industrial (countries) societies, hegemonic cultural tools, such as compulsory schooling, mass media, and popular culture, indoctrinate workers to a 'false consciousness.' Gramsci described cultural hegemony as a form of control by the dominant economic and ruling groups that consisted of permeation throughout society of an entire system of values, attitudes beliefs and morality.[30] Cultural hegemony is present today within schools, pop culture and the media. It appears as the contested culture that meets the minimal needs of the majority, while serving the interest of the dominant class.

Here is an example of pop culture as part of cultural hegemony. Activist Reverend Al Sharpton challenges Rap artists to clean up the word "nigga", "bitch" and "ho" (slang for whore) in popular music. He finds it necessary to address three entertainment conglomerates, Viacom (Inc), Time Warner (Inc) and Vivendi. The protest consists of urging public divestment from the music industry until Rap singers stop employing the n-word and terms degrading to women. The initial response from Time Warner was to point out it sold its music business, including such labels as Atlantic and Reprise, to a private equity group in 2004. Apologists for the pension funds noted that their job is to maximize returns, not make moral judgments.[31] This is an example of industry wearing the cloak of 'free speech' while defending cultural hegemony in pop-culture.

In Tom Hine's *Populuxe* the media is supplanting the community as the dispenser of trusted advice.[32] In fact, mass media is a significant part of life today and, in many respects, provides significant support to the dominant class. Today with the press, media and advertisers, lifestyle now takes on religious connotations. Nike does not sell shoes but "enhances people's lives through sports and fitness." IBM stopped selling computers and began selling business solutions. Diesel Jeans doesn't sell a product, but sells a lifestyle.[33] Advertizing, which is all around us, has normalized consumption as a way of life. The advertisers offer ideal images of us to sell as products. Most of us will find ourselves pitifully inadequate when we compare ourselves with such images.[34]

Culture can now be tailored to our requirements, and the choices available are adapted to fit our desires. We now have personalized media consumption. There are choices of portable media and 100s of TV channels to choose from. For a long time, people have welcomed the chance to express their individuality through exercising choice. The ultimate goal of this individualism and personalization is commonly known as self-actualization- the development and expression of a personal identity unique to the individual. While there is a strong relationship between self-actualization and spirituality, today, it is being replaced through consumer oriented ways. This includes using personal trainers and life coaches to help 'live an ideal life.' Instead of the extended family being around to influence an individual, it is done on a professional relationship between two people. People now reach a level of economic freedom that pressures them to feel that they must identify and accomplish what they most want and thus 'actualize' themselves. In some instances that means having to be seen to have certain things.[35]

The media is for profit, with the majority owned by large corporations. Large corporations are managed by business elite who share common interests with managers of other corporations. The managers of the media are dependent on other corporations for advertising. The products they produce are not shows, rather audiences that they sell to advertisers. Advertisers target wealthier audiences with products geared towards the wealthy. The shows developed tend to go along with the prejudices and beliefs of the wealthier group. The media depend disproportionately upon government as a news source, and the information is open to the practice of manipulation and therefore, the process of hegemony. This makes it easy for powerful groups to manipulate the media through various means to magnify the effect of a story.

In a world of hundreds of satellite and cable channels, virtually all are owned by one of nine companies: AOL-Time Warner, Disney, Bertelsmann, Viacom, Rupert Murdock's News Corporation, Tele-Communications Inc (TCI), General Electric, Sony and Seagram.[36] The mass media and advertisers are part of the dominant culture in the West. This drives an individualistic consumer society. What dominates the media? Determination, single-mindedness, wealth, status, influence, sexual prowess, and celebrities breaking the law dominate. Mainstream media has latched onto celebrities and teens.[37] We are in a celebrity-obsessed culture, and such a culture is never in finer form than when one of its most loved icons is mired in scandal. Teens became an important demographic; 1992 was the first year since 1975 that the number of teenagers increased. The cult of individualism drives the need for attention. Venues available for attention seeking include MySpace, YouTube, Facebook, Twitter and Reality TV.

People have a need for order and consistency in their lives; cognitive dissonance is the tension created when beliefs or behaviors conflict with one another. This process occurs when people make purchases. For example, people will collect more information after they have bought a product than before the purchase, because they want to confirm they made a good choice. This tends to reduce the tension from cognitive dissonance. Warranties also reduce cognitive dissonance. Marketing and advertising feed into the cult of individualism. Products appear as a choice. The product can be distinctive which has a value for being unique. This in turn leads to 'self-confidence.' A fashionable product provides social recognition and a sense of security. Television tends to feed an information diet (self-approval) similar to consuming too much sugar inducing short-term euphoria and happiness while distracting from reality. The weakness of mass media remains an inability to transmit tacit knowledge and inability to deal with complex issues, so there is a need to simplify. Consequently they tend to focus on the unusual or sensational, and the promotion of anxiety and fear.

Individualism is the view that the individual, rather than society as a whole, is the most important entity. Individualism, a positive force supporting the development of democracy and free enterprise, is about the pursuit of individual rather than common interests. Capitalism is based on individualism and making free choices. In the American vision of this system, the harder you work, the more money you make. Individualism fuels the American dream – the hope for a better quality of life and a higher standard of living than their parents. This is part of an inherent belief that any one can "pull themselves up by the bootstraps" and raise themselves from poverty.[38] Today, more and more people are into instant gratification – participating in large prize television game shows, big jack-pot lotteries and compensation lawsuits.[39] Conservative foundations in America fund free-market-oriented programs at universities and subsidize the research of right wing intellectuals to develop free market rhetoric, in language that is elaborate and intellectually vacuous.

3

Cognitive Dissonance

The engine that drives self-justification, the energy that produces the need to justify our actions and our decisions, especially wrong ones, is an unpleasant feeling that social psychologists call "cognitive dissonance." In 1957 Leon Festinger described the theory behind cognitive dissonance. There is a perception of incompatibility between two cognitions where cognition is defined as any element of knowledge including attitude, emotion, belief or behaviour.[40]

In cases of discrepancy between attitudes and behaviour, it is most likely that attitude will change to accommodate behaviour. Dissonance occurs most often in situations where an individual must choose between two incompatible beliefs or actions. The greatest dissonance is created when the two alternatives are equally attractive. Attitude change is more likely in the direction of less incentive, since this results in less dissonance. In this respect, the dissonance theory is contradictory to most behaviour theories, which would predict greater attitude change with increased incentives (i.e. reinforcement).

Cognitive dissonance occurs after making an ethical decision when there is a discrepancy between what a person believes, knows, and values, and persuasive information that calls these into question. There are negative aspects. Dissonance can lead to rationalization of unethical conduct, as when the appeal and potential benefits of a large amount of money makes unethical actions to acquire it seem less objectionable than if they are applied to smaller amounts. It affects how one processes information. For example, within political debates when the talking head is analyzing the debate, we believe the person with whom we agree provided the best opinion. In such debates, partisans also believe that partisans on the other side are far more ideologically extreme than they actually are.

The drive to avoid cognitive dissonance can be so strong that people sometimes react to discomforting evidence by strengthening their original beliefs and creating rationalizations to dismiss the discomforting evidence. While we might be able to spot these behaviours in other people, we are less likely to detect them in ourselves. An example in science is the story of Alfred Wegener who, in 1915, published a shocking new theory that the Earth's continents had once been contiguous. He claimed that over millions of years, this continent split into separate segments, which drifted apart into their current arrangement. This theory dubbed "continental drift" was supported by extensive geological evidence. The leading geologists of the day dismissed the idea as impossible, and Wegner died in 1930 as an intellectual pariah. Today, Wegener's theory is taught in schools and when one looks at a map of the world we consider this once impossible theory to be self-evident.[41] Our beliefs can dictate what we see. Cognitive dissonance is the uncomfortable feeling people experience when confronted by things that 'should not be, but are.' Some react to the situation with anxiety, but others will develop even stronger convictions of their previous belief.

There are three basic strategies employed to reduce cognitive dissonance:

(1) Adopt what other people say, noting that peer pressure can lead to some irrational needs.
(2) Apply pressure to people who believe differently because he/she is in error. This has been the source of religious and other types of persecution throughout history.
(3) Make the person who believes differently significantly different from oneself. Examples of this would be the treatment of religious heretics and ethnic cleansing.[42]

People are quite capable of spotting cognitive dissonance in people with opposing beliefs, but seem utterly unable to recognize it in themselves. It can occur with a belief system, whether it be scientific, religious or political. To identify cognitive dissonance within one's self, one would need to identify situations which cause one to react in an extreme manner or take a step to make a group of people significantly different from one's self (politics, religion or sports). Cognitive dissonance is so unpleasant that many individuals would rather be closed-minded than be informed and deal with the repercussions of cognitive dissonance. However, it can be a tool for education in general. Firstly, pointing out the conflict of what people know and do. Secondly, point out contradictions. An example is the contradiction between religious beliefs and the violence of terrorism. In order to justify the violence it is necessary to dehumanize the other side. To counter, one could introduce new information to both sides.

In the summer of 2008, polls showed 28% of people still approved of President George W. Bush's performance in office.

This is not based on competency to run a war or manage the economy. Francis Bacon would have found nothing surprising in the disinclination of core Bush voters to judge the president harshly. "The human understanding when it has once adopted an opinion...draws all things else to support and agree with it," he wrote in Novum Organum (1620). "And though there be a greater number and weight of instances to be found on the other side, yet these it either neglects or despises...in order that by this great and pernicious predetermination the authority of its former conclusions may remain inviolate." To maintain our former conclusions inviolate, we will ignore, deny, even despise numerous and weighty instances that chafe up against them.[43] People choose not to change in order to minimalize their cognitive dissonance. Cognitive dissonance also occurs in the pairing of unrelated facts to create correlation. An example of this is President Bush's speech in which he mentioned Iraq and the September 11th attacks in the same sentence. The close proximity of the mentions is designed to create a correlation in peoples' minds even when the reality is different. By insinuating, people subconsciously take the idea and turn it to a possibility. Through repetition, the correlation becomes fact based upon misinformation.

The use of cognitive dissonance to persuade voter groups occurred in the 2008 presidential race in America. To create dissonance in a significant part of the undecided voters, the Republican strategists used specific messages to make the Democratic nominee, Barack Obama, seem different from these voters. They built on the fact that Obama was already different in a couple of aspects from the majority of these undecided voters – being black and having an unfamiliar name was a source for some dissonance. A series of calculated messages over several months were used to increase this dissonance. This was achieved by making Obama appear different from the targeted voters (who are mainly white and blue collar). These messages included statements that 'Obama doesn't wear a flag pin, so he must not be that patriotic'; his popularity during his visit to Europe made him a celebrity who is out of touch with ordinary people, plus an attack ad including footage of Brittany Spears and Paris Hilton along with the large crowds who welcomed Obama in Europe – trying to enforce the celebrity label by insinuation. The Republican strategists continually promoted pictures of his pastor, Reverend Wright, who has made somewhat controversial statements in some of his sermons, and pictures of Obama in his youth visiting Africa wearing traditional clothes, all in an effort to present images to make Obama appear significantly different. Conservative talk show hosts delighted in mentioning Obama's middle name, Hussein. These are topped up with misinformation in blogs that subsequently were discussed in mainstream media, that Obama is a Muslim and not a Christian. When rational analysis is applied to each of these 'attacks' separately, none by itself would easily sway how someone voted. However, the cumulative effect of these messages in the subconscious could create enough cognitive dissonance to prevent an individual from voting for Obama. News analysts noted during the summer of 2008 that Obama needed to reach out to undecided voters and communicate to them that he is just like them and shares their concerns of community and country, and in this manner make these voters comfortable with him.

The cult of individualism makes us particularly prone to cognitive dissonance because our personal identity is very important. We see ourselves as stable, self-contained beings. The multinational corporations have responded by branding – creating an image around a particular brand. The successful corporation today produces brands as opposed to products. Brands are about "meaning" not product attributes.[44] Advertising targets the right brain where the long-term memory resides. The messages include the product plus a jingle or phrase that gets by the logical centre of the brain. They establish credibility through repetition.[45] Advertisers create dissonance in the consumer by planting a contradictory cognition to one's belief that he or she is complete and self-fulfilled individually, so that he or she will likely feel the desire to reduce the dissonance by purchasing the advertised product or service. Highlighting the negative aspects of the other alternatives can create dissonance. The media creates cognitive dissonance by advertising that we may be missing out on something, or not fitting in. This creates anxiety. Increased cognitive dissonance is a source of psychological suffering and the vast amounts of stress we see today.

Dissonance is most powerful when it is about self-image. It appears in virtually all evaluations and decisions. The narcissist lives with considerable cognitive dissonance. One basic drive is pathological envy, an integral part of narcissism, brought on by the realization of some lack, deficiency or inadequacy in oneself. This is the result of unfavorably comparing themselves to others with respect to success, reputation, luck, possessions and/or qualities. The cognitive dissonance results in devaluing their frustration and envy by finding faults. The result is a spectrum of reactions to this pernicious emotion. The reactions include shunning or relational aggression. In covert bullying, the victim may not know the abuser is lying or gossiping about them. The abuser may even pretend to befriend the victim. The abuser chooses to destroy the object that gives them so much grief by provoking in them feelings of inadequacy and frustration. Onlookers wonder why the two people seem to hate each other so intensely.[46]

4
Self-esteem and Narcissism

athaniel Branden declared that self-esteem was the most important facet of a person in his 1969 publication of *The Psychology of Self-esteem.* This book promoted the belief that one must do whatever he can to achieve positive self-esteem. Self-esteem has become a movement with broad societal effect. Education departments adopted this mantra. The world will be saved from crime, drug abuse and under-achievement through bolstering self-esteem. Accordingly, school systems lowered educational standards to protect children from failure.[47]

Abraham H. Maslow (1908-1970), American psychologist, developed a theory of human needs, focusing on human potential, believing that humans strive to express their capabilities fully, and that this is the basis for happiness. Maslow took a humanistic approach to behaviorism. He developed a system of hierarchy of needs by studying healthy people. In his initial work he identified five levels: (1) physiological, (2) safety, (3) love and belonging, (4) esteem, (5) self-actualization. The first four make humans anxious if they are not met. Physiological need is about food and sustenance. Safety is about shelter and protection from environmental threats. The third, love and belonging, deals with a person functioning within a group, family, community, work place. After belonging, people seek to climb the hierarchy or maintain their position in the group.[48]

Under modern humanism, every human being has worth independent of what they can do. They have an intrinsic worth supporting the concept behind human dignity and universal rights. This supports the self-esteem movement. Esteem is described as feeling of moving up in the world and self-confidence, with few doubts about the self. There are two ways to establish self-esteem. The first way is internally; judge one's self and find one's self worthy by one's own defined standards. The second way is from other people. This includes seeking social approval and esteem and judging themselves by what others think of them. Maslow's self-actualization is the level at which humans try to make the most of their abilities and strive to be the best they can.[49]

From the 1970s to the 1990s, individualism thrived in the school system. Rights replaced responsibilities. Self-criticism, self-denial, self-control, self-sacrifice were no longer in vogue. Self-expression, self-assertion, self-indulgence, self-realization and self-approval, all which blend into self-esteem, became important.[50] Surveys identified that self-esteem correlates with self-reported happiness. Vincent Ryan Ruggierio reports that a culture of selfness produces bad attitude among students and stops them from learning. Supported by mass culture and teachers imbided with attitude leads the following visions: "Being myself makes self-discipline unnecessary," and "I have a right to my opinion, so my opinions are right." This can lead to extreme individualism and the problems of self-tolerance. In New York a fourteen year old was murdered by a fifteen year old for his sneakers and beeper. Designer shoes and carrying a beeper had become a way for poor kids to "feel important."[51]

Narcissism has been on the rise and now influences many aspects of our lives, and along with it appears a heightened sense of entitlement. With this sense of entitlement has come expecting well-paid employment and not having to work hard. In an individualistic consumer society, there is a strong focus on rights. Along with these rights are expectations of entitlement to goods and services. This has led to a culture of complaint. In complaining, the individual establishes an image of himself that he knows what's going on (even if it is wrong) and therefore establishes an image of himself as alert and knowledgeable. Complaining amidst a group of like-minded whiners forges a sense of togetherness and community.

Narcissism is described as extreme individualism. Kohut described narcissism as part of normal development; without narcissism we are unable to feel good about ourselves and other people.[52] The narcissism associated with extreme individualism is associated with poor relationship skills. Such individuals focus on short-term relationships and activities correlated with risk taking and sensation seeking. Materialism is part of this system. Entitlement is part of their belief system – they believe they deserve special treatment. They lack empathy for others and selfishly take advantage of others. There is a lack of respect for authority. Rules do not apply to them –they are special – 'can't you make an exception?' Problems are not their fault and they don't take criticism well. Dysfunctional narcissist traits continually interfere with their own and other's lives.

During the past decade, there have been reports of more and more children being diagnosed with Attention Deficit Disorder (ADD) and being medicated. Recent reviews suggest that

ADD has been over-diagnosed in children, that children with significant behaviour problems were being labeled ADD. This change coincides with the self-esteem movement in schools that has created a population of children with an exaggerated sense of entitlement who can become enraged with little provocation. The ADD diagnosis has no definitive medical or psychological marker, so it is often made exclusively on the basis of a patient's history. The child can behave or perform quite normally in the doctor's office yet meet DSM criteria for diagnosis from reports of difficulties at home or school. This shift from stricter criteria has created a large pool of concerned parents available for recruitment to support groups.[53]

Psychiatry identifies behavior problems in adults as personality disorders when they cause emotional upsets and trouble with other people at work and in personal relationships. There are about a dozen behaviour patterns identified with personality disorders. However, many disorders overlap and this creates an epidemic of co-morbidity. For example, two personality disorders, narcissist and psychopath, share some personal and behavior traits; both lack empathy and both share a disregard for societal conventions and cues. The narcissist is a psychopath preoccupied with building a false and often grandiose self-image. Following the massacre at Virginia Tech, some commentators attributed the actions of Cho Seung-Hui to extreme narcissism.[54] Did he actually have this diagnosis? Psychiatry is not an exact science; psychiatric diagnosis is subjective. The Diagnostic and Statistics Manual of Mental Disorders (DSM-IV) consists of a checklist of signs and symptoms and provides a list of psychiatric disorders. It is supported by academic psychiatry to create some consistency in diagnosis for research purposes and the insurance industry for practical reasons. It is difficult to measure narcissism in the community. This is illustrated by the fact the most commonly diagnosed personality disorder is 301.9 Personality Disorder not Otherwise Specified. Fortunately, psychiatric medications are aimed at symptoms, not diagnosis.[55]

Alienation is the dark underside of modernity in general, and individualism in particular. In this situation, individualism becomes isolation, freedom becomes rootlessness, and egalitarianism becomes destruction of all values as rationality disappears. This person becomes a wild animal pacing in a cage. Generally, such individuals no longer coexist with family, community, country or church.[56] Cho lashed out at "rich brats" with their trust funds, gold necklaces and Mercedes. His parents were emigrants from Korea who worked hard and appeared to be the essence of the American Dream. Cho sent out plenty of body language that he could be a problem. While some of his classmates tried to reach out to him, the outcast needed a strong cohesive group to rescue him – individualism does not provide that system. His actions were consistent with alienation.

The Narcissist's Vocation

Narcissism appears as a spectrum. There is the narcissism associated with extreme individualism and there is the narcissism correlated with good psychological health. In this system, there is less sadness and anxiety and more subjective well being associated with a significant level of narcissism. Self-love exists on the edge of dysfunction because it's motivated first and foremost by emotions and desires. Psychiatric practice is aware of the arbitrary distinction between normal personality, personality traits and personality disorder as identified in the Diagnostic and Statistic Manual of Mental Disorders (DSM-IV), psychiatry's official nomenclature of mental illness. Despite interpersonal deficits, such people meet the definition of being psychologically healthy. The cult of self-esteem associated with extreme individualism can have very negative consequences for society, when people live with these belief systems. The psychopath is on the pathological end of the continuum of narcissism.

The cult of individualism creates the milieu for excessive narcissism and the accompanying mental manipulation. This manipulation is a subtle thing. Mental manipulators manipulate reactions to things; as reactions come from within, they are manipulating thoughts. Narcissists are excellent at manipulation because they have been practicing from childhood. Typically they share personal information of themselves to make people feel sorry for them. Initially this may appear that they are sensitive and perhaps vulnerable, but this is only part of their system. Everything they say and do is for effect; to get the reaction they want. The truth is irrelevant; it is whatever works as they play for the reaction they want. This activity makes them extremely observant and perceptive; they can appear to be smart. They will tend to agree with people, that is, tell them what they think they want to hear, and then find subtle ways to undermine it. They do not deal with things directly, but go behind people's backs and put others in the position of telling what they would not say themselves. The cult of individualism affects day-to-day decision-making and interpersonal interactions. It is necessary to recognize its existence and measure the effect of extreme individualism in daily activities.

Vocation is defined as an inclination to a particular state or course of action. The idea of vocation is central to the Christian belief that God has created each person with gifts and talents oriented toward a specific purpose and way of life. The idea of a vocation or 'calling' has been pivotal within Protestantism. Martin Luther taught that each individual is expected to fulfill his God-appointed task in everyday life. In Lutheranism, there was no particular emphasis on labour beyond what is required for one's daily bread. Luther, in reacting to abuses propagated by church officials, argued that vocation was a call to serve neighbours in the world, rather than withdrawing from the world as a priest or monk. John Calvin joined Luther in affirming that all work could be rightly considered a vocation.[57] Over time, the concept of vocation has evolved, growing increasingly inclusive.

In the DSM-IV, five or more of nine criteria, including such criteria as "requires excessive admiration," and "show arrogant, haughty behaviour or attitude", indicate the diagnosis of narcissistic personality disorder. There will be many individuals with three or four of these criteria who have extreme individualism and are very adept at manipulating their environment, and caught up in their cognitive dissonance on how they compare themselves to others. Such behaviour is associated with creeping traits of narcissism, but because of uncertainty in psychiatry, most of these individuals would not be labeled with a mental health problem. These people expect everything to work for them; if it doesn't then someone must be to blame. Whoever is at fault, it's not them. With the focus on self-esteem and the accompanying lack of accountability, a new needy person has appeared. This person is not the narcissist with his/her fixed fantasy, but one who manipulates their environment daily. A metaphorical description of their mental function is a person living a narcissist's vocation. This metaphor consists of the Lutheran version of a vocation as "no particular emphasis on labour beyond what is required for one's daily bread" combined with the traits of narcissism incorporated into daily activities.[58] The behaviour of the person living a narcissist's vocation causes distress and dysfunction in their own and others' lives.

The appearance of the cult of individualism creates the milieu for individuals to live a narcissist's vocation. The person who lives a narcissist vocation is addicted to the attention of others for admiration, applause and affirmation. They are driven by a need to uphold and maintain a false self projected to the world. Behind this façade they only care about appearances. They feel omnipotent; there is nothing he/she cannot achieve. They rarely admit to ignorance and regard his/her intuition and knowledge as superior to objective data. They are impervious to consequences of their actions; and have an ability to find scapegoats while others see them as 'getting away with it.'

With this belief system, the narcissist conditions the people around them using intimidation, positive and negative reinforcement, and ambient abuse, covert or controlling abuse. They survive in the system by manipulating policies in place to address bullying in the work place, any time their system is challenged. They only seek physicians for help for the anxiety caused whenever there is a significant challenge to their system.[59] Within this bubble universe others are recruited, play a role assigned by the narcissist who rewards compliance with pandering and punishes deviation from it with severe abuse. This abuse consists of putting them in their place, humiliating them, and demonstrating to them how inadequate they are in comparison to values/issues that he/she has established. They can socially ostracize a person with groupthink, bringing the individual under pressure not to express arguments against any of the group's views. In the work place, this manifests as subtle forms of intimidation and other activities such as guilt making and shunning.

Individuals living the narcissist's vocation constantly lie about his/her life – self, history, work, and emotions. They believe this false information provides advantage or edge in relationships and encounters. They measure life by events, difficulties and negative predictions and projections related to them. They avoid their own feelings, lack empathy and do not recognize boundaries: personal, corporate or legal. Everyone and everything is a mere instrument and object available for pursuit of narcissistic gratification. These actions regulate a sense of self worth and feed the all-important self-esteem. The narcissist hungers for everything in and out of reach: money, property, power, adulation, fame, and dominance over the lives of others. They can become enraged and defensive at the slightest hint of criticism, disapproval or dissatisfaction with their performance. As narcissists think highly of themselves, they will seek out leadership positions and take charge. They tend to exaggerate their abilities and, not surprisingly, group members see them as people who can really run the group. Narcissists generally do not perform better than others in a leadership role.[60] Corporate narcissism occurs when the narcissist becomes the leader and recruits co-dependents into his bubble. Corporate narcissism gives free reign to materialistic impulses. This is the same narcissist who drives the company towards risky business decision-making. The narcissist is stunned by society's insistence that he should be held accountable for his deeds and penalized accordingly.

5

The Early Church

By the beginning of the 5th century CE, after just 400 years, the church had grown from a fledgling mystery cult into a power on nearly equal terms with the Roman Emperor himself. The Pax Romana, (from 27 BCE to 180 CE), two hundred years of peace within the Roman empire, which united a great variety of cultures and peoples into a world-state, provided security and advanced civilization. Latin became established as the common language of the empire, allowing the communication of new ideas. One of the new ideas, Christianity, slowly spread from east to west. The cruelty of the Roman emperors assisted in spreading the Christian faith, because of the oppressed nature of the subjects of the Roman Empire, the message of Christ appealed to the lower classes. Chance and circumstance, and the influence of important characters and events, secured the rise of Christianity to dominate western religion.[61]

The Roman Empire experienced a period of turmoil from 235 to 284 CE, known as the Imperial Crisis of the 3rd century CE that was associated with external invasions, internal civil war, plague, and economic collapse. During that time, there were 20 to 25 emperors claiming the title at the same time, but very few who ever ruled the entire empire. Most of them were prominent generals who assumed Imperial power over all or part of the empire, only to lose it by defeat in battle, murder or death, ruling on average only two or three years. For a while the empire broke into competing states. One long-term consequence was the disruption of Rome's extensive internal trade network. In order to finance their armies, money was debased which subsequently created havoc in the economic system. Diocletian, emperor from 284 to 305, brought changes to end the political chaos that plagued the empire: he introduced reforms to stabilize the administration of the empire. He concluded that the empire was too large and complex to be ruled by only a single emperor, and introduced a co-emperor and established two capitals, Milan in the west and Nicomedia in the east, with one emperor in each region.[62]

Constantine, emperor from 306 to 337, continued with reforms in the empire in order to strengthen the empire. The Praetorian Guard was disbanded as their status had been considerably reduced under Diocletian. The mounted guard, largely consisting of Germans, introduced under Diocletian, took their place. The army was divided between frontier garrisons and mobile forces consisting largely of heavy cavalry, which could move quickly to troubled spots. To address economic issues, Constantine introduced new coinage; his gold solidus (struck at 72 to the pound) became the western world's standard coin for the next 1000 years. He established a new capital named Constantinople at the site of the Greek town of Byzantine.

Constantine's reforms included the Christians. One story says that on the eve of battle against the rival emperor, Maxentius, Constantine had a vision of the sign of Christ, the "chi-rho", in a dream. Following the defeat of Maxentius at the Battle of Milvian Bridge in 312 CE against considerable odds, he became emperor of the west and a champion of Christians. To strengthen the empire and to help consolidate his power among diverse people of his empire, Constantine issued a series of decrees giving Christians the right to build churches, to accumulate property and to establish courts with jurisdiction over clergy. This marked the beginning of the institutional church.[63]

In 380 CE Emperor Theodosius declared himself a Christian of the Nicene Creed. He called the Council of Constantinople to counter the Arian and Macedonian heresies. In 391, Theodosius outlawed the pagan religions and closed the pagan temples. Severe punishments were introduced for people who disagreed with the official version of Christianity. He was angered by a riot in Thessalonica that was triggered by the arrest of a popular charioteer involved in public games, and retaliated having his soldiers kill 7,000 citizens. One of the most influential men of the 4th century was Saint Ambrose (340-397), bishop of Milan, who composed religious hymns, and wrote books on scripture, dogma and morality. Ambrose, Theodosius' spiritual advisor, required him to do penance for killings in Thessalonica, which he did. Theodosius changed the course of history in two ways, by decreeing orthodox Christianity on the empire and placing his power under the church, setting a standard for more than 1000 years.[64]

Augustine (354-430 CE), philosopher and theologian, and an important figure in the development of Western Christianity, converted to Christianity in 386 at the hands of Ambrose. Christianity had just become the state religion and Theodosius had outlawed pagan religions in the Roman Empire. Early

Christianity was primarily a religion of salvation, rather than a moral system. Augustine used his skill sets honed as a philosopher, developed before his conversion, to counter competing viewpoints. He created over 1000 pages of writing taking on competing view points to Christianity that included Greek and Roman philosophy, Manichaeism and Christian heretical viewpoints. His writings became authoritative, right into medieval times.[65]

Augustine's writing was affected by the events of his time, the crumbling empire and the apparent demise of civilization. The early Christians believed in the imminent end of this world, and put all their thoughts in the 'next' world. This is the Christian worldview of the 'second coming' through the apoplectic end of history. The arrival of the Kingdom of Heaven, an event most early Christians expected would take place in their own lifetime, would eliminate material and social forms of the old order. The need to keep holy and blameless in anticipation of Christ's imminent coming was the foremost imperative for the early Christians. The sack of Rome by the Visigoths in 410 CE brought forth criticism of the Christians. The pagan Romans claimed that the new set of values and vision of history of the Christians undermined the integrity of Roman imperial power, and thereby opened the way to the success of barbarian invasions. Augustine countered with a new version of history: all true progress was necessarily spiritual and transcended this world and its negative fate; what was important for man's welfare was not the secular empire but the Catholic Church. Because divine Providence and spiritual salvation were the ultimate factors in human existence, the significance of secular history, with its passing values and its fluctuating and generally negative progress, was accordingly diminished. The particulars and achievements of secular history were of no ultimate importance in themselves. Actions in this life were significant mainly for their afterlife consequences, divine reward or punishment. The individual soul's search for God was primary, while history and this world merely served as the stage for that drama. Escape from this world to the next, from self to God, from flesh to spirit, constituted the deepest purpose and direction of human life.[66]

On the death of Emperor Theodosius in 395, the empire was divided into Eastern and Western Empires. During the 5th century CE, there were three offices of political power interacting during the fall of the Western Roman Empire. These offices were Master of the Soldiers (the general in charge of the army), the Western Roman Emperor, and the Eastern Roman Emperor. During the 5th century CE, most of the garrison in Italy consisted of German mercenaries, and the office of Western Roman Emperor consisted of a series of weak emperors.

In 475, Oretes, Master of Soldiers, removed Julius Napos (backed by Byzantine Emperor, Leo I), and made his son Romulus Augustus, Emperor (his mother was Roman). However, the German mercenaries had been promised land in return for their support of Orestes who failed to deliver on his promises of land grants, the German soldiers, led by Flavius Odoacer, marched on Ravenna and removed Romulus Augustus. Flavius Zeno, Eastern Roman Emperor (474-491), presided over the official end of the political structures of the Western Roman Empire. Odoacer ruled Italy as an agent of the Eastern Roman emperor, Zeno. As the relationship with Zeno deteriorated, Theodoric the Great (leader of the Ostrogoths) was invited to invade Odoacer's kingdom in 488. Theodoric the Great ruled Italy from 493 to 526, also as an agent of the emperor in Constantinople.[67]

Pope Leo I, pope from 440 to 461, was known for extending the power of the church in the West. At the same time, suppression of heresies was in full force. Many Manichaeans, who had fled from the Vandals in Africa and had settled in

Rome, were persecuted as heretics and driven from Rome, under Leo's direction. The weakness of the imperial power forced the Bishop of Rome to assume defensive, financial, civil and political responsibly for the city, because the imperial government was unable to do so. In 452, Pope Leo met Attila the Hun outside the city and with persuasion and likely some gold convinced Attila not to sack Rome. In 455, Genseric, king of the Alans and Vandals, who had established a significant Mediterranean power centered in Carthage, met Pope Leo at the gates of Rome who implored them not to destroy the ancient city. Genseric agreed, the gates were thrown open and the Vandals helped themselves to gold, silver and hostages for ransom while sparing significant destruction of Rome.[68]

The reasons for the decline of the Roman Empire have been the subject of considerable debate. Weak leadership of the German mercenaries played a key role in the failure to hold back the advance of the Ostrogoths. There were other factors in play. The Justinian plague was associated with a steep decline in population followed by crop failure and severe weather. Recently weather tree ring evidence from Irish bogs indicates colder than average summers from 535 to 555. Some believe a catastrophic event triggered the weather changes that subsequently ended the classical world and brought in the Middle Ages.[69]

Christianity was the state religion of the Roman Empire and had power to suppress dissention and heretics, and organize wealth. As the state religion of the Roman Empire, the church was able to ban other translations of the Bible and to restrict it to only one language, the Latin Vulgate. This meant authorities refused to allow the scripture to be available in any language other than Latin. In Western Europe, this made the Catholic Church of Rome the only organized and recognized church at that time in history. As the seat of the empire and the site of the martyrdoms of Apostles Peter and Paul, Rome held a primacy of respect and honour throughout the church. The Bishop of Rome slowly acquired the rights to resolve disputes in other diocese, to define doctrine and to exercise administration and discipline throughout the church. In *The Passion of the Western Mind,* Richard Tarnas observed:

"The church's conception of humanity's relationship to God as a judicial one strictly defined by moral law was partly derived from Roman law, which the Catholic Church, based in Rome, inherited and integrated. The effectiveness of the Roman state's religious cult was based upon meticulous use of a multitude of regulations. More fundamentally, Roman legal theory and practice were founded on the idea of justification, transposed to the religious sphere; sin was a criminal violation of a legal relationship established by God between himself and man.... As the Christian religion evolved in the West, its Judaic foundation readily assimilated the kindred juridical and authoritarian qualities of the Roman imperial culture, and much of the Roman Church's distinctive character was molded in those terms: a powerful central hierarchy, a complex judicial structure governing ethics and spituality, the binding spiritual authority of priests and bishops, the demand for obedience from church members and its effective enforcement formalized rituals and institutionalized sacraments, a strenuous defense against any divergence from authorized dogma, a centrifugal and militant expansiveness aimed at converting and civilizing the barbarians, and so forth." [70]

With the collapse of the Western Roman Empire, the church was the only central organized force in Western Europe. Only the priests were educated to understand Latin, and this gave the church the power to rule without question. Nobody could question their 'Biblical' teaching, because few people other than priests could read Latin. Tarnas noted, "...against a growing number of sects and doctrines, leading early Christians concluded that the beliefs of the faithful must be established, disseminated, and sustained by an authoritative Church structure. Thus the institutional church, as the living embodiment of the Christian dispensation, became the official guardian of the final truth and the highest court of appeal in any manners of ambiguity – indeed, not only the court, but also the prosecuting and punitive arm of the religious law." [71]

Initially, persecution of heretics was to prevent the appearance of rival churches, but it evolved into a system to suppress any new ideas. Those who hold an opinion contrary to that which was generally accepted by the established church were known as heretics. Heretics existed from the early days of the formation of the Christian Church, but once religion became tied to the state, the church had the power to systematically persecute them. As the church grew in power and wealth, the suppression of heretics was part of maintaining the status quo. The story of the heretics is the painful history of Christians, which is important for understanding the development of individualism and today's politics.

The Dark Ages

After Theodoric the Great died in 526, his daughter ruled until her death in 535. Things changed with the accession of the new Byzantine Emperor, Justinian, who had ambitious plans. Justinian had concluded a peace treaty with the Persian Empire in 532 which allowed him to concentrate his army in the West. With the appearance of a leadership vacuum in Italy in 535, he decided to take advantage. Justinian had expended large amounts of money against the Ostogoths in Italy and the Vandals centered in Carthage. The Vandals were defeated in 533. Then the bubonic plague struck the Byzantine Empire from 541 to 542 CE, with a subsequent precipitous drop in population. This had a dramatic effect on tax collection. However, the plague weakened the Byzantine army just as they had nearly completed the invasion of Italy. The over extended troops could not hold on, and this led to a series of wars from 535 to 552 that devastated the urban society of Italy. The last Ostrogoths were removed from Italy in 552.[72]

The economic destruction of Italy was so total, that it took centuries for the cities to recover. The prolonged fighting left the Byzantine finances in ruin. Russel suggests a total European population loss of 50% to 60% from 541 to 700.[73] The pandemic did not appear again until the 14th century. The effect of the plague on the Christian Church system was the emphasis on guilt, sin, and a wrathful God. Imperial gains were fleeting. In 568, just three years after Justinian's death, the Lombards (a new German people who had crossed the Danube into the Eastern Empire when the East Goths moved into Italy) invaded Italy and gradually took over the countryside.

The Umayyad dynasty (661-750) was the second of the four Islamic caliphates established after the death of Muhammad. Damascus was the capital of their Caliphate. The Umayyads established the largest Arab-Muslim state in history, making it the largest empire the world had yet seen. They crossed Gibraltar in 711 with the conquest of the Iberian Peninsula by 719. By 719 they had taken Narbonne, the capital of the Visigoth province of Septimania (on the Mediterranean coast of present day France). They met reverses, their first defeat at the Battle of Toulouse in 721, which prevented their advances into Aquitaine. The second reverse came in 732, when Charles Martel, grandfather of Charlemagne, out maneuvered the Moors in the

Battle of Tours, defeating their heavy cavalry with an experienced infantry. Charles Martel failed to take Narbonne by siege in 737, but managed to destroy the relieving army. These events helped establish Charles Martel as the de facto leader of the Franks. The Umayyads' reign in the Middle East ended when the Abbasid caliphs chased them out of the Middle East. They moved their headquarters to Cordova, Spain and ruled southern Spain from 756 to 1031 CE.[74] Pepin III captured Narbonne in 759, bringing Narbonne into the Frankish dominions. The Umayyad Dynasty was expelled from France, driven back over the Pyrenees. The Moorish Calvary used stirrups, which were unknown to the Franks prior to Tours. After the Battle of Tours some believe there is a direct relationship to the introduction by Charles Martel and his descendants of the stirrup for cavalry to the appearance of feudalism and knights in Western Europe.[75]

In 751, Pope Stephen II asked Pepin III (father of Charlemagne) for help against the Lombard King who had captured Ravenna, the last enclave of Byzantine rule in Italy. Previously, popes had relied on the Byzantine emperors for protection and any necessary intervention. At this time, the Byzantine Empire was preoccupied with invasions from Bulgars on one front, and Muslims on another. Pepin sent in his army, and Ravenna and other conquered territories were recovered and given to the pope as the Papal States. In return, the pope declared Pepin, King of the Franks. This marked an important shift; Rome was no longer subservient to the Eastern Emperor for support.[76]

The last King of the Lombards, Desiderius, came into collision with the Papacy while trying to extend his territory. In 772 the new pope, Adrian I, implored the aide of Charlemagne (778-814) against him. Charlemagne invaded and took over the Lombard kingdom. Charlemagne restored the territories of the papal states to the pope (a band of territories across Italy). Charlemagne, as King of the Franks, was noted for expansion of territory into an empire that included much of Western and Central Europe. This included a protracted war with the Saxons, bringing them into his realm and forcibly converting them to Christianity. He expanded Christianity by bring monks from Ireland and England to improve the schools and monasteries of his dominions resulting in educated clerics who could connect with the papacy. He standardized schools, monasteries and writing – his many battles resulted in a consolidation of Christian Europe. Charlemagne began the Reconquista, establishing the Spanish Marsh south of the Pyrenees, forming a buffer zone against the Moors' lands across the Pyrenees. His actions were a forerunner to the religious wars that bloodied Europe and Asia for centuries in the future.[77]

The next leader in Western Europe with enough power and authority to be considered the successor to Charlemagne's heirs was the Saxon, Otto I, who had come to power in 938 as the Holy Roman Emperor. Otto supported the church, using it as a unifying force in his German territories. Through the German Church he was aligned with the rich and powerful bishops and abbeys. A rich silver mine was discovered in Saxony during his reign, which provided resources for his campaigns. These mines provided much of Europe with silver, copper and lead for the next 200 years. The time of Pope John XII was a low point in the organization of the papacy. Pope John II, fearing Berenger II of Italy and the plots of the Roman aristocracy, invited Otto to Italy to intervene. Otto obliged and for his efforts was crowned Holy Roman Emperor. This action joined the affairs of Italy and Germany for centuries.[78]

The Eleventh Century

The destruction of the barbaric invasion was not as bad in Tuscany as in the rest of Italy. This was a major factor leading to the pre-eminence of the Tuscan cities (Lucca, Pisa, Siena and Florence) during the Middle Ages. During the barbarian invasions, the people in the province of Venetia established their city on marshy islands separated by canals. The barbarians left them alone and they stopped farming and became great traders. In 1002, Venice won a great victory over a Muslim fleet and this enhanced Venetian trade with Byzantium.[79]

This period was also the medieval high point for Islamic science, technology and literature. In 1086 the Moorish princes invited the Almoravid Empire in Africa to help defend them against Alfonso VI (1040-1109), King of Castile and Leon. Their leader, Yusuf ibn Tashfin defeated Alfonso's army at the Battle of Sagrajas in 1086, and immediately after the battle, Ibn Tashfin returned to Africa because of the death of his heir. Castile retained Toledo, which they had won the year before, while Christian advances were halted for several generations.[80]

By the 11th century, the Viking raids had ended and they had settled in Normandy, Sicily and England. Normandy was created in 912 when a deal was struck between the French king and the Viking settlements in northwest France. The French recognized Viking possession of the area, and made Rollo, their leader, a French noble. In return, the Viking duke converted to Christianity, acknowledged the French king as his overlord, and protected France from other Viking raids. With the death of Edward the Confessor, of England, in 1066, there were three claimants to the throne. The English noble, Harold, defeated the invading army of the King of Norway. But later that year, he was defeated at the Battle of Hastings by William, Duke of Normandy. The Normans took control of England and set up a system that would develop into a strong monarchy. In 1046 the Normans moved into Sicily, encouraged to come by the pope to help control the Muslims in southern Italy. By 1053 they had taken over Sicily and the southern part of Italy, and in 1059, they took Messina,

Bari, Palermo and Salerno from the Byzantines. With a population of 300,000, Palermo was one of the most important ports of trade between East and West. This began a 100-year Norman occupation of enlightenment and learning during which art flourished. The court in Palermo became known for its support of philosophy and translations of Greek classics, and became an important source of learning for Western Europe.[81]

The Holy Roman Emperors were a significant force in Europe during the 11th century. Henry II, Holy Roman Emperor from 1014 to 1024, the last of the Saxon (Ottonian) Dynasty, lead three campaigns by invitation of the church to support stability in Italy. During the Salian Dynasty (1024-1125), there was a significant shift in the political climate. The Holy Roman Emperor went from a staunch ally to bitter rival of the pope. Henry IV, the third emperor of the Salian Dynasty, quarreled with Pope Gregory VII over investiture (the control of appointment of church officials). The emperor controlled the appointment of bishops and abbots, which were a significant source of revenue as these positions were available upon payment of money. Gregory VII considered restoring the power of investiture to the church an important area of 'reform' and the quarrel lead to the undercutting of the imperial power of the Salian dynasty in Germany. In 1076, the German king, Henry IV, called a council, which deposed Pope Gregory VII and referred to him as a 'false monk.' Pope Gregory responded by excommunicating the king, removing him from the church and deposing him as German king. Gregory released Henry's subjects from their oaths of allegiance to him, and Gregory used the fact that Pope Zacharias had given permission to Pepin to depose the last of the Merovingian kings (Clideric III) precedence for the notion popes can depose sovereigns. This controversy with the papacy stirred up revolt in Germany and created a climate of civil war for fifty years. These activities laid the groundwork for the strong papacy that appeared during the following two centuries and the subsequent increasing involvement of the papacy in the secular affairs of Europe. It set in motion the events that lead to the disintegration of Germany as a country.[82]

The Eastern and Western churches gradually grew apart. Theodosius the Great was the last to rule over a United Roman Empire. On his death in 395, the empire was divided again into western and eastern empires which led to a Latin/Greek linguistic split. The precipitating event occurred with Pope Leo IX claiming authority of the four eastern patriarchs with respect to insertion of the filioque clause (a combination of Latin words meaning "and from the son" added by the Third Council of Toledo in 589 that the Eastern Church did not accept) into the Nicene Creed by the Western Church.[83] The disagreement led to the excommunication of the Patriarch of Constantinople by the pope in 1054. This event triggered the Great Schism. On another front, a group of Turkish tribes, the Seljuk Turks, came out of central Asia and captured Baghdad in 1055. They made the caliph their nominal leader – the caliph made their leader his deputy. They conquered Armenia, then struck at Byzantine power in Asia Minor. In 1071, the Byzantine army was defeated at the Battle of Melasgrid, and the Turks overran the Byzantine lands in Asia. The Byzantine emperor, Michael VII wrote to Pope Gregory VII appealing for aide, but Gregory VII was involved with the Investiture Controversy and unable to call on the Holy Roman Emperor. Michael VII's successor, Alexius I Comnenus, wrote more urgently to Pope Urban II for help. Urban II saw this as an opportunity of reassuring the supremacy of the Latin Church over the Greek Church and of resolving their differences around the Great Schism.[84]

6

The Medieval Church

The Crusades

The Crusades were a series of military campaigns usually promoted by the pope, waged by Christian Europe against external and internal opponents. While the Crusades were fought mainly against Muslims, they were also against Christian heretics and enemies of the pope. The First Crusade, called by Urban II in 1095, in a "most moving sermon" to the faithful asked the nobles of Europe to stop fighting amongst themselves and take up the fight with the Turks in the East. If they were to lose their lives, they would receive immediate remission of their sins. The First Crusade (1095-1099) established four Crusader states. The Crusaders used the Christian cross as a symbol, and became known as the 'War of the Cross.'[85]

The Second Crusade, announced by Pope Eugene III in 1145, was in response to the fall of one of the Crusader states (the County of Odessa) to the Muslims the year before. The only success of this crusade was the liberation of Lisbon in 1147 from Crusaders heading to the Mediterranean via the Atlantic. The Third Crusade was caused by the capture of Jerusalem in 1187 by Saladin, the sultan of Egypt. This crusade involved Richard the Lion Heart who was a strong soldier, as well as a capable negotiator and Philip-August of France. Richard sold the northern counties of England to Scotland in order to raise money for the crusade. Philip-August's planning included writing his will and designating the treasurer of the Knights Templar as executor. The royal income during his absence went directly to the Templars. While Jerusalem was not captured, agreements allowed Christian pilgrims to visit. This crusade saved the principality of Antioch, and Christians remained in possession of the seacoast of Palestine.

The Fourth Crusade had as its goal the liberation of Jerusalem. The Italian Count Boniface of Montferrat in 1200 negotiated with the Dodge of Venice to transport the crusaders to Egypt. Support for the action fell short, resulting in a shortfall in monies to pay the Venetians. Boniface struck a deal with Alexius IV Angelus, the son of the recently deposed Emperor Isaac II Angelus, whereby Alexius offered to reunite the Byzantine Church with Rome, pay the crusaders an enormous sum, and join the crusade to Egypt with a large army, if the Crusaders would sail to Constantinople to restore his throne. The crusaders succeeded in taking Constantinople but Alexius failed to raise the moneys required to meet his promises, so the Latins took over Constantinople. The crusaders never attacked Egypt as planned.

The Albigensian Crusade or Cathar Crusade (1209-1229) was a twenty year military campaign initiated by the Roman Catholic Church to eliminate the religion practiced by the Cathars of Languedoc, which the Roman Catholic hierarchy considered heretical. This was the first time a crusade was called against dissidents who called themselves Christian. The Languedoc area was one of the more urbanized areas of Europe at the time. The northern French called the Cathars 'Albigensians' because of the strong representation of the belief's adherents in the town of Albi.[86]

During this time, the Inquisition had come of age. The violence inflicted was extreme; the church offered legally sanctioned dominion over conquered lands to northern French nobles and the King of France, acting as essentially Catholic mercenaries, who then acquired the region for France, which at the time had closer cultural and language ties to northern Spain. This offer enticed many knights from far who needed, or merely sought, more land. Simon de Montfort, 5th Earl of Leicester (1160- 1218) who had participated in the Fourth Crusade (1202 -1204), was made Captain General of the French forces in the Albigensian Crusade. Simon was rewarded with the territories of Raymond IV of Toulouse. Known for his treachery and harshness in dealing with the Cathars, by 1229 the area had been seized, and the Inquisition was used to crush the remaining Cathar resistance.

Waldo (1181-1226) preceded Saint Francis in adopting a life of poverty to be free to preach. He gathered a group known as the 'poor men of Lyons', and the Waldensian movement spread quickly. 'Waldenses' was the name given to heretical Christians in the south of France about 1170. The difference was that the Waldenses preached the doctrine of Christ while the Franciscans preached the person of Christ. His beliefs were founded on the Bible, especially the gospels, which he thought so self-explanatory they needed no interpretation. He thought all that was needed was to make the Bible available to the people, so he commissioned two priests to translate the Bible into Provençal, starting with the gospels.[87]

In 1184, Pope Lucius III (1181-1185) excommunicated Waldo and all his followers, and they were driven from Lyons to the high valleys of the Piedmont and the southeast of France. The Synod of Verona declared groups that included the Cathars and Waldenses as heretics and formally started the Inquisition administered by local bishops. Innocent III preached a crusade against them in 1208. In 1211, more than eighty Waldenses were burned for heresy. This was the beginning of centuries of persecution. In spite of this, somehow the itinerant Waldensian preachers were able to maintain links throughout Europe, by going underground and withdrawing to other countries, especially Italy, Switzerland, and Austria. These valleys were too inaccessible for the inquisitors, and Waldenses took refuge there. It became the center of their religion. As late as 1487, Pope Innocent VIII issued a Bull for their extermination.

The Fifth Crusade (1217-1221) was an attempt to take back Jerusalem by attacking Egypt. It failed. The Sixth Crusade seven years later involved Frederick II of the Holy Roman Empire. Frederick II (1138-1254), from the House of Hohenstaufen, was Holy Roman Emperor from 1220 until his death in 1250. Frederick II was considered one of the foremost European Christian monarchs of the Middle Ages, ruling from Palermo, the capital of his lands. He spoke six languages and was a patron of the arts and science. Upon being crowned Holy Roman Emperor, he agreed to lead a crusade. There was controversy that he was delaying the crusade and as a consequence, the pope excommunicated him. The successes of the Sixth Crusade were due to Frederick's negotiations with the Sultan Malik al-Kamil of Egypt. Christians gained access to Jerusalem; it was the most successful crusade since the First Crusade. It was a bittersweet victory, as he did not have the blessing of the pope.[88]

The Seventh Crusade, lead by Louis IX of France, from 1248 to 1254, attacked Egypt. In 1250 Louis was captured by the Muslims and ransomed for 400,000 livres. The Templars paid part of it. The Pope allowed him to tax the church (an ecclesiastical tenth, mostly from church tithes) to pay for the crusades. Louis returned to France without accomplishing his goal.

The Eighth Crusade was a crusade launched by Louis IX of France (who was by now in his mid-fifties) in 1270. Louis landed in Africa in 1270, and participated in the siege of Tunis. There was much illness within the armies and Louis died. In the agreement of withdrawal, the Christians gained free trade with Tunis, and residence for monks and priests in the city was guaranteed so that the Crusade could be considered a partial success. The attack on Tunis had been called off by the time Edward of England arrived. He continued on to Acre, the last crusader outpost in Syria. Philip III, son of Louis IX, tried to launch another crusade – the Aragonese Crusade. It was a disaster. Philip III died and this Crusade left France with considerable debt. Philip IV became king of France in 1285 at the age of seventeen, inheriting this enormous debt.[89]

In 1190, a field hospital was founded by support from German merchants for the duration of the siege of Acre. Pope Celestine II recognized the order in 1192, granting them Monk Augustine Rule. Modeled after the Knights Templar; it transformed into a military order known as the Teutonic Knights. In 1226, Konrad I, Duke of Masovia in west-central Poland, appealed to the knights to defend his borders against the pagan Prussians. The knights agreed as this was considered good training ground for knights to gain experience for the fight against Muslims in the Holy Land. Emperor Frederick II, with the Golden Bull of Rimini, gave the order special imperial privileges to conquer Prussia. Following fifty years of bloody fighting, the Teutonic Knights conquered Prussia. With the fall of the Kingdom of Jerusalem in 1291, they directed an increased program against pagan Lithuania. Knights from England and France journeyed to Prussia to participate in the seasonal campaigns against the Grand Duchy of Lithuania.[90]

In 1386, Grand Duke Jogailia of Lithuania was baptized into the Roman Catholic Church (and married Queen Jadwiga of Poland) becoming the King of Poland. The crusading rational for the Order of Teutonic Knights ended when Prussia and Lithuania became officially Christian, however, the Order's feuds with Lithuania and Poland continued. During the first two decades of the 15th century Lithuania-Poland grew stronger, while the Teutonic Knights grew weaker. By 1425, Prussia was lost and all that remained in the control of the Teutonic Knights were scattered territories in the Holy Roman Empire.

In 1382 Richard II married Ann of Bohemia, which brought to the English court couriers from Bohemia. Knowledge of Wycliffe's writings spread to Bohemia, and Jan Hus, initially began to study Wycliffe's works in order to refute them. Soon, however, he accepted Wycliffe's ideas, challenged the tradition of providing the mass in Latin and began to preach in the vernacular to the people. He translated many of Wycliffe's works into Bohemian. The archbishop of Prague was unable to control the ideas of Hus, so the Council of Constance responded to the challenge by burning Jan Hus at the stake in 1415, and John of Prague the following year. These deaths triggered a five year war of rebellion against the Roman Church by the Hussite movement. There was an uprising in 1420 and Martin V, the new pope, proclaimed a crusade against the Hussites. In the ensuing engagements, the Imperial armies were repeatedly defeated. Both sides finally came to terms in 1433 with the Compacts of Prague, which established a state Bohemian church.[91]

For the most part, the crusades were a series of wars taken by Christians between the 11th and 14th centuries to recover the Holy Land from the Muslims. In fact, various popes called for crusades against Christians who had been declared heretics. One significant consequence was the crusades allowed Western Europe to control the Mediterranean – Black Sea trade routes. This allowed trade and the economy of Europe to advance.

The Knights Templar

The Knights Templar were founded in 1118, as an aftermath of the First Crusade in 1096. By the 1140's, the Templar knights appeared with short-cropped hair, bearded, and in white garb emblazoned with eight point red crosses. As many other religious orders, the Templars acted as bankers from the very beginning.[92] It was normal at that time for peasants to entrust their money and properties to churches and abbeys to benefit from the 'Protection du Dieu' given to these houses. Some people gave themselves and all their properties to a religious house in exchange for protection and security. In addition, other people deposited their movable properties, money and jewels with the same religious houses without losing ownership. The then treasury of churches and abbeys were the equivalent of present day bank strong boxes. The valuables were in this way under the protection of trusted persons, always present and in a place untouchable according to the common view. In the case of the Templars, having houses in many places, this depository function helped the pilgrims who could cash money in the Middle East against a proof of deposit in Europe. This was a kind of checking account, as we know them now. The Templars were also able to transfer money and valuables in their own boats more safely than an ordinary man or knight could do.[93]

The double aspect of the Order – military and religious – gave a guarantee of safety to the customers. In addition to money, jewels and other valuables, the Templars were also the custodians of the standard weights. They offered guard and caution in many fields. For instance, many pilgrims deposited their fortune with the Templars to be transferred to their heirs in case of death during the trip. In 1135, the Templars were lending money to Spanish pilgrims going to the Holy Land.

Their immense resources allowed them to lend money on a large scale, in particular in the Middle East. They played an important role in financing the crusades and all the needs of the Holy Land. Among their numerous customers were the Italian traders present everywhere in Palestine and in the commercial fairs of Champagne, Flanders and the north of France. The Paris Temple became the depository of the royal treasure of France and remained such until the end of the 13th century. It was transferred to the Louvre under Philip IV for a while and then came back to the Templars in 1303. The King had an open account that he used for his needs and those of the administration of the kingdom.[94]

In 1307 the Muslims drove the crusaders from the Middle East. As one of the defenders, the Templars took much of the blame for the fall. Philip IV, King of France from 1285 to 1314 was a cold and calculating person in need of money to build his country. Determined to strengthen the monarchy at any cost, he developed a professional bureaucracy of legalists to help justify his actions, and his quest for money led to the persecution of groups such as Jews, Lombard bankers and the Templars. He first went after the Jews and the Italian bankers (Lombards). He expelled the Jews from France after systematically extracting money from them. He recalled the coinage, had it melted down and replaced with coins of lesser value. (This was one of the first recorded examples of debasing currency.) He needed the help of the church to bring down the Templars. It is generally agreed that Philip was motivated by his quest for money, as he was hugely in debt, rather than his belief that the Templars were corrupt.

As the Templars were free of all authority save for that of the papacy, the only way Philip could lawfully seize Templar assets was to accuse them of magic and heresy, which he did through his right hand man, Guillaume de Nogaret, King Philip's chancellor. Philip tried to get Pope Boniface VIII to excommunicate the Templars but was refused. Philip sent his agent, Guillaume de Nogaret, to 'persuade' the Pope who refused, but who later died of wounds inflicted at the hands of de Nogaret and his agents. The next pope, Benedict XI, lifted the excommunication of Philip IV from Pope Boniface, but refused to absolve his agent de Nogaret. He refused to cooperate on the Templars and died in 1304 after only eight months as pope.

Clement V was elected pope in 1305 after an interregnum of a year because of disputes (between French and Italian cardinals who were nearly equally[95] balanced) in conclave. His first action was to add nine more French cardinals. In 1306 Clement V removed the bulls of Boniface VIII, which were particularly offensive to Philip IV.

Philip IV's agents pressed charges of improper conduct and heresy against the Templars. The Order had become corrupt and greedy and increasingly unpopular, and the West had lost interest in the crusades. When Philip IV attacked the Order, no one came forward to defend it. On Friday 13, 1307 (the real reason the day carries bad luck) hundreds of Templars in France were arrested on a variety of charges and accusations. The trials of the Templars lasted from that date through until March 19, 1314. On March 18, 1314, Jacques de Molay, last Grand Master of Knights Templar died, burnt at the stake. Allegedly, as he was dying, he placed a curse on Philip and Clement that they would be dead within the year. On April 20, 1314, Pope Clement V died. On November 29, 1314 Philip IV died following a hunting accident.[96] With these events the legend of the Templar secret power remained intact.

The Weakened Church

Pope Gregory VII laid the groundwork for a strong papal monarchy throughout medieval Europe. Gregory VII allied himself with the reformers attacking simony, the selling of ecclesiastical offices, and married clergy. He had a long-standing quarrel with Henry IV (King of the Germans from 1056, Holy Roman Emperor 1084-1105) over lay investitures, the right of lay rulers to grant church officials the symbols of their authority. His excommunication of Henry IV led to the king asking for the pope's forgiveness as he faced revolt from the German princes. Gregory VII used papal legates for business and insisted on their precedence over local bishops. The setting up of Latin kingdoms in Syria and the Holy Land in religious communion with Rome, and the conquest of Constantinople during the Fourth Crusade, expanded the influence of the church in the eastern Mediterranean. By the 13th century, the control of the Roman Catholic Church was wide spread in Europe – with Constantinople in Latin hands (from 1204-1261), from Bulgaria to Ireland, from Norway to Sicily and Jerusalem, the pope was supreme.

The papal monarchy reached its height under the pontificate of Innocent III (1198 -1216). By means of interdict, Innocent compelled Philip Augustus to take back his wife that he had repudiated. Similarly, he forced King John to recognize England and Ireland as fiefs of the pope. After the death of Henry VI (Holy Roman Emperor) in 1197, Innocent became the tutor and sponsor of Frederick II of Sicily, allowing him to reassert papal power in Sicily. He sponsored the Fourth Crusade

(1198) and the Albigensian Crusade. He convoked the Fourth Lateran Council, considered the most important council of the Middle Ages. This council commented on such things as the requirement that every individual must make an oral confession of his sins to a priest at least once a year, and then undergo the punishment imposed before becoming eligible to partake of the Eucharist, and enforced the decree of duty of bishops to search out heretics in their dioceses and hand them over to the secular power.[97]

Innocent III sent numerous preaching missions to the Cathars, not only including the likes of St. Bernard, but also St. Dominic, who tried to counter the Cathars with his own band of followers who adopted a life of simplicity and poverty that the Albigenses and Waldenses practiced. Saint Dominic founded the Dominicans in 1215 during his preaching tours against the Albigenses in southern France. The Dominicans were friars, receiving rigorous theological training in order to preach and answer objection against the Christian faith. They were founded with the purpose of counteracting, by means of preaching, teaching and example of austerity, heretics present at the time. The first House of Friars was established in Toulouse, in the heart of Cathar lands. The Dominicans were closely associated with the development of Scholasticism during the 13th century. They became prominent teachers in the great universities of Europe. The Dominicans, known as dedicated preachers and combatants against any departure of the teachings of the Roman Catholic Church, went on to play a significant role in supervision of the Inquisition.[98]

As H.G. Wells notes: "while in the time Urban the power of faith was strong in all Christian Europe, in the time of Innocent III, the papacy had lost its hold on the hearts of princes, and the faith and conscience of the common people were turning against a merely political and aggressive church."[99]

Boniface VIII who was pope from 1294-1303, proclaimed that it "is absolutely necessary for salvation that every human creature be subject to the Roman pontiff", pushing papal supremacy to its historical extreme.[100] These views and his intervention in 'temporal' affairs led to many bitter quarrels with Emperor Albert I of Hapsburgs, the Colonnas (Roman aristocrats) and Philip IV of France (1285–1314). Boniface VIII clashed with Philip IV of France who demanded a new tax on ecclesiastical revenues. Philip IV desired these funds for his debt relief. Philip's agents attacked Boniface who died shortly after. This event led to considerable erosion of the Church's prestige.

In 1305, Clement V became pope with the support of Philip IV. In 1309, under Clement V, the entire Papal Court settled in Avignon (an enclave surrounded by French territory). This was justified at the time by French apologists on the grounds of security, with much fighting and unrest amongst the Roman aristocrats. This marked the beginning of the Avignon Papacy or in Petrarch's words, "Babylonian Captivity" (1309 -1377). During this time the papacy's reputation suffered. The Pope was considered a puppet of the French government, unable to stop the Hundred Years War between France and England. In addition, the church suffered because it was unable to provide sacraments necessary for salvation for the many dead during the Black Death.[101]

In 1310, John XXII was called from Naples to Avignon to advise on the affairs of the Templars and condemn the memory of Boniface VIII. After becoming Pope in 1316, he involved the papacy in politics and religious movements. He developed prescriptive rules for benefices that would provide more funds for the central church. He burdened Christianity with new taxes and future irritants and upheld the absolute religious power of the papacy. In 1323, he forbade recognition of Louis IV of Bavaria as Holy Roman Emperor. His attacks on the writings of Marsilius of Padua and William of Ockham drove these two thinkers to the court of Louis IV for support.

The power of the Roman Catholic Church was based in part on the ability of the church to enforce the use of Latin as the language of the worship of God. As long as the church could maintain this link, and as long as it controlled who learned to speak and write Latin, the church could maintain its position in the world. With Latin as the only language for religious texts, the priest represented the only true path to God and the only way to salvation. Through that link, the church maintained its political power in the world.

Johannes Gutenburg introduced his revolutionary moveable type printing press in 1440 in Mainz. Printing spread rapidly from Gutenberg's print shop in Mainz.[102] One event, which facilitated the spread, was an attack on Mainz by the soldiers of the Archbishop of Mainz in 1462, to destroy the town. However, by sending soldiers into Mainz, the Archbishop forced the printers to flee, taking their newfound skills with them and hastening the spread of printing throughout Europe. By the year 1500, just sixty years after its invention, printing had become established in more than 250 cities on the continent. The first printing press in England was established in 1477, and London soon became one of the most important centres for printers. William Claxton learned the trade in Europe and set up his press in Westminster. His first book printed in England was *Dictes or Sayengis of the Philosophirs.*[103] Gutenberg's machine brought down the cost of printing dramatically, and enabled the free exchange of ideas and the spread of knowledge – themes that helped define Renaissance Europe. It was no longer necessary for written material to be copied laboriously by hand, and no longer could the clergy, who had been occupied in this copying process for a thousand years, claim a monopoly on written information. As a direct result of the loss of the monopoly, the church was destined to lose yet more of its grip on power.

7

Humanism

The Averroists

The Moors began their invasion of Portugal and Spain in 711 and quickly subdued most of the Gothic kingdom. Islamic Spain was known as Al-Andalus. Until 756 Al-Andalus was ruled from Damascus, and afterward Spain became an independent Muslim state under the last remaining member of the Umayyad Dynasty. From 756 to 1031 the Umayyad rulers, located in the capital of Cordova, made many cultural and economic advances. Waterpower was harnessed to drive mills, and new crops, such as rice and sugar cane, were introduced. Other new important products included wine, olive oil, leather goods, weapons, glass works and tapestries. The Muslims of Spain were the most cultured peoples of Western Europe and scholars from northern Europe flocked to Cordova to study.[104]

Al-Andalus became one of the great Muslim civilizations reaching its summit with the Umayyad caliphate of Cordova by the tenth century. In 10th century Cordoba, the capital of Umayyad Spain was a leading city of wealth and arts of civilization, not only in the Islamic world but also in the Christian lands of the West. It was an intellectual centre boasting seventy libraries. Cordova rivaled Constantinople as the largest city of Europe. This rich and sophisticated society took a tolerant view towards other faiths. This was at a time when tolerance was unheard of in the rest of Europe. It was Cordova's civilization that enlightened Europe and played an important role in bringing it out of the Dark Age.

Averroës (Ibn Rushd, 1126-1189), a Muslim scholar born in Cordova, wrote commentaries on Aristotle, likely based on Syriac and Arabic translations. His major work consisted of interpretation of Aristotle and his reconciliation of Aristotelianism and Islamic faith. His work started to spread across Europe after 1230 and European philosophers applied these ideas from Aristotle's writings to Christian theology. These philosophers were labeled Averroists. Averroist attempts to harmonize religion and philosophy led to accusations of accepting the doctrine of 'double truth', that something can be true in philosophy according to reason, while its opposite is true in theology according to faith. In the late 13th century, these ideas came under systematic attack from the established church. From the 13th to 17th centuries, scholars read Aristotle with Averroës' commentaries.[105]

Marsilius of Padua (1270-1342) studied in Paris and was a contemporary of the leading Averroists, Peter of Albano and John of Jandun. He wrote the book, *Defensor paci*, published in 1324, considered the most important political treatise written in the late Middle Ages. He attacked many of the arguments used to support the political and temporal authority of the papacy, his message that all power is derived from the people, and their ruler is the only delegate. The church should be under the ruler, its only providence being worship. His contemporaries who supported the Catholic Church fiercely rebutted this thought. After 1326, when John XXII in Avignon criticized his work, he left for Bavaria under the patronage of Louis IV, the pope's main enemy. There he worked on papers that declared John XXII a heretic. Two centuries later Luther was accused of resurrecting Marsilius' ideas. Thomas Cramer became a champion and had the book translated into English to be studied when constituting the English Church during the reign of Henry VIII.[106]

Dante Alighieri (1265-1321), a Florentine poet, wrote *De Monarchia*, an anti-papalist and secularist thesis based on Averroës' theory of the 'possible' intellect. His writing supported the restoration of Imperial rule in Italy. This book was associated in time with Pope Boniface VIII issuing his famous Bull, *Unum Sanctum*, which advanced the broadest claims to the supremacy of the church over temporal authority, particularly over the Holy Roman Empire. He participated in the turbulent politics of Florence serving as a member of the governing council. When the White Guelph's lost power to the Black Guelph's (Papal Party), Dante spent the last two decades of his life in exile. In 1327, Dante's work was condemned as Averroist and *De Monarchia* was burnt at the public square in Bologna by order of John XXII. His greatest work, *The Devine Comedy*, is considered the greatest literacy statement produced in Europe in the Medieval Period, and the basis of the modern Italian language.[107]

William Ockham, born in Surrey, England, entered the Franciscan order and studied and taught at the University of Oxford from 1309 to 1319. He challenged the Dominican school. He was a critic of scholastic philosophical position, as their theories grew more and more elaborate, without corresponding increase in predictive power. He is famous for the principle of parsimony– "entities are not to be multiplied beyond necessity". He applied this principle to scholastics defending the church dogma and concluded theology was not a science and should be separated from philosophy (the established knowledge of his day). He went to France to answer charges of heretical doctrine and was held in house detention for four years (1324-28) at the papal palace in Avignon while the orthodoxy of his writings was examined.[108]

While in Avignon, Ockham reviewed the dispute against the pope over Franciscan poverty and came down on the side of the Franciscan general. He fled with the general to Munich in 1328 to seek the protection of Louis IV, Holy Roman Emperor, who had rejected papal authority over political matters. One of Ockham's writings declared: "A Christian is not bound to believe, as necessary to salvation, anything which is not contained in the Bible, nor be plainly and of necessity inferred from what is contained there." Martin Luther took this concept to the next level.[109]

The Council of Toulouse forbade the laity to read vernacular translations of the Bible. John Wycliffe, an Oxford scholar, translated the Latin Vulgate into English so that the ordinary person was able to hear Christ's teachings of equality and love. In 1376 he wrote *Civil Dominions*, calling for reform in the church. He advocated a church dedicated to simple charitable life without wealth. In 1377 Pope Gregory XI condemned the writings of John Wycliffe and ordered him seized and imprisoned. The order was ignored as John of Gaunt protected Wycliffe with the death of Gregory XI in March 1378, and interest of Wycliffe in Rome waned.

In 1378 the Papacy returned to Rome. With the death of Gregory XI, two popes were eventually elected, one in Rome and one in Avignon. Urban VI was elected pope (1378-1389) in Rome, and was recognized by England, Scandinavia, Germany and northern Italy. This was followed shortly by a dispute and Clement VII was elected pope at Avignon (1378 -1394). Clement was the leader for France, Scotland, Naples, Sicily and the kingdoms in Spain. This was the start of the Western Schism and contributed to considerable weakening of the church. During this time John Wycliffe was ignored. When Wycliffe died in 1384 his work was carried on throughout England by the Lollards. The Lollards operated without interference from the crown until the death of Richard II in 1399.[110]

The new king of England, Henry IV found the church in conflict, as the Lollards had sympathy at the previous court and continued support from some knights of the realm. The king attacked the Lollards accused of heresy. He issued *De Haevetico Comburendo* making it legal to burn heretics at the stake. Also, he decreed it illegal to preach without a license from the bishop of a diocese, and preach, teach or write a book contrary to Catholic faith or the Holy Church. In 1401 the burnings began.

In 1417, Henry V of England came to power with plans to ready his country for the upcoming fight with France. To settle religious discontent and threat of rebellion, the Lollard leader, Sir John Oldcastle, was executed. In his other government reforms he ordered all government documents to be written in the vernacular English. While the ruling classes had used Latin and French for centuries, he encouraged cross-class use of English. He was the first king to use English in his personal correspondence since the Norman conquest, which occurred 350 years earlier.[111]

From 1378 to 1409, there were two popes. In 1409 there were three popes, and one of them sold indulgences in Prague to finance his campaign against the other two. The Council of

Constance (1414-1417) was called by Sigismund, Holy Roman Emperor, mainly to resolve the challenge of the three popes, and to deliberate on other manners important to the church. The three popes were deposed and a new pope, Martin V was elected. The Council invited Jan Hus, the accused, to defend his thoughts. In 1415, Hus was burnt at the stake as a heretic and his ashes thrown into the Rhine River. The Council also called for Wycliffe's bones to be burnt. In 1428 Monks dug up the bones of John Wycliffe, had them burned, and threw the ashes into the River Swift. This was to ensure that there would be no relics from these two heretics.[112]

The death of Jan Hus and John of Prague the following year, triggered a five year war of rebellion against the Roman Catholic Church by the Hussite movement. This was aggravated by anti-German sentiment and move by Sigismund, to press his claim to the throne of Bohemia with the death of his half-brother, Wenceslas IV(whose sister had married Richard II of England), in 1419. There was an uprising in 1420 and Pope Martin V proclaimed a crusade against the Hussites. In the ensuing engagements the Imperial armies were repeatedly defeated. Both sides finally came to terms in 1433 with the Compacts of Prague, which established a state Bohemian church. The terms granted a degree of ecclesiastical freedom that included allowing the conduct of services in Czech rather than Latin, permission to give sacrament with both wine and bread, a clergy committed to poverty together with expropriation of church property in their territories (to meet requirements for poverty), and an independent church under an elected archbishop.[113]

The Fifth Ecumenical Lateran Council was called by Pope Julius II and sat for twelve sessions from 1512 to 1517. The last seven sessions of the council were presided over by Leo X. One hundred and twenty Bishops and representatives of Kings and

Princes met to consider challenges facing the Roman Catholic Church. The sessions made declarations on many issues that included money, power sharing, book publishing and condemning a philosophical standpoint. Specific decisions included such things as provisions to raise money to fight the Turks and abolishing the Pragmatic Sanction in France (which had limited the authority of the pope over the church within France) and a decree legalizing the charitable pawnshops the Franciscans had been establishing. The council ratified the censorship of books introduced earlier by Alexander VI, and condemned the Averroist philosophy of Neo-Aristotelians. Martin Luther's promulgation of the ninety-five theses occurred just seven months after the close of the Council.[114]

Humanism

Humanism was the philosophical backbone of the Renaissance, emphasizing the potential for individual achievement and stipulating that humans were rational beings capable of truth and goodness. All humanist movements had the study of the classical literature as well as the learning of Greek and Latin in common. The guiding principal of the humanist is *"Ad Fontes!"* – back to the source – back mainly to the Greek writings from the classical period. Works by classical authors, lost to the West for centuries, were rediscovered, and with them a new, humanist outlook that placed man and human achievement at the centre of all things. Renaissance scholars celebrated the works of the ancient Greeks and Romans for their own sake, rather than for their relevance to church doctrine.[115]

In the 14th century, three Italian writers, Dante, Petrarch and Boccaccio, were important in setting up the climate for humanism. Petrarch (1304-1374) had an inquiring mind and love of classical authors leading him to travel, visit men of learning and search for classical manuscripts. This earned him the support of powerful men of the time. These thinkers expressed an interest in individuality and believed the height of human accomplishment had been reached in the Roman Empire, and since that age there had been social decline. In his writing he studied human thought and actions. As a devout Christian he did not see a conflict between realizing humanity's potential and having religious faith.[116]

Boccaccio (1313-1375), a friend and correspondent of Petrarch, was an author and a poet who inspired humanist philosophy. He lived through the plague as it ravaged the city of Florence. The uncertainty of daily survival during this time created a general mood of morbidity, influencing people to 'live for the moment'. His book, *Decameron*, used the appearance of the Black Death in Florence as the setting for the story. In the introduction to the book he gave a graphic description of the effects of the epidemic on his city. His writings shifted focus from God and the afterlife to the 'here and now'. He emphasized enjoyment of the present moment and solving problems of the human condition. He wrote in the vernacular, and he, along with Dante and Petrarch, was the reason the Tuscan dialect was to become the official language of Italy.[117]

As a member of the king's household, Geoffrey Chaucer was sent on diplomatic errands throughout Europe. Chaucer (1340-1400), while on a diplomatic mission to Italy in 1372, came under the influence of Dante and Boccaccio, and wrote in the vernacular English rather than French or Latin. His masterpiece was *Canterbury Tales*. In 1476, when William Claxton set up the first printing press in England, one of the 96 books he printed was *Canterbury Tales*.[118]

The centre of gravity through out the Renaissance was Florence. It was here that the rulers both hidden and explicitly, sought to glorify their wealth and power by subsidizing literature, philosophy and science, architecture and the arts. It is an old given in Renaissance studies that the phenomenal growth of wealth in these small city states was directly responsible for the flowering of literature, scholarship and the other arts during the Italian Renaissance as the aristocracy and the powerful sought to praise and legitimate their power by patronizing the arts and scholarship.

Italian humanists saw Roman history as a glorious episode in their nationalist past. Many turned to Plato, rather that his pupil Aristotle. Northern Europeans did not identify as strongly with Rome, and retained stronger ties to Christianity (than Italy). Northern humanists were less hostile to scholasticism. These Christian humanists studied the Bible directly and also read biblical texts in the original Greek and Hebrew. Their work in translating and analyzing original sources often uncovered discrepancies among these sources, which led to questions about the Catholic Church's practice and encouraged efforts for reform. Humanists inspired the spirit of questioning and skepticism that characterized the Reformation.

Desiderius Erasmus (1466-1536), born in Rotterdam, made a Latin translation of the New Testament from the original Greek. He condemned overly rigid belief systems, favouring flexibility and tolerance. Erasmus advocated a tolerant Christianity and was highly critical of the abuses of the Catholic Church, and his ideas helped to prepare the way for Martin Luther and the Protestant Reformation. However, Erasmus disapproved of Luther's radical methods and criticized him in his book *De Libero Arbitrio* (1523). He would not support Luther's notion that major doctrines of the Catholic Church could be proved wrong with absolute certainty.[119]

Frederick the Wise appointed Martin Luther (1483-1546) and Philipp Melanchthon to the University of Wittenberg. Melanchthon, a young professor of Greek who arrived at the University in 1518, became Luther's close friend and fellow reformer. The University of Wittenberg was the first university in Germany to be founded without the permission of the church. It was advertised as offering up to date humanist learning compared to the church founded universities down the road.

In 1520, Pope Leo X condemned Luther's Protestant views as heretical. Consequently, Luther was summoned to appear at the Diet of Worms on April 17, 1521 to defend his ideas. He refused to recant. On May 25, 1521 the Emperor issued the Edict of Worms, declaring Martin Luther an outlaw and an enemy of the state. Luther went into hiding and Frederick the Wise provided him with protection. Frederick the Wise died in 1525, and his bother John became Elector of Saxony. He requested that the Wittenberg theologians write a statement of what the churches of his land believed and practiced. An imperial diet met in Augsburg Germany, in April of 1530. Emperor Charles V desired a united empire against the Turks and intended that all religious disunity come to an end. He hoped to bring Catholics and reformers together to resolve their differences. However, at Augsburg the princes and cities that held to Luther's teachings decided to make a common confession rather than just a Saxon confession. It was also determined that the Lutherans did not want to be identified with other opponents of the Roman church. The document was to include agreements along with differences. Under the preparation of Philipp Melanchthon and the consultation of Martin Luther, who was not present in Augsburg, the confession was completed and signed by seven princes and the representatives of two free cities, and delivered to Charles V on June 25, 1530.[120]

The Renaissance inspired the spirit of questioning and skepticism that characterized the Reformation. Luther borrowed from the humanists the sense of individualism, that each man can be his own priest, and that the only true authority is the Bible. Luther's translation of the Bible in 1522 into the vernacular allowed many to see that a great part of the teachings of the Catholic Church had no basis in the scriptures, and that did not bode well for the church. The Augsburg Confession became the description of the Lutheran faith. It is one of the most important documents of Lutheran reformation. While 1517 marked the beginning of the Reformation, 1530 marked the beginning of the Lutheran Church. John Calvin died in Geneva in 1564. In less than fifty years after Luther posted his ninety-five theses against indulgences on the church door in Wittenberg, Protestant reformers had established original systems of Christian doctrine and new churches in opposition to the Church of Rome.

Copernicus et al.

At the beginning of the 16th century, the Ptolemy theory was still used to explain the movement of the planets in relation to the Earth and sun. The Ptolemy theory had problems explaining the backward and forward movements of the planets relative to the fixed stars and their varying degrees of brightness. Ptolemy and his successors developed solutions based on the geocentric Aristotelian comos that require the use of numerous mathematical devices – deferents, major and minor epicycles, equants, eccentrics to make observed positions consistent with uniform circular motion.

Copernicus (1473-1543) developed the first explicitly heliocentric model of the solar system. In 1491, he began his initial studies at the Krakow Academy. While studying canon and civil law in Bologna, he met the astronomer Domenici Maria di Ferrara who initiated his interest in astronomy. He finished his studies in Padua in 1504 and returned to work in Frombork. Frombork, at this time, was an important city of the Prince-Bishopric of Warmia that was part of the Kingdom of Poland.

In 1514, Copernicus made available to a small group of friends his *Comentariolus (Little Commentary)*, a short text describing his ideas of the heliocentric hypothesis. The heliocentric theory placed the order of the planets circulating the sun: Mercury, Venus, Earth and Moon, Mars, Jupiter and Saturn. Copernicus did not publish the book *De revolutionbus orbium coelestrum (On the Revolution of the Celestial Spheres)* until 1543, the same year as his death. The Catholic Church condemned, in no uncertain terms, the heliocentric hypothesis of *De Revolutionibus* and placed it on the Index of Forbidden Books. The theory conflicted with parts of the Bible. It posed a fundamental threat to the entire Christian framework of cosmology, theology, and mortality. The moral drama of human life pivotally centered between spiritual heaven and corporeal Earth – all would be cast into question or destroyed altogether by the new theory.[121]

The second major player was Galileo. He had heard of the invention of the telescope in the Netherlands and developed his own. Using his new telescope to study the skies, he observed the moons of Jupiter and the phases of Venus, which suggested Venus orbits the sun. In 1610, he published his results of the moons of Jupiter and observations of mountains on the Earth's moon under the title *Starry Messengers*. With his newfound fame, he became the court mathematician at Florence. With his protected time, he continued to study the skies. His observation of the phases of Venus convinced him of the validity of the heliocentric theory of Copernicus.[122]

The Jesuits analyzed Galileo's work for the church and reported to Cardinal Bellarmine who was the leading theologian in the church and the Guardian of Orthodoxy. He had been one of the Inquisitors who had tried Giordian Bruno for heretical views on the Immaculate Conception and conflict-ing philosophies that included support for Copernicus' theory. Bruno was burnt at the stake in 1600. Bellarmine did not want another case, so Galileo continued to publish his discoveries. In 1614, a Florentine priest denounced him from the pulpit. These controversies lead Cardinal Bellarmine to intervene. In 1616, the church requested that Galileo no longer speak and write publicly about the policy that the Earth moves, which conflicted with the teachings of the Catholic Church.

In 1632, Galileo published *Dialogue on Two Chief World Systems* in which he discussed the Ptolemaic and Copernican hypothesis in relation to the physics of the tides. Soon after, he was summoned to Rome to face the Inquisition and stand trial for 'grave suspicion of heresy.' The charge was grounded on a report that Galileo had been ordered not to discuss the Copernican theory orally or in writing since 1616. In 1633, he was compelled to recant the theory and sentenced to life imprisonment that was commuted to house arrest. Imprisoned on his farm outside of Florence, he wrote *Discourses Concerning Two New Sciences,* his most important scientific work. The man-uscript was smuggled to Holland and published in 1638.[123]

It remained for Kepler to develop the theory further. Kepler was an assistant to Tycho Brahe, court mathematician to Emperor Rudolf II in Prague. Tycho died in October 1601 and Kepler became Imperial mathematician. He inherited Tyco's observatory and papers. From studying the orbit of Mars, he developed the first law of planetary motion: all planets move in ellipses, with the sun at one focus. His second law states: plan-ets sweep out equal areas in equal times. His third law reads, the square of the periodic times are to each other as the cubes of the mean distances. He developed an improved version of the refracting telescope and validated the discoveries of Galileo Galilei.[124]

Isaac Newton (1642-1727) tied together Kepler's laws of planetary motion and Galileo's laws of terrestrial motion in one comprehensive theory. This included that the planets are pulled toward the sun with an attractive force that decreases inversely as the square of the distance from the sun and that bodies falling toward Earth – not only a nearby stone but also the distant moon – conform to the same law. Thus all the major cosmological problems confronting the Copernicans were at last solved – what moved the planets, how they remained in their orbit, why heavy objects fell toward the Earth, and the basic structure of the universe –the issue of the celestial – terrestrial dichotomy. In 1686 the Royal Society of London published Newton's *Principia Mathematicus Philosophaie Naturalis*. During the following decades, his achievement was celebrated as the triumph of the modern mind over ancient and medieval ignorance. Voltaire called him the greatest man who ever lived.[125]

8

Money and Individualism

The stable currency of the Byzantine Empire was the solidus. From 690 it was joined as a hard currency by another gold coin, the dinar (from Latin denarius), first minted by Caliph Ald-al-Malik in Damascus. In the 8th century, the Frankish King, Pepin III (father of Charlemagne) introduced a silver denarius, or penny, which became the standard medieval coin in Europe. Later kings of the Carolingian Dynasty standardized the penny, decreeing that 240 were to be struck from a pound of silver. Subsequently, it was established that twelve silver pennies were to be considered equivalent of the Byzantine gold solidus or shilling. This monetary scale-pound/shilling/penny = 1/12/20, prevailed in much of Europe until the introduction of decimalization during the French revolution, and 1971 in Britain.[126]

By the year 1100, Venice had established a huge trading empire. It controlled the entire Adriatic coastline and was an economic superpower of Europe. Other cities in northern Italy also developed. As they grew wealthy, many became centres of banking long before the rest of Europe had discovered this lucrative area of commerce. Lucca (85 kilometers west of Florence) was a principle city of Tuscany and gained prominence as it commanded one of the important roads between Lombardy and Rome. It became prosperous through the silk trade that got a start in the 11th century. The currency of Lucca was highly valued in Europe as a means of exchanges and trade. The Crusaders relied on Lucca's coins to pay for whatever services they required (equipment, food, logistics, transportations, ransoms, fees, soldiers salaries, rights of passage). The privilege to mint was confirmed by Frederick Barbarossa and by Frederick II Hohenstaufen, and also by the popes. When Pisa tried to counterfeit Lucca's coins, the Pope issued a terrifying 'anathema' against the Pisani and brought them to order. After the 11th century, Lucca began to lose importance to Florence.[127]

The success of the First Crusade was part of the age of optimism and rebirth of the 12th century Renaissance, along with the exposure to new ideas and culture. However, the most important effect of the Crusades was economic. Trade between Italy and the ports at the eastern end of the Mediterranean were tremendously increased. By the time European nobility had begun to look upon such imports as Oriental rugs and perfumes as essentials, the growing middle class of merchants and artisans was already demanding the new commodities. This included foodstuffs, such as cane sugar, rice, garlic and lemons, and textiles such as muslin, silk and satin from the East, which became less expensive as the shipments increased in size. Trade passed through Italian hands to Western Europe at a handsome profit. Goods brought into Europe had to be distributed, and as trade increased, the towns and cities along the inland trade routes grew. This commercial power became the economic base of the Italian Renaissance.

Black Death

The bazaars of the East taught European merchants new ways of doing business. As early as the very beginning of the 13th century, the Pisan merchant Leonardo Pisan, better known as Fibonacci, traveled and traded throughout the Arabic east, where he gained the ability to calculate profit and loss using Hindu-Arabic numerals. In his revolutionary book, *Liber abbaci* (1202), he introduced Europe to the Arabic methods of subtraction, addition and multiplication, explaining how he was "marvelously instructed in the Arabic-Hindu numerals and calculation," and how they helped him in his business.[128] Other European merchants openly traded with Muslim, African and Hindu businessmen, regardless of religious and cultural differences. They were introduced to numerous Islamic products that they took back to their countries: embroidered silk, textiles known as brocade, damask cotton fabric from Damascus, and carpets from Baghdad, as well as paper, soap, ceramics, glass, jewelry and medicines.

Europeans also learned the commercial usefulness of algebra from the Persian astronomer al-Khowarizmi, and adopted the word "cheque" from the Arabic "sakk". International finance became increasingly liquid and intricate during the 13th -15th centuries, and Florentine merchants based in the Medici bank opened offices throughout the east from the early 15th century onwards. They used bills of exchange, forerunners of the modern cheque, to secure lucrative contracts with Muslim merchants, who possessed the luxury objects desired by the élite of 15th-century Italy.

Coming out of the East, the plague first appeared along the trading routes of Europe. Infected people first broke out with red ring shaped marks with dark center spots on their arms and necks, and usually died within a week. The dark markings on the skin provided the other name, Black Death. The plague, spread by the fleas on the rats that accompanied the trading ships, hit Western Europe in 1348 decimating its societies and population. It killed indiscriminately, striking at rich and poor alike. Over ten years, one-third of the population of Western Europe was wiped out and towns were the hardest hit. The economy was devastated, and the social structures of Europe changed. The church lost prestige, spiritual authority and leadership over the people. The people wanted answers, but the priests and bishops did not have any.[129]

Black Death wiped out half the population of Florence and set the city on turbulent times. However, this led nicely to the rise of a business class to power. Only a few strong businessmen escaped the Black Death and the crash of the economy. Many of the small banks failed. Of the oligarchy that formed, rising to the top of the new governing class was a family of bankers called the Medici. The Medici became 'God's Bankers' in 1410 when John XXIII established his papacy at Rome. They continued as the church's banker after the Council of Constance and Pope Martin V. This arrangement put the Medici in the forefront of international banking. They collected all the papal incomes and paid out vast papal expenditures. The Medici Bank, centered in Florence, became the most profitable business in Europe. By 1434, a significant portion of the bank's revenue came from the Rome 'branch,' which was in fact little more than a mobile bank that followed the pope's activities around the world. Italy was particularly hard hit by the plague; it has been speculated that the familiarity with death that this brought caused thinkers to dwell more on their lives on Earth, rather than spirituality and the afterlife.[130]

Rise and Fall of Bruges

Bruges is a city in the Flanders region of northwest Belgium. Because of Bruges' intricate network of canals, it has been described as the Venice of the north. Baldwin I, Count of Flanders, fortified Bruges in the 9th century because of the Viking raids. His son, Baldwin II (868-918) married Elfrida, daughter of King Alfred the Great of England.[96] This marriage was motivated by the common English-Flemish opposition to the Vikings and was the start of an alliance that was a mainstay of policy for centuries to come. Flanders was known for the seasonal trade fair, which lasted two months each summer. The main commodity was cloth – silk, wool and linen, and as trade with England and Scandinavia developed, Bruges had become an important wool market and weaving centre by the 12th century. It became the southern terminus of the Hanseatic League.[131]

The Hanseatic League was a mercantile league of medieval German towns, a group of merchants banding together for security. The Hansa was founded in the twelfth century by an alliance between the northern towns of Hamburg and Lübeck, which lay on opposite sides of the base of the Danish peninsula. Lübeck fishing boats had easy access to the herring spawning grounds off the coast of Scania (the lower tip of Sweden, which at that time was Danish territory). A large portion of the diet of Christian Europe was made of fish since there were many 'fast' days and the church forbade the eating of meat on Friday. Lübeck was in a position to capitalize on a large commodities market in herring, but one thing held Lübeck back; with no refrigeration or canning, the shipping of a highly perishable commodity like fish was problematic. Hamburg, on the other side of the Jutland peninsula, had easy access to the salt produced in the salt mines at Kiel, and salting and drying of meat and fish made transport and distribution possible. It was in the best interest, then, for the merchants of these two towns to open trade along the "salt" road. A major impetus to the league's development was the lack of a powerful German national government to provide security for trade. In order to obtain mutual security, exclusive trading rights and, wherever possible trade monopoly, the towns drew closer together. In 1241, Lübeck and Hamburg concluded a treaty of mutual protection. Ports and inland towns from Holland to Poland entered the league, but the northern German cities remained the principal members. The league vigorously extended its operations, founding principal foreign branches at Bruges and Bergen. The Hansa towns reached the height of their power in their victories over Waldemar IV of Denmark in 1370, gaining a virtual trade monopoly in Scandinavia. Their Baltic hegemony continued through numerous wars, until their defeat by the Dutch in 1441.[132]

By the 13th century, Flanders was one of the most urbanized areas of Europe, after northern Italy. In 1277, the first fleet from Genoa arrived in the harbour of Bruges. This opened up the trade in spicies and led to the improvement of banking. All the Italian banking houses eventually established offices in Bruges, which became the main link to trade in the Mediterranean. A significant weaving industry developed. In 1282, the guilds declared only English wool would do for the top class Flemish weavers. This emphasized important trade with England.[133] William Claxton, the first printer to produce works in English, published the first book in English in Bruges. New walls were thrown up in 1297 trebling the size of the city, which was quickly filled in with new palaces and warehouses. The old moats were now used as canals, facilitating the transport of goods.[134] In 1309, the Bruges bourse opened, the money market from which all stock exchanges are named. It was probably named after the wealthy merchant of Bruges, Van de Burse, whose house became a meeting place where product traders met regularly. Around the 1340s the population of Bruges was equal to London's. Bruges became the commercial capital of Northern Europe in the late 14th century as a centre for wool, cloth (linen) and gold trade.[135]

India remained the main producer of diamonds until the 18th century. In the 13th century, Venice had been the centre of diamond trade in Europe and was the gateway for silk and diamonds to Bruges, however, in the 15th century, the art of diamond polishing was invented in Bruges, and quickly Bruges became the centre of diamond trade.[136] By 1500, the Zwin channel had silted up and Antwerp took over as the economic centre and became the most important port in Europe. The pattern established by Bruges as a commercial centre was imitated by Antwerp and Amsterdam, which included public investment in infrastructure, waterworks, street building, and monumental civic structures to encourage the processes of exchange from which the population would gain residuals.

In *False Economy,* Alan Beattie noted, trading groups tended to set up monopolies. Those with monopoly power often tended to abuse it, and "the creation of a trading system or trade route all too often was followed by an attempt to milk it for profit by keeping out competition." The Baltic Sea monopoly led to the Hanseatic League clash with the Dutch. In turn, the Dutch, by the brutal use of military force, managed to establish exclusive supplies of spices from East Asia. There were various interventions by governments to strike a balance by moderating a company's power with early versions of anti-trust law. For example, the Hudson's Bay Company, which traded furs from North America, was allowed to sell the furs it brought back only in small lots in fixed auctions, to prevent its manipulating the market by creating shortages and driving up prices.[137]

The Renaissance

The money pouring into the cities from trade and banking fueled the growth in power of the city-states in northern Italy. Little was done to stop the growth of these autonomous states during the 13th and 14th century as both the Pope and the Holy Roman Emperor strived for influence in the area. Each was so intent on the other that both permitted the growth of powerful autonomous regions to further their own aims. By the beginning of the Renaissance, there were five major players in city-state politics: the Papal States ruled by the Pope, the republics of Florence and Venice, the Kingdom of Naples and the duchy of Milan.[138]

The Medieval Church restricted individual expression and demanded implicit faith and unquestioning obedience. There was a rediscovery of the Greek classics during the Renaissance. Hellenic philosophy was designed to teach men how to live successfully rather than how to die with the assurance of ultimate salvation. Individualism spread with many of the new ideas during the Renaissance, including humanism. Humanism emphasized that people should think for themselves rather than just trust authority, thus introducing healthy skepticism. Reliance on faith and God weakened. These new ideas were incubating three centuries prior to the Renaissance of the 15th century. Milton Viorst observed, "The seminal notion that the Renaissance introduced to the West was that mankind, not God, is the hub of the social universe." As there was no Catholic Counter Reformation in America, the Reformation carried on longer in America than Europe, and this accounts for a great deal of the influence that developed the unique American character of individualism.[139] Sociologist Emile Durkheim noted more than 100 years ago "the development of rationalism does not come about without a parallel development of individualism."[140]

The appearance of individualism is intertwined with the story of heretics and money in the Western world. Money is traced from the global economy under the influence of the mass media and the advertisers back to the emerging economy appearing during the 300 year warm period in Medieval Europe. From the 12th to 17th century, spices constituted the most profitable and dynamic element in European trade. The phenomenal growth of wealth in the small city (states in northern Italy) is directly responsible for the flowering of literature, scholarship and the other arts during the Renaissance. During the Age of Enlightenment the ideas of the Renaissance continued to grow and become more widespread. In particular, advancement in science led to the emphasis on the power of human reasoning.

The Spice Islands

The Republic of Venice controlled the spice trade through the monopoly of trade with the Middle East up to the 15th century. This trade was very profitable. The Portuguese developed trading posts along the west coast of Africa in the 15th century. Vasco da Gama illustrated the logistics of a trade route around Africa to India. In order to secure the overseas route and secure the monopoly on the spice trade, it was necessary to prevent Muslim shipping from gaining access to India. Alfonso di Albuquerque (1453-1515) secured the route; in 1506, he took the Island of Socotra in the mouth of the Red Sea; in 1507, he took Ormaz in the Persian Gulf and, in 1510, Goa from India and Malacca on the Malay Peninsula in 1511. This effectively cut out Muslim traders from the majority of the trade.[141]

The centre for spice trade was the Spice Islands or the Moluccas Islands – famous for nutmegs, cloves and mace. The Moluccas were the source of the most valuable spice of all, the clove, coveted for many different purposes – as a flavor in food as a preservative, as a mild anesthetic, as an ingredient in perfume, even to mask stinking breath. The Dutch controlled the trade in cloves with ruthless efficiency. During the 17th century, clove trees were eradicated on the Spice Islands except for two, Amboina and Ternate – to limit production and keep prices high. Strict measures were taken to ensure the plants were not exported for propagation elsewhere (a restriction successfully maintained until the late 18th century).[142]

This chain of small islands west of New Guinea, comprising about forty square miles, was the source of large fortunes for the Europeans. The Portuguese never controlled the Spice Islands, as they were always in conflict with one part of or another of the native population. The Dutch noted this conflict when they arrived in 1599. The collapse of Spanish power after the Thirty Years War in 1648 opened the colonial empire of the Spanish and Portuguese up for grabs. While the Thirty Years War started as a conflict between Protestants and Catholics in Germany, Catholic France under the de facto rule of Cardinal Richelieu supported the Protestant side to weaken the Hapsburgs, furthering France's position on the continent. By the mid 17th century, the Dutch had the largest mercantile fleet in the world and conquered most of the Portuguese colonies in the East Indies. This included the near-by Banda Islands which were the sole source of nutmeg and mace up to the 19th century.

In *The Ascent of Money*, Niall Ferguson observes that the rise and fall of the stock price of the Dutch East India Company over 150 years followed the rise and fall of the Dutch Empire. The Dutch East India Company was chartered in 1602 to enjoy a monopoly on all Dutch trade east of the Cape of Good Hope and west of the Straits of Magellan. It became the world's first big corporation. The original charter called for the company to be dissolved and profits taken after ten years, but this was suspended in 1612. This meant shareholders who wanted their cash back had to sell their shares to another investor. Thus the joint stock company and the stock market were established within a few years of each other. The Amsterdam Exchange Bank had opened in 1609. Soon the bank started accepting shares of the Dutch East India Company as collateral for loans, and the link between the stock market and supply of credit began to be forged. Eventually the banks lent money so that shares could be purchased with credit. This was the dawn of a new economy. Ferguson observes, "the history of the Dutch East India Company…shows that, with the sound money of the sort provided by the Amsterdam Exchange Bank, stock market bubbles and busts can be avoided." [143]

A Frenchman stole nutmeg and cloves seeds that allowed plantings on French controlled islands in the Indian Ocean. The Dutch monopoly was broken by the end of the 18th century. Similarly, in 1698 Zanzibar came under the control of the Sultanate of Oman who moved to develop plantations to grow spices. Hence this archipelago in the Indian Ocean also became known as the Spice Islands and continues as a world leader in the production of nutmeg, cinnamon and pepper.

9

The Reformation

The Universities

The universities of Europe came into existence during the Middle Ages. In 1079 Pope Gregory VII issued a papal decree mandating the creation of cathedral schools that would be responsible for educating the clergy. This decree ultimately led to the proliferation of educational centres, which evolved over time into the universities of Medieval Europe. In the later half of the 12th century, the cathedral schools in Paris and Bologna became universities. They received a form of self-government, but universities could not grant degrees without the approbation of pope, king or emperor. Pope Innocent IV officially granted this privilege to Oxford University in 1254. For universities equipped with approval of the pope, the degree was recognized throughout Christendom. For example, masters degrees from Oxford or Paris were entitled to teach anywhere in the world.[144]

The 10th to 13th century coincided with global warming in Europe. This extended the growing season three to four weeks. The vineyards extended further northwards, well into England and Germany (compared to today). Food was easier to obtain and the population increased dramatically. From 11th century to 1300 the population of Western Europe doubled.[145] The renaissance of the 12th century involved massive translation works. By 1200, students started entering schools with no intention of becoming clergy. The rise in lay education caused a loss of church control over education.

A typical medieval university's curriculum consisted of the trivium of grammar, rhetoric, and logic, and the quadrivium of arithmetic, music, geometry, and astronomy. This breakdown of the liberal arts was focused mainly on the philosophical and theological implications of the subjects. Grammar, rhetoric, and logic were all related to the discipline of reading and writing Latin, the common international language of the Middle Ages. The study of arithmetic, geometry, astronomy and music concerned the 'secrets of nature.' These represented the basic rounded education of a person with higher education.

German and English universities emphasized arts and theology. In Italy, Spain, and the south of France, where the curriculum might have been called more career-oriented, study centered more on law and medicine. Students could enjoy the benefits of the clergy. It needed to be an extra ordinary crime to lay a hand on them, as they were potential clerical candidates. In 1237 Gregory IX provided the Master of Paris, the right to self-government for the University of Paris. In this model, grievances at the university were brought to the pope in Rome. Medieval towns loved the money, but hated the students.[146]

In 1085 Alfonso VI conquered Toledo, in central Spain, from the Moors, and made it a tolerant city where Christians, Muslims and Jews peacefully coexisted. In the reign of Alfonso

X, in the 13th century, the 'School of Translators' was established. Translations of Arabic and Greek texts made Toledo a European intellectual hub. From these translated works the rest of Western Europe was able to obtain Arabic and Greek culture and beliefs, and rediscover the classical Greek teachings. The flood of new Latin translations (from Greek and Arabic) of classical philosophers, including all of Aristotle, occurred throughout the second half of the 12th century. This new work, Aristotle's natural philosophy, became part of the curriculum for the Faculty of Arts in the universities across Europe. It became important because a Bachelor of Arts degree was required of all students for graduation. An arts degree was a prerequisite for higher faculties of theology, medicine or law.[147]

Saint Dominic founded the Dominicans in 1215 during his preaching tours against the Albigenses in southern France. The Dominicans were friars, receiving rigorous theological training in order to preach and answer objection against the Christian faith. They were founded with the purpose of counteracting by means of preaching, teaching and example of austerity, the heretics present at the time. Dominicans sought doctrinal purity and became leading university professors throughout the West. Assimilation of this new learning took place in the universities of the 13th century through the genius of the Dominicans Saint Albertus Magnus and his great pupil Thomas Aquinas. A use of Aristotelian logic was called the scholastic tradition because its advocates were university teachers or 'schoolmen.' Scholastics prove truth; they do not discover it.[148]

St. Thomas Aquinas (1225-1274), who sought to resolve the dispute between the Averroists and the Augustians, held that reason and faith constitute two harmonious realms in which the truth of faith complements that of reason, both being gifts of God, but reason having an autonomy of its own. He produced a synthesis of Aristotle and Christian thought and established a method for scholastics to support church teachings. Aquinas claimed when reason is used correctly it affirmed what God had revealed in Scripture. He introduced definitions on natural law to be used with his system. For Thomas Aquinas, natural law was that part of the eternal law of God (the reason of divine wisdom) which is knowable by human beings by means of their powers of reason. Positive law, the formal legal enactments of a particular society, is the application of natural law to particular social circumstances. Aquinas believed that a positive law that violates natural law is not true law.[149]

Franciscan friars appeared who countered some of the dominance of the Dominicans. Roger Bacon (1214-1292) was an English friar who became an expert on Aristotle at Oxford. Aristotle had been banned from the University of Paris for a few years on the grounds he was not a Christian. In the 1240's the study was reintroduced and Bacon was invited to lecture on Aristotle. He studied optics and astronomy. He calculated that the calendar year was eleven minutes longer than the solar year. This amounted to an error of one day every 125 years. Since the introduction of the Julian calendar, there was now a surplus of nine days. He communicated this to the papacy but nothing was done. It would not be addressed for another 300 years, until the introduction of the Gregorian calendar.[150]

Fredrick the Wise was one of the seven Electors and ruler of Saxony. He endowed the University of Wittenberg in 1502. German universities were structured to make it possible for the university to introduce change into religion and society. The term scholasticism then began to be used in a derogatory sense. In 1511, Luther was sent by his order to teach at Wittenberg. Under the influence of Philipp Melanchthon, building on the works of Martin Luther, the university became a centre of the Protestant Reformation. As the students were chiefly from Northern Germany the university was an important factor in the spread of Protestantism. The appearance of humanism as a program and philosophy at universities separated the Middle Ages from the Renaissance.[151]

The Florentine Medici Popes

The church lost a great deal of authority during the Renaissance with the involvement of the pope in numerous secular activities. Caesare Borgia (1475-1507), son of Pope Alexander VI, used an alliance with France and the patronage of his father to set up control of territories in northern Italy. A diplomat and realist of political theory, Niccolo Machiavelli (1469-1527), (who met Cesare Borgia while on diplomatic functions and spent two years as the court representative of Florence), captured these exploits in a book. He used Borgia's exploits and tactics as examples in his book, *The Prince*. Written in 1513, but not published until 1532, the book covered insightful and shrewd methods for aspiring rulers to establish and maintain power. This book promoted the justifiable use of force rather than fairness, and became responsible for the term 'Machiavellian' as a pejorative term. Machiavelli dedicated *The Prince* to Lorenzo de' Medici, Duke of Urbino, to gain favour from the ruling Medici family.[152]

Leo X, pope from 1513 to 1521, born Giovanni di Lorenzo de' Medici, was the second son of Lorenzo de' Medici, the most famous ruler of Florence. Following the expulsion of the Medici from Florence in 1494, Leo traveled Europe as a cardinal until 1500 when he returned to Rome under the protection of Cesare Borgia and his father, Pope Alexander VI. Restored to respectability by Pope Julius II, he eventually gained control of Florence. Following the close of the Fifth Ecumenical Lateran Council in 1517, Leo was involved in a series of wars in northern Italy. In the war of Urbino, Leo helped set up his nephew,

Lorenzo de' Medici, as the new Duke of Urbino. The war was expensive and wrought havoc on papal finances. While Leo was engaged in these activites, he was not focusing on the Reformation occurring in Germany and Scandinavia.

Leo arranged the marriage of a royal French princess, Madeline la Tour d'Auverge to his nephew, Lorenzo. Their daughter Catherine de' Medici, (1519-1589) married Henry, second son of Francis I of France. They had three children - Francis II, Charles IX, and Henry III. Their first son, Francis II married Mary Queen of Scots, niece of Francis, Duke of Guise. When Henry II died, Francis II became King of France at age fifteen, on July 10, 1559. Cardinal Lorraine and the Duke of Guise took control of the court. They set about persecuting Protestants with zeal. Francis II died December 5, 1560, and 10-year-old Charles IX became king with his mother as consort. Initially there were conciliatory overtones to the Huguenots, but the Guises opposed as dangerous any "consensus to the heretics". Catherine de' Medici could not control many events, but she was blamed for the St. Bartholomew's Day massacre in which thousands of Huguenots were butchered throughout France. Charles IX died in 1574, and Catherine's third son came to power as Henry III. A great deal of influence continued to be exerted by Henry I, Duke of Guise and the Catholic League to persecute Protestants. Philip II of Spain provided funds to the Catholic League to maintain a civil war in France.[153]

The principle attributes of the Catholic faith in the 16th century included the dogma 'only the Church, through its priest, can interpret God's will to man'. There is a point part way between Heaven and Hell called Purgatory, where a person's sins are purged to make him/her worthy of Heaven. The prayers of the living can shorten a soul's stay in Purgatory, so it is good to pray for the dead. The saints were more virtuous than they needed to be to get into Heaven, so there was a reserve of left over grace available. Drafts on this reserve were called indulgences, and they were for sale.

Leo X spent lavishly on everything from charity to culture. He set out to make the capital of Christendom a centre of culture. His generous support of art, building construction, personal expenses and political ambitions exhausted the savings set aside by Julius II within two years. His need for money was extensive. Many devices were developed to raise money, such as creating new offices that were sold, and encouraging the sales of indulgences.

One of the seven Imperial Electors, Albert of Mainz (1490-1545), represented the culture of the Catholic Church in the 16th century. As one of the electors he voted for Charles V in 1519 for Holy Roman Emperor, for which he received a large amount of money. He held a bishopric and a second archbishopric, in addition to Mainz. Although plurality is against cannon law, Pope Leo X agreed to overlook the irregularity in turn for a large donation to the building costs of the new St. Peter's. Leo made it possible for Albert to recover his costs by granting him the concession for the sale of indulgences towards the building of St. Peter's. Half the money from each indulgence went to Rome; the other half paid off Albert's debts. He borrowed the money for the original donation from the Fuggers of Augsburg who had one of the biggest banks and business firms of their time.[154]

Albert recruited a monk, John Tetzel to sell the indulgences. Tetzel was a slick salesperson, who shocked many with his glib sales – promises of the immediate release of love ones from the pain of Purgatory as soon as the purchase was made. Martin Luther, teaching at the University of Wittenberg, had spoken out prior to 1517 on the sale of indulgences. Upset with stories from parishioners returning in October to Wittenberg who told of indulgences bought from Tetzel, Martin Luther penned 95 theses and nailed them to the church door on October 31, 1517.[155]

The second Florentine Medici pope was Giulio de 'Medici. When his cousin Leo X was pope, he was his main confidant looking after Medici interests in Florence, as archbishop of the city. He became a cardinal in 1513. Giulio de 'Medici, as Clement VII, was pope from 1523 to 1534. When crowned pope, Francis I of France and Charles V of Spain were at war. Charles V supported his candidacy for pope as he saw the empire and the papacy as a partnership. Clement VII's concern over dynastic interest of family drove him to Francis' Court. The French were defeated at Pavia in 1525. Because of the subsequent intrigues, Charles V kept his armies in northern Italy for four years. During this time the sack of Rome and the six-month imprisonment of Clement by the Emperor (1527-1528) occurred. Following the sack of Rome, the city never recovered its Renaissance luster.[156]

Clement relied on the support of Charles V for the security of the Italian lands. This reliance is why, in 1533, Clement refused to sanction the annulment of the marriage of Henry VIII to Catherine of Aragon. Catherine was the youngest surviving child of Ferdinand and Isabella, making Charles V her nephew. In 1534, the Act of Supremacy established an independent Church of England. This set the climate for the development of the Anglican Church and the loss of England to the Catholic Church. Clement was indifferent to what was going on around him. His actions were those of an Italian prince, as he failed to understand the spiritual movement convulsing the church.

As the Anglican Church was being established in England, Protestantism was spreading on the continent. Luther challenged the concept of Latin as the only language appropriate to worship in, or the only path to God. Learning was no longer unique to the clergy. Printing allowed a much broader audience to read Luther's German translation of the Bible. The new translations identified contradictions between the scripture, and what the priest taught. This opened the people's eyes to new ideas and freed them from the powerful grip of the institutional church. Luther's protests spread throughout the German countryside on printed sheets that were widely copied, discussed, and argued about. The flames of the Reformation spread rapidly.

The English Bible

Jerome, who was commissioned by Pope Damascus, translated the Latin Vulgate from Hebrew and Aramaic between 382 and 405 CE. It became the standard version of the Bible for Roman Catholics for over 1400 years. The first English Bibles were hand written, produced in the 1380's by John Wycliffe and his followers. Wycliffe opposed the teachings of the organized church, which he believed to be contrary to the Bible. He used the Latin Vulgate as his source for translation. The organized church opposed his activities.[157]

Thomas Linacre was one of the first Englishmen to study Greek in Italy. As well as studying Greek at Padua, he obtained a degree in medicine. He became the physician to Henry VIII. He brought back 'new learning' to Oxford and founded the Department of Greek Studies. He discovered that the Greek manuscripts were significantly different from the Latin Vulgate. He wrote in his diary "Either this (the original Greek) is not the Gospel...or we are not Christians." [158] In *Misquoting Jesus The Story Behind Who Changed the Bible and Why* Bart D. Ehrman observes,

> "...most of the changes found in our early Christian manuscripts have nothing to do with theology or

ideology. Far and away most changes are the result of mistakes, pure and simple – slips of the pen, accidental omissions, inadvertent additions, misspelled words, blunders of one sort or another. Scribes could be incompetent: it is important to recall that most of the copyists in the early centuries were not trained to do this kind of work but were simply the literate members of their congregation who were (more or less) able and willing. Even later, starting in the fourth and fifth centuries, when Christian scribes emerged as a professional class within the church, and later still when most manuscripts were copied by monks devoted to this kind of work in the monasteries, - even then some scribes were less skilled than others." [159]

Another Oxford scholar, John Colet, spent a two-year sabbatical in Italy studying Greek. On his return to England he assisted Linacre in the production of the first Greek grammar book published in England. The work of Colet and Linacre contributed greatly to public awareness that the Roman Catholic Church's Latin Vulgate text could not be trusted, and called for Christian scholars to return to the original Greek manuscripts to translate, or at least understand, the Gospel, as it was originally meant to be communicated. Under the influence of Linacre and Colet's ideas, Erasmus went on to produce the Greek-Latin New Testament. It was based on half a dozen partial old Greek New Testament manuscripts that he had acquired. In 1516 this new non-Latin Vulgate Bible was published in Basel. It focused attention on how inaccurate and corrupt the Latin Vulgate had become. He received no praise from Rome for this important work.[160]

William Tyndale was a scholar and theologian fluent in eight languages. At university he became interested in the ideas of Wycliffe. Like Wycliffe he became convinced the church had become corrupted and selfish. Tyndale wanted to translate the Bible into English. Under the 1408 Constitutions of Oxford, it was strictly forbidden to translate the Bible into the native tongue. During this time, individuals were burnt at the stake for saying the Lord's Prayer in English rather than Latin. With opposition to his work in England, he moved to the continent to pursue his plans.

One of the first published Bibles in the vernacular was the German translation published in 1522 by Martin Luther. Luther used Erasmus' new Greek-Latin New Testament for much of his work. In 1524, Tyndale went to Hamburg where he met Martin Luther, and the following year moved to Cologne where his translation of the Bible was printed in English. Tyndale came under attack from the likes of Thomas More (who, as Lord Chancellor, had a number of people burnt at the stake for heresy), because he changed the meaning of certain words in the English translation that undermined the authority of the Catholic Church. For example from the Greek, he translated 'congregation' instead of 'church.' This change challenged the Catholic belief that priests and members of the clergy make up the institution known as the church. It tended to support the views of leaders of the Reformation that the church was made up and defined by the believers, or congregations.

As Tyndale's Bibles were illegal, they were smuggled into England in bales of cloth. The established church struck back. In 1530, Henry VIII gave orders that all English Bibles be destroyed. Agents of the church in Antwerp arrested Tyndale in 1535, and in 1536, he was strangled and burnt at the stake. He is frequently referred to as the 'Architect of the English language' (even more so than William Shakespeare) as many of the phrases Tyndale coined exist in the language today.[161]

Two of Tyndale's disciples, Myles Cloverdale and John Rodgers, carried on Tyndale's work. In 1535, Myles Cloverdale finished translating the Old Testament with the use of Luther's German text and Latin sources. This was the first complete Bible in the English language. In 1537, John Rodgers printed the second complete English Bible under the pseudonym "Thomas Mathew." He made use of Tyndale's version and it became the first English Bible translated from the original Greek and Hebrew.

In 1539, Thomas Cramer, the Archbishop of Canterbury, hired Miles Cloverdale, at the request of Henry VIII to publish the "Great Bible." It became the first English Bible authorized for public use. It was distributed to every church and chained to the pulpit. The name came from the fact that the pulpit version measured over 14 inches tall. This was just another step of Henry VIII taking control of the Church of England in his fight with the Pope.

The reign of Queen Mary (1553 to 1558) saw an attempt to return England to the Catholic Church. Reform at the top saw John Rodgers and Thomas Crammer burnt at the stake. At the bottom, anyone caught reading an English Bible was burnt at the stake. This five-year period created the Marian exile.

In the 1550's reformer refugees were welcome in Geneva, Switzerland. Calvin had developed the Reform Church in Geneva and turned it into a training ground for reformers across Europe. Here a group from England, that included Miles Cloverdale and John Foxe, began work on producing a Bible to educate their families while they were in exile. A complete version of the new Bible was published in 1560 and became known as the Geneva Bible. It was the first Bible to add numbered verses to chapters. Each chapter included marginal notes and references so that it was considered the first English study Bible. The Geneva Bible contained 90% of Tyndale's original English translation. It became the Bible of choice for the next 100 years.

Under Queen Elizabeth, (in 1568) there was a revision of the 'Great Bible' introduced that became known as the 'Bishop's Bible'. It never became popular compared to the Geneva Bible. The challenge of the 1611 King James Bible was to equal the scholarship and accuracy of the Geneva Bible without the controversial marginal notes (such as proclaiming the pope the antichrist). The Geneva Bible, more than any other in format, influenced the 1611 King James Version, and remained more popular for decades after the release of the King James Version. The Geneva Bible was the first Bible taken to America, and was the Bible of the Puritans and Pilgrims.[162]

The Presbyterian Assemblies

Martin Luther's concept that individuals are justified, are made able to meet God's justice by faith alone, removed the need for a priestly hierarchy to mediate between God and the individual. He advocated a priesthood of all believers. By removing the power of the priest and the coercive power of the Catholic Church, it made Christianity a deeply personal religion, emphasizing the faith of the individual over formal rituals and social practices.

Ulrich Zwingli (1484-1531), a Swiss theologian, read Erasmus' edition of the Greek text of the New Testament which led him to question Catholic teachings. He went further than Luther in simplifying the liturgy and rejecting all ostentation in worship. Calvin was a French theologian who joined the Reformation in 1533 and became one of its most influential leaders. He established a theocratic state in Geneva, which became the centre of a missionary movement spreading Calvinism widely by mid 16th century. Calvin's followers created many churches that included French Huguenots, English Puritans, the Scottish Presbyterians, and the Dutch Reformed

Church. Calvin accepted the basic tenets of Lutheranism, but placed greater emphasis upon the evil nature of humans and the predestination of the soul. He went further than Zwingli in banishing doctrines and practices of Catholicism. He replaced the old hierarchical structure of government with assemblies of elected ministers and "elders." All citizens of Geneva were provided with at least elementary education so that they might read and understand the Bible.[163]

By the 16th century the church in Scotland had accumulated half the country wealth and all the vices that accompany such power. The nobles invited John Knox (1513-1572) to return from Geneva to lead the reform party in the country. He organized Calvinism as the national Church of Scotland. During a lull in the tension in the country with the death of Mary of Guise in 1560, Knox persuaded the Scottish parliament to adopt a confession of faith and book of discipline modeled after those in use in Geneva. The Parliament created the Scottish Presbyterian Church, which provided governance of the church by local church sessions and by a general assembly representing the local churches of the entire country. The Presbyterian Church promoted new ideas: the prayers of the priests were no more perfect, and no more important to God than others. Testifying, or preaching and interpreting the Scripture, was encouraged and expected of both the minister and congregation. The prayers of noblemen were no more valuable to God, either. Everyman was equal in the sight of God. This was revolutionary thinking against the hierarchical structures of secular and religious governance of the day.

The Council of Trent was the missed opportunity of the 16th century to re-unite the Christian factions, as the established hierarchy of the Church of Rome was unwilling to give up the necessary power and wealth to bring the Protestants back to the fold. Luther set forth the powerful doctrine of spiritual individualism that changed Western Europe forever, based on two core elements: God's promise to man as set forth in the Scripture, and man's faithful acceptance of that promise. This concept weakened the control of the established church over the laity. The counter-reformation organized by the Catholic Church included some much-needed reforms, but also created activities that led to the Thirty Years War that destroyed large parts of Germany as well as sewed the fear of plots. The English parliament was wary of attempts to change the monarchy to Catholicism. The English Bill of Rights following the Glorious Revolution, which made William and Mary king and queen in 1688, was designed to prevent the abuse of power by the monarchy. In particular, it blocked the crown from passing to a Catholic for fear of creating religious conflict that was engulfing the continent. The English parliament assumed more power, but did vote the necessary monies for William to carry on the fight for Protestants on the continent.

The Renaissance helped learning spread through Europe and provided support for the ideas of the Reformation. The Roman Catholic Church did not move quickly enough to adapt to the new forces released by Renaissance thinking, that the evolution of democracy included separation of church from the state. Protestant Churches multiplied. Jurisdictions, such as the British Parliament, put even more limits on the power of the monarchy in order to ensure separation of church from government. One of the consequences of the Protestant movement was the ability of the people to interpret the Bible directly. The Presbyterians rejected the governance of hierarchies as represented by bishops and chose authority being exercised by bodies of elected delegates to co-ordinate church activities. They developed assemblies to organize the congregations of these new churches, and used covenants when they established congregations in the Old World. Many of these new religious groups moved to America to escape prosecution as heretics and the Presbyterian assemblies that organized the new congregations that left the Old World for the New World facilitated the development of democracy in America.[164]

10

Holy Roman Emperors and the Hapsburgs

Charlemagne was crowned Roman Emperor by a grateful Pope Leo III for his aide against the Lombards. Similarly Otto I, King of the Germans, was crowned Holy Roman Emperor in 962, in gratitude for protecting Pope John XII, from the aggressions of the King of Italy. This event linked the destinies of Germany and Italy for centuries. The German king, elected by the German princes, automatically sought imperial coronation by the pope. However, not every German king became emperor because the popes often claimed that the selection of the emperor was their prerogative. The subsequent history of the papacy and the Holy Roman Emperors was mostly a series of conflicts for control of Italy, and church interference in secular activities in Germany.[165]

The Hapsburgs were first elected Holy Roman emperor in the late 13th century. The disorder in Germany with the death of the direct heir to the Hohenstaufen Dynasty allowed Rudolf I (1273-1291) to increase his territory and position himself to be elected king of the Germans. He renounced any claim to Sicily and was recognized by Gregory X as Holy Roman Emperor. As emperor he consolidated his territory, including Hapsburg claims to the duchies of Austria and Styria – laying the foundation of the House of Hapsburg. Albert I, the eldest son of Rudolf I, was as an efficient administrator of Austria. However, after Rudolf's death the electors rejected Albert's candidacy in order to check the growing power of the Hapsburgs. The electors chose Adolf of Nassau as king of the Germans. Albert later engineered Adolf's deposition and replaced him. His attempt to expand his territories to the west brought him into conflict with Pope Boniface VIII. Albert was able to reach an agreement with Boniface, who recognized his title in 1303. A nephew, John of Swabia, whose inheritance Albert had withheld, murdered Albert, and Henry of Luxemburg, Holy Roman Emperor as Henry VII, from 1312 to 1313, succeeded Albert.[166] Henry led an army into Italy to pacify the warring factions, and many Italians celebrated his arrival. Dante paid tribute in his letters and his thesis, *De Monarchia*, however, Henry died of malaria before he could achieve his goal.[167]

Louis IV, Duke of Bavaria, was elected Holy Roman Emperor in 1314 with four of seven votes of the imperial electors. He did not have the support of the pope who used this opportunity to strengthen papal rule in the Holy Roman Empire and in particular, restore papal authority in Italy. In 1322, Louis defeated his rival (Frederick I of Austria, House of Hapsburg, Rudolf I's second son) in battle, but Pope John XXII still refused to ratify the election. With these ongoing conflicts with the papacy over the choice of Holy Roman Emperor, the imperial electors decided in 1338 the candidate receiving the majority of the votes would be king of the Germans and automatically be Holy

Roman Emperor without being crowned by the pope. The controversy between Louis and the popes caused the publication of many books and pamphlets, notably the *Defensor pacis* by Marsilius of Padua, which supported Louis' claims. Louis was successfully resisting rival claims when he was killed in a hunting accident.[168]

Pope Clement VI, seeking a more malleable emperor, sponsored Charles of Moravia, King of Bohemia (grandson of Henry VII). In 1355, a papal representative crowned Charles in Rome. In the Golden Bull of 1356, Charles identified seven electors, the Archbishops of Mainz, Tier, Cologne, Count Palatine of the Rhine, Duke of Saxony, Margrave of Brandenburg, King of Bohemia and formalized their roles: electors lands were indivisible, they were granted control of monopolies and tolls, and secured gifts from all imperial candidates. As a result, these seven rulers became the strongest of all German princes. This arrangement did not cover all areas of Germany as it left out such jurisdictions as Bavaria.

Charles' son, Sigismund (Holy Roman Emperor, 1411-1437), successfully recruited one of the papal claimants, John XXIII to call the Council of Constance that ended the Great Schism of the popes. Sigismund died without an heir and the electors chose his Hapsburg son-in-law, Albert of Austria. The Hapsburg line of Holy Roman Emperors began with Emperor Albert II in 1438 and remained continuously except for a short period (1742-1745) until 1806. Frederick III (1440-1493), Albert II's son, spent most of his energy defending the empire against the intrigues of the Ottoman Empire. In the Siege of Neuss (1474-1475), he forced Charles the Bold of Burgundy to give his daughter Mary of Burgundy as wife to Frederick's son, Maximilian. Maximilian, Holy Roman Emperor from 1493 to 1519, arranged the marriage of his son, Philip of Burgundy, with Joanna of Castle, the daughter of the Spanish monarchs,

Ferdinand and Isabella. As a result of the Battle of Dornach and the 1499 Treaty of Basel, Maximilian was forced to acknowledge the de facto independence of the Swiss confederacy from the Empire.

For the most part, only a few Holy Roman Emperors had enough power to influence events significantly. The first emperor, Otto I, linked the history of Italy and Germany together for centuries. Louis IV, a main opponent of the Pope John XXII, became patron of the two great thinkers of the age, Marsilius of Padua and William of Ockham. Sigismund organized the Council of Constance that ended the Great Schism of the popes and the life of Jan Hus who was burnt at the stake. The Hapsburg marriages created the largest empire of the world, to that time. Charles V (son of Philip of Burgundy and Joanna of Castile) was the most powerful ruler of Europe in the 16th century. The Hapsburgs were at the zenith of their power. Shortly after that, three great struggles emerged that sapped the Hapsburg strength: (1) defense of Central Europe against the Turks, (2) support of the Catholic Church against Protestantism and (3) a series of wars with Louis XIV of France whose territory faced the prospect of Hapsburg encirclement. The Ottoman Empire sought out advantage with the Protestants and a 16th century alliance with France against the Hapsburg empire. Also, the French allied themselves with Protestant Sweden and the Lutheran princes in Germany to achieve their ends.[169]

Rebellion in the Low Countries

Philip the Fair, Duke of Burgundy and Brabant (1478-1506), son of Holy Roman Emperor Maximilian I and Mary of Burgundy, succeeded to his mother's dominions in the Low Countries before marrying Joanna, daughter of Ferdinand of

Aragon and Isabella of Castile. Their son, Charles V, was born in 1500. His aunt, Margaret of Austria, acted as regent on his behalf in Burgundy, after the death of his father in 1506. In 1515, on the death of Ferdinand, Charles V became the King of Spain, founding the Hapsburg Dynasty in Spain.

The Low Countries held an important place in the Empire. Because of trade and industry along with the rich cities, they were also important for the treasury. After Charles V left the Low Countries for Spain, one of the main changes was the effect of the Calvinist influences moving down the Rhine. In the heavily urbanized Low Countries, new religious ideas spread quickly. Efforts to repress religious dissent soon followed, and this repression clashed with the regions' traditions of independence. Prior to 1553, Protestants had moved between communities in the Seventeen Provinces and bases in England and East Friesland (Emden) ahead of the Hapsburgs authorities persecuting religious dissention.

The ascension of Philip II to the Spanish throne in 1555 brought on the next crisis in the history of the Spanish Netherlands, as King Philip's strident Spanish Catholicism coincided tragically with the rise of Protestantism in northern Europe.[170] In the Flemish cities especially, Protestantism was a deeply political movement, linked to the long tradition of resistance to aristocratic domination. In 1557 Spain declared bankruptcy. The Low Countries were the richest of Philip II's dominions and he had heavy taxes levied to help alleviate the financial difficulties. Philip II's administration further alienated the Low Countries by organizing the church into more bishoprics and increased activity of the Inquisition, seeking Spanish heretics who had fled Spain. This activity came up against the limited freedoms that the Dutch had gained from the Dukes of Burgundy (local power that was theirs by right). By 1562, Protestant activities came into the open with public services.[171]

In 1566, a group of noblemen petitioned the Regent Margaret to mollify the heresy laws. She yielded, Protestants abandoned their caution, and exiles returned home. Preachers excited mobs to sack churches and attack iconoclastic symbols. In response, Philip II sent the Duke of Alva to suppress the activity which saw much violence and large numbers of the community in Antwerp dispersed. William of Orange was the largest landowner in the Netherlands after Philip II. He refused to swear a reformulated oath to Philip in 1567, and fled the country, withdrawing to his possessions in Nassau.

Heavy taxes and abuse of privileges kept the spirit of resistance active leading to open rebellion in 1572. William of Orange returned from exile to lead the revolt. In 1579 the Northern Provinces signed the Union of Utrecht, bringing together the cities and provinces committed to carrying on resistance to Spanish rule. While initially developed to facilitate the military capacity and conduct the war of independence, it became the foundation of a separate state and distinct nation in the northern Netherlands. Before the Low Countries could be completely reconquered, war between England and Spain broke out, forcing the Spanish troops under Philip II to halt their advances. Meanwhile, Philip's Spanish troops had conquered the important trading cities of Bruges and Ghent. Antwerp, which was then arguably the most important port in the world, had to be conquered.

Antwerp, the cultural and economic centre of the Seventeen Provinces, fell against the Spanish army under Duke of Parma on August 17, 1585. This ended the Eighty Years War for the southern Netherlands and sent the Protestant citizens into exile. Half of the population of Antwerp went north, as did the rich Calvinist merchants of the southern cities. Many migrated to Amsterdam, at the time a tiny port, but quickly transformed into one of the most important ports in the world during the 17th century.[172]

The Spanish invasion of the Netherlands was interrupted periodically by other events in Europe. One such event was the Spanish Armada that set sail from Lisbon in 1588 with the goal of invading England to shut off the support of the English for the Dutch rebels. Pope Sixtus V, who treated the invasion as a crusade, supported Philip II. Prior to the undertaking, Pope Sixtus V allowed the king of Spain to collect crusade taxes and granted his men indulgences. The Spanish fleet - the Armada – hounded by Dutch and English ships, was destroyed in the waters around the British Isles, with the majority of the damage due to a succession of storms.

The United Provinces (the Netherlands Proper) fought on intermittently. From 1588 to 1598, the army of the Northern Provinces, under the command of Maurice of Orange, drove back the Spaniards such that the borders of present day Netherlands were defined. During the peace from 1609 to 1621, the Dutch built up their fleet. When war resumed, the Dutch fleet crippled the maritime trade, which Spain relied on after its economic collapse. This fighting was part of the Thirty Years War occurring in the rest of Europe, and concluded with The Peace of Westphalia in 1648. Part of the Treaty of Westphalia, the Treaty of Munster, ended the Eighty Years War; Spain and the Holy Roman Empire recognized the Republic as a free and sovereign state. This treaty closed the Scheldt to navigation and destroyed Antwerp's trading activities. The treaty ended Spain as a major power. Portugal and Spain had been under the common throne from 1580 to 1640, but in 1640 the Portuguese restoration war commenced, and Portugal would wait another twenty-nine years to get its colonies back. During this time the Dutch found it easier to attack the poorly defended Portuguese outposts than Spanish.[173]

The Hapsburgs inherited one of the richest areas of Europe. The Hapsburg marriages created the largest empire of the world, to that time. Charles V (son of Philip of Burgundy and Joanna of Castile) was the most powerful ruler of Europe. His son, Philip II of Spain, chose to reinstitute the Catholic faith in the Low Countries even though it meant frittering away the richest part of his empire. The trade was chiefly in the hands of Calvinist merchants, many of who moved north after the 1585 siege of Antwerp. The inflow of merchants set the scene for Amsterdam to become the largest trading port of Europe in 17th century. The northern provinces of the former Hapsburg territories became the Protestant United Provinces. The revolt of the Spanish Netherlands led to the collapse of Spain as a major European power.

Tulipmania

While a small ruling class of aristocratic origin ruled Venice, the United Provinces were ruled by a small oligarchy consisting of merchants. In the United Provinces, the small ruling class of merchants were Protestants, and formed the pillar of the community. Calvinism predominated. Calvinism encouraged the purposeful investment of money, by presenting luxury and self-indulgence as a vice and thrift as a virtue. In the 17th century, the Dutch were the most urban population in Europe, as two-thirds lived in towns and had the highest wages in Europe. Prosperity was based on overseas trade.

Dutch trade with the orient began with one ship in 1595, and subsequently expanded up to ten ships sent out annually by merchants to trade in the East. In 1602, the Dutch India Company was formed. It had a tax-free monopoly for twenty-one years, power to build forts, establish colonies, mint coins and maintain an army and navy as required. The Dutch East India Company established a capital in 1619 at Batavia, Java.

In 1609 the Bank of Amsterdam was founded. It was the first exchange bank established in northern Europe. It had full reserves and operated without fear of failing. Coins held in the bank were secure against theft and did not need to be repeatedly assayed. The two main benefits were that merchants could carry out business transactions by transferring deposits between accounts and it provided a system to discourage the circulation of debased coins. It covered 800 foreign coins. The bank served an important role in maintaining the prosperity of Amsterdam.[174]

During the 17th century the Dutch could build wooden ships faster and cheaper than any of their rivals in Europe. The lumber came from countries around the Baltic Sea. These Dutch vessels were very important in carrying the trade that was the lifeblood of the economy. The Dutch maintained the largest merchant fleet in the world in the 17th century.

Tulips were popular in the courts of Suleiman the Magnificent, Sultan of the Ottoman Empire from 1520 to 1566. This was at the height of Ottoman power when the Ottoman Empire stretched from Tripoli to the Persian Gulf to Hungary. Ogier Ghiselian de Bushecq, the Austrian ambassador of Emperor Ferdinand I to the Ottoman Empire, first saw the magnificent tulip blooms in Constantinople. In mid-1550's he brought back some bulbs and seeds to Vienna where he gave them to his friend Carolius Clusius, then Prefect of the Imperial Herb Garden. Carolus Clusius successfully raised the first European tulips in the 16th century. He fled to Holland for religious sanctuary, where, in 1553, he became Director of the botanical garden at the University of Leiden. He took his bulbs with him and both thrived in the Dutch climate. In early 17th century horticultural experimenting created many new breeds of tulips. At this time Dutch merchants were at the centre of the lucrative East Indies trade. The rich merchants paid high prices for rare bulbs with intense colours, that were akin to art trading. Initially, they chased beauty and status. The most spectacular and highly sought after tulip had vivid colour lines and flames on the petals as a result of being infected with a tulip specific virus known as Mosaic virus. During the 1630's, the middle class moved into tulip trading and speculation in full force, which was discouraged by government but driven by the economy. In 1637 the bubble burst and the tulip market crashed with the price of tulips dropping 100 fold. The fall out of the bubble burst damaged the code of honour that underlay Dutch capitalism.[175]

In the 17th century, the Dutch empire spread around the world. By 1658, the Dutch had ousted the Portuguese from Ceylon (Sri Lanka). Ceylon's importance came from it being a half-way point between their settlements in Indonesia and South Africa. The island itself was a source of cinnamon and elephants, which were sold to Indian princes. India was twice as large a market as Europe. The Banda Islands were the only place in the world where nutmeg was found, at this time the most valuable spice in the world. As a commodity it could be sold for over 300 times its cost.[176]

Dutch sea captains discovered that it was feasible to sail directly northeast across the Indian Ocean from the southern tip of Africa. This made the Cape a very important port of call for taking on water and fresh supplies. In 1651, the company decided to meet this need by establishing a small Dutch settlement on the bay beneath Table Mountain. The Dutch were successful in keeping other European powers out of the Spice Islands, but in expelling the English from the Moluccas, the Dutch unwittingly did them a favour. The English East India Company decided to concentrate its efforts on India.

The Dutch Republic became known for its relative religious tolerance. Jews from the Iberian Peninsula, Huguenots from France, prosperous merchants and printers from Flanders, as well as economic and religious refugees from the Spanish controlled parts of the Low Countries, found safety in Amsterdam. The influx of Flemish printers and the city's intellectual tolerance made Amsterdam a centre for the European free press. In the 17th century, the United Provinces emerged as a commercial and maritime power. The Dutch East India Company established the Dutch empire extending from Cape of Good Hope, east to trading posts in India, Ceylon and Indonesian Spice Islands, and policed the area to control the trade. Amsterdam became the financial centre of the world and emerged as Europe's leading trade centre and, in turn, became the cultural capital of Europe.

11

Age of Enlightenment

The Growth of Democracy in England

The development of the English parliament is intertwined with the story of the church and tax money in England. The first significant intervention was by Pope Innocent III, during the height of the power of the church, supporting King John in his fight with the barons. This intervention coincided with the signing of the Magna Carta - one of the earliest documents designed to define the power of the monarch. During the period of turmoil in Henry III's reign, Simon de Montford, in an attempt to secure popular support for his plan to limit the power of the crown, increased representation in parliament and introduced two knights from each county and two burgesses from each town. Edward I convoked the Model Parliament in an effort to make the crown less dependent on the nobles. Elizabeth I used the parliament to introduce any changes to the church – ensuring input from all sides. Charles

I triggered a civil war with the parliamentarians by raising a standing army without the consent of parliament. The 1689 Bill of Rights reaffirmed parliament's claim to legislation and taxation. The deposition of the Roman Catholic James II ended any chance of Catholicism becoming re-established in England. The 1701 Act of Settlement ensured when the last Protestant heir of James II, Queen Anne, died, the crown went to a German Protestant. With foreign kings, the British parliament became more powerful.

Henry II (a great grandson of William the Conqueror) was one of the most effective administrators of England's monarchs. He reformed the finance, justice and administrative systems of the country. The church courts instituted by William the Conqueror became a safe haven for criminals of varying degree and ability, for one in fifty of the English population qualified as clerics. During the efforts to reform the church courts, there was a clash with the church that led to the death of Thomas Beckett, Archbishop of Canterbury. In the resolution of this conflict, the appeals from the church courts in England went to the pope's court. This remained in place until the Reformation.

In 1189 Henry II died, and his son, Richard the Lionheart, succeeded. Richard sold the three northern counties of England to King William of Scotland for 10,000 crowns and took off for the crusades. For various reasons he was absent from England most of his reign. John succeeded Richard in 1199, and became the first Duke of Normandy to reside in England. John faced two powerful enemies, King Philip Augustus of France and Pope Innocent III. At the beginning of his reign, John clashed with the pope over the appointment of the Archbishop of Canterbury. The Pope had favoured Stephen Langton, John refused and the Pope closed down the churches of England for over six years – no baptisms, no marriages, no last rites, no church tithes.

Normandy was lost in 1205. John needed money to continue the fight in France but received push back from the barons. The barons rebelled in 1212 but John easily dispersed them. He had been excommunicated by the church in Rome, and in order to repair the relationship he gave England and Ireland to the church in Rome. The northern Earls rose in rebellion again in 1215, and there were chases around the country. Finally he met the barons in June 1215 at Runnemede. John made small concessions and agreed to rule England with a council of twenty-five barons. The barons were to receive their confiscated lands and parks back. The document recording this was stamped with the royal seal and known as the Magna Carta. Pope Innocent annulled and abrogated the Magna Carta and described it as conspiracy against and persecution of his vassal, King John of England. Pope Innocent excommunicated all the Surety Barons; the result was armed conflict. The Barons refused to leave London after the signing, and invited France to intervene. The Dauphin of France led an invasion force that landed at Stanhope on May 21, 1216. Rather than full engagement, John retreated across England. The Dauphin and the barons held much of England for almost a year. The pope excommunicated the King of France, the Dauphin and all accomplices. John fell ill and died October 1216. John's son Henry III descended the throne at the age of nine years. William Marshall, the new protector and Regent of England, pulled together forces to support Henry III, and, in 1217, Marshall led an army that defeated the Dauphin and the northern barons at Lincoln. After signing a pact, the Dauphin was allowed to return to France.

On November 12, 1216 the Magna Carta was reissued with some of the contentious clauses (such as the council of 25 barons) removed. It was reissued in 1225 when Henry III became of age. With his fifty-six year reign the Magna Carta became established. Henry III's failed attempt to place his youngest son as King of Sicily led to bankruptcy and threatened excommunication. Henry III (1207-1272) was met by nobles under Simon de Montford in 1258 who presented the king with the Provisions of Oxford. Power was placed in a council of 15 members who were to supervise ministerial appointments, local administration and custody of royal castles. Parliament was to meet three times a year to monitor the council. The barons pressed Henry III with the Provisions of Westminster in 1259 in a futher further attempt to define common law in the spirit of the Magna Carta. For the first time the English crown was forced to recognize the rights of power of parliament. A Papal Bull of 1261 exempted the king from the oath. Civil war broke out and the king was taken prisoner. In 1265 Simon de Montfort, wishing to secure popular support for his plans to limit the power of the crown, called the Great Parliament with increased representation: two knights from each county and two burgesses from each town. This was the first elected parliament. De Montford was defeated and killed at the Battle of Evesham in 1265. By the Statute of Marborough in 1267, the king promised to uphold the Magna Carta and part of the Provisions of Westminster. Henry III adopted de Montford's expanded parliament that he called from time to time during his reign. The Great Council of Nobles, which consisted of barons and bishops, was known as Lords. The group consisting of knights and burgesses was known as Commons. This became the basis for the House of Lords and House of Commons in the present British parliamentary system.[177]

Edward I (1272-1307) convoked the Model Parliament in 1295, not for the purposes of democratic reform, rather to broaden political structure and thereby make the king less dependent on the nobles. This parliament reissued the Magna Carta for the final time in October 1297. The Magna Carta was an early attempt at separation of church and state. The first clause stipulated that the Church of England would be free from the influence of the king. The dispute of King John over the choice of Archbishop of Canterbury was fresh in their minds. This document became important in the 17th century as Parliament tried to control the power of the monarchs.

Elizabeth I ruled from 1558 to 1603, the longest reigning monarch of England in two centuries. She was the first woman to successfully occupy the throne. She was called "Good Queen Bess", and enjoyed enormous popularity during her lifetime. Her mother, Ann Bolyn, was beheaded for treason when she was age two. She was raised as a Protestant in the household of Catherine Parr, Henry VIII's sixth wife. She received a rigorous training in Greek, Latin rhetoric and philosophy from her tutor, Roger Ascham. When her half-sister Mary was ruler, she spent some time in the Tower of London because she was Protestant.

The reign of Elizabeth I was known for the defeat of the Spanish Armada, the English Renaissance of literature with the outpouring of poetry and drama by William Shakespeare, Christopher Marlowe and the establishment of Protestant religion in England. With respect to religion, Henry VIII terrorized Catholics and Mary I terrorized Protestants while Elizabeth took a more tolerant approach. Protestants who had fled during Mary's reign, returned with the new ideas of John Calvin. Throughout Elizabeth's reign, Catholics challenged her on one side and Puritans on the other. She used Parliament and the Privy Council to ensure input from all sides. The significance of her religious settlement was that she was able to hold a great majority of people together despite being a compromise few would have chosen.

Charles I became king in 1625 with the death of his father James I. There was tension early in his reign over finances and religious suspicion, when he married a Roman Catholic, Henrietta Maria of France. He clashed with the first four parliaments, then reigned for eleven years starting in 1629 without parliament. He engaged in ill-fated wars with both France and Spain at the same time. There was rebellion in Scotland when he tried to force the high Anglican liturgy on the Scots, so Charles had to call a parliament, which queried the need for funds for war against the Scots. This Parliament refused to vote the king funds unless royal abuses were addressed, and was dissolved within weeks. Charles I was forced to call another parliament in 1640 - which became known as the Long Parliament. He had to agree that parliament could not be dissolved without its own consent and the Triennial Act stipulated no more that three years could lapse between parliaments. An Irish uprising in 1641 led to a clash between king and parliament over command of the army. The plots against Elizabeth I and the Gunpowder Plot in James' I reign was still fresh in collective memories, when the Protestant course was going badly in the war in Europe. Parliament did not want Charles to raise his own army; the result was the Militia Bill in which troops could only be raised under officers approved by parliament.

In August 1642 Charles raised an army without permission of parliament. Parliament responded by raising an army and controlling the navy and making an alliance with the Scottish Presbyterian group. Following some military reverses, Charles placed himself in the hands of the Scottish army, tried to rally the Scots around him but failed, and was turned over to the English. In 1648, Cromwell's final victory at Preston set up Charles' trial and subsequent beheading and establishment of the Commonwealth. His two sons, Charles II and Duke of York (later James II) fled to France.

Charles II (1660-1685) restored the monarchy with concessions to religious tolerance and general amnesty. On his watch, England lost a naval war with the Dutch, the great plague hit London (1665), and the Great Fire destroyed 450 acres of

London in 1666. Charles II patronized the arts and sciences by inviting Van Dyck and Ruebens to work in England and buying a collection of paintings by Raphael and Titian. He helped organize the Royal Society - a scientific group whose early members included Robert Hooke, Robert Boyle and Isaac Newton.[178]

When Charles II died in 1685, his younger brother became king at the age of 52. James II made a series of mistakes in political and religious spheres: he turned from Anglicism to Catholicism, he acted recklessly and attempted to restore royal prerogative and turn England back to the Catholic faith, and he married a Catholic, Mary of Modena. Charles II had James' children from Anne Hyde, Mary and Anne, raised as Protestants. From Parliament, royal lineage was still of major consideration, but Protestantism became a major factor in choosing a monarch. The birth of a male heir to Mary of Modena interfered with parliament's plan for James' Protestant daughter, Mary, to succeed him to the throne.

William III, son of William II, Prince of Orange, and Mary, daughter of Charles I, was born at the Hague. As leader of the Protestants in Europe, he led campaigns to drive the French out of Dutch territory and spent his life addressing the aggressions of Louis XIV. He married Mary, daughter of James II. With the birth of a son to James II and his Catholic wife, parliament invited Mary and William to become rulers of England. William and his army landed at Torbay, Nov 5, 1688. There was no fighting in England and this became known as the "Glorious Revolution." Resistance in Scotland ended with the defeat of Dundee at Killiecrankee. Forces of the French, Irish and James were defeated at the Battle of Boyne by an army led by William.[179]

After 1688, parliament met more often and developed into the two party system of Whigs and Tories. In 1689 Parliament passed the Bill of Rights, which limited the sovereign's rights, reaffirmed parliament's claim to legislation and taxation, the King was forbidden to maintain a standing army in time of peace without parliament's consent, and prohibited Catholics or anyone married to a Catholic from becoming sovereign. This was part of the Glorious Revolution as parliament became a permanent feature of life. In 1694, The Bank of England was established to raise money for war by borrowing. It was set up as a guaranteed loan to the monarch by a group of business-men with all the privileges of a bank. It provided transparency to parliament on government expenditures. William's policy of intervention in Europe was costly in terms of finance and popularity, as William spent much time abroad, engaged as the leader of Protestants fighting France to contain French expan-sionism by Louis XIV.

The Toleration Act of 1689 gave all non-conformists (Prot-estant denominations outside Anglicanism), but not Roman Catholics, freedom of worship. The Act of Settlement in 1701 was designed to secure Protestant succession to the throne and strengthen guarantees of ensuring a parliamentary system of government. According to the Act, the throne went to Sophia, Elector of Hanover, and a granddaughter of James I, and her Protestant heirs. This was a reaction to the Catholic counter-reformation proceeding on the continent and the conspiracy theories swirling about in England. With the death of Queen Anne, the youngest Protestant daughter of James II, the Brit-ish crown went to George of the House of Hanover. He was a Protestant who spoke not a word of English, only German.

The council of barons established by the Magna Carta grew over the centuries into a parliament representing the church, wealthy noblemen like the barons, commoners and people from the emerging middle class. William signed the English Bill of Rights, assuring the power of parliament and indirectly denying that kings have the divine right to rule. The Glorious Revolution event marked the beginning of modern English parliamentary democracy. It was called glorious because it achieved its goals without bloodshed in England. This struggle between king and parliament ended in victory for the people. The revolution permanently established parliament as the ruling power of England. Some describe the Enlightenment as beginning with Britain's Glorious Revolution.

Age of Reason

The 18th century is called the "Age of Reason" or the "Age of Enlightenment." In the Western world a philosophical, cultural and political movement tried to institute the law of reason in all areas of life. The enlightenment aimed at a future for humanity that was characterized by sober rationality, scientific investigation, improved technology, popular democracy, universal peace and the progressive improvement of people's lives both in terms of physical comfort and intellectual sophistication. Gone in particular would be the fanatical and bloody wars fought in the name of religion, the dogged adherence to opinions and customs, the persecution of so-called heretics, the oppressive rule of absolute governments and the general ignorance and backwardness of a population that had been kept in the dark by worldly and spiritual authorities for too long. In 1751, Denis Diderot recruited a group of intellectuals in France to write and publish the first systematic encyclopedia of human knowledge. This group included Voltaire, d'Alambert, La Mettrie and Rousseau. They hoped to enlighten the public by encouraging critical thinking, promoting scientific research and by publishing information that people could use to understand their world and improve their material existence. Initially a twenty-eight volume encyclopedia was published. The

Catholic Church in France banned the books because of some articles that criticized religious persecution. The books were translated into other languages and spread to the rest of the world, including the American colonies.

The over-all ideal and goal of the Enlightenment was rational self-determination. On a personal level, it was the idea that every individual had the right to determine for himself or herself how to live and what to live for; a person's own reason and conscience was the ultimate arbiter of right and wrong. This commitment to human self-determination had a profound effect on the religious life of the West. The Enlightenment thinkers reduced the role of God in the explanation of things and the influence of religion in public life as much as possible. A massive shift towards the secularization of life was a crucial development in the Age of Reason. The established religion (in France the Catholic Church), which continued to insist it was the only source of truth, was one of the main targets of the Enlightenment. Religion became merely a personal and private affair, the separation of state and church an accepted principle. While the ideas of the Enlightenment were the focus of thinking in the salons of Paris and Berlin, the practical application of ideas was carried out in the American colonies.[180]

David Hume (1711-1776), a Scottish historian, philosopher and economist, was born in Edinburgh. After studies at the University of Edinburgh, he traveled England and France for a few years. From 1763 to 1765 he served as secretary to Lord Hereford in Paris where he met Voltaire and Rousseau. He was part of the "Scottish Enlightenment." His writings influenced others like Immanuel Kant, who wrote, "I freely admit that it was the remembrance of David Hume which, many years ago, first interrupted my dogmatic slumber and gave my investigations in the field of speculative philosophy a completely different direction." [181]

Immanuel Kant (1724-1804) became one of the greatest Enlightenment thinkers. In his 1784 essay *What is Enlightenment?* he declared:

> "Enlightenment is man's release from his self-incurred tutelage. Tutelage is the inability to use one's own reason without direction from someone else. The tutelage is self-incurred when its cause does not lie in the lack of reason, but in the lack of resolution and courage to use it without direction from someone else. Sapere aude! *'Have courage to use your own reason!'* —that is the motto of the enlightenment."[182]

Kant developed a unique moral philosophy: a moral person has to determine rationally for himself or herself what is right and wrong; a moral person has to be autonomous. To keep this philosophy of personal autonomy or individual self-determination from becoming subjective, or veering off into egotistic arbitrariness, he designed a system of ethics. One important aspect required testing whether a particular judgment or action is morally all right or not. Kant declared: "Act only on that maxim which you can at the same time will to be a universal law."[183] A maxim is a personal rule that someone might follow in his or her life. The moral test of the validity of such a maxim consists of asking whether one would accept it as a universal law, i.e. as something every rational being would follow. If the answer is yes, then the rule of conduct in question is morally all right. If the answer is no, then the rule is morally irrelevant or even immoral. It is an individualism that is embedded in a community of other individuals who are all equally autonomous and beholden to the consideration of the interest of others.[184]

Adam Smith (1723-1790) met David Hume, about 1750, and they became good friends and shared a close intellectual alliance. Adam Smith toured France from 1764 to 1766, where he met many of the intellectual leaders of the country, and he published *Wealth of Nations* in 1776, which established him as the "Father of Modern Economics." "The invisible hand" is an often-quoted metaphor that appears in Book IV of the *Wealth of Nations*. It implies that in a free British market, the self-interest of the capitalist, an individual pursuing his own good tends also to promote the good of his community. The free competitive market ensures these goods and services perceived as most beneficial, efficient or of the highest quality will naturally be those that are most profitable. In this free price system the prices were not set by government or a central planning board, but by the interchange of supply and demand.

The ideas of the Age of Enlightenment included the premise that science can explain everything, where previously God had controlled the universe. The philosophers thought they had discovered a simple formula for perpetual human happiness. They sought to deliver individuals from restraints so that they could act freely in accordance with their nature. On the one hand, the formula promised that pursuit of self-interest would benefit society; on the other, it promised that a free human reason would produce sound moral judgments. In other words, individual freedom permitted the operation of natural laws. Believing they had learned these laws, eighteenth-century rationalists thought they had found the secret of never-ending progress.[185]

These thinkers and writers believed that human reason could be used to combat ignorance, superstition, and tyranny, and to build a better world. These attitudes shaped events in America – the American Revolution would not have happened when it did without these ideas. These ideas also enabled the French revolution twenty years later. The Reign of Terror under Robespierre, that included beheading 15,000 suspected enemies and dissenters marked the end of this age. People blamed the Enlightenment attacks on tradition and challenging norms for the excesses during the time of the revolution.

The American Colonies

The development of the American colonies was dictated by various waves of emigration during the 17th and 18th centuries. The first permanent colony was established at Jamestown, Virginia. The town was named in honour of King James I and Virginia in honour of the "Virgin Queen", Elizabeth I, who never married. Charles II, at the time of the restoration, gave the colony the title of "Dominion" because they had remained loyal to the crown during the English civil war. (This became the source of the name "Old Dominion.") In 1689, the capital was moved to Middle Plantation, which was renamed Williamsburg in honour of William of Orange.

Charles I dissolved Parliament in 1629, and proceeded to raise royal finances without parliament. In parallel, William Laud continued the plan to turn the church to high Anglican. This upset many who wanted the church to move closer to continental reform ideas. Subsequently, 20,000 Protestants left Britain immigrating to New England. This ushered in the era of the first governor of Massachusetts, John Winthrop. University trained clergy were part of this group and, in 1636, they founded a university college that was soon named Harvard after an early benefactor.

Charles I granted a charter for Maryland (named after his Catholic wife, youngest daughter of Henry of France and his wife Maria de Medici) to Lord Baltimore who was a recent convert to Catholicism. Lord Baltimore sought to make a haven for Catholics and sought a policy of religious toleration. This allowed Protestants and Catholics to work together harmoniously. Protestants still formed the majority of the colonists throughout the history of colonial Maryland.

In 1609, Henry Hudson, under the employ of the Dutch East India Company, was sent to look for a shorter route to the orient via a northern route, rather than around the Cape of Good Hope. During this search he explored Manhattan Island and the Hudson River up to Albany. This gave the Dutch their claim to the region. In 1614 a Dutch fur trading post was established at the southern end of Manhattan. A decade later thirty Dutch families arrived at Albany and built a settlement named Fort Orange. In 1626, the governor of the colony purchased the Island of Manhattan from the local Indians and built a fort at the lower end named, New Amsterdam. Charles II did not have a good rapport with his parliament, therefore, he was always searching for ways to finance his court. His brother, the Duke of York was a partner in the East India Company. The main cause of the Second Anglo-Dutch War was the plan to seize Dutch colonies and control world trade. The British seized Dutch colonies in West Africa, the Caribbean and New Amsterdam in North America, and, in 1664, the British conquered New Amsterdam and renamed it New York after the Duke of York and Albany. At the peace settlement the Dutch preferred to obtain control of the small Island of Run, in exchange for Manhattan and the surrounding area. This was considered a more valuable asset as it consolidated the Dutch control of the Spice Islands and gave the Dutch the world monopoly on nutmeg.[186]

Charles II granted the Charter of Pennsylvania in 1681 to William Penn as a payment of 16,000 pounds that the crown owed his father, Admiral William Penn, a hero of the Second Anglo-Dutch War. William Penn, the founder of Pennsylvania (which was named after his father) was a Quaker. The Quakers were not welcome by the Church of England, and Penn used his connections to set up the colony that would be home for his persecuted friends. The territory was set between Lord Baltimore's province of Maryland and the Duke of York's province of New York. This colony was known for religious freedom and tolerance with native Americans. The area was also open to people fleeing religious wars in central Europe which led to a population represented by Lutherans, German Reformed, Moravian, Amish and Mennonite churches. The population grew quickly, and Philadelphia became the most important city in colonial America - the intellectual hub of American life, strongly influenced by European thoughts. Philadelphia became the intellectual nerve center of revolution in the mid-1770s. The Continental Congress convened there. The Declaration of Independence was drafted and first posted there, six weeks before the news reached the royal court in London at which it was directed. By 1776, it was the largest English-speaking city in the world outside of London. New York did not overtake Philadelphia until 1835 after the opening of the Erie Canal provided access to the rich agricultural land of the interior.

A significant number of early emigrants to the American colonies were Protestants who wanted more changes than were occurring in the Anglican Church. There was no counter-reformation in America. This meant the Reformation carried on longer in America and accounts for a great deal of the influence that developed the unique American character of individualism. Because of how the colonies evolved, no one church could dominate the new state.[187]

Money was an important aspect of many of the causes of the American Revolution. The conclusion of the French and Indian wars in 1763 removed a long-standing threat to the colonies, and marked a watershed in events between England and the American colonies. The British parliament made a decision to tax the colonies to pay for the war debt and the ongoing defense. The mercantile policy of trade, requiring the colonies to almost only trade with England, was an irritant whenever it was enforced to any degree. Over the ensuing decade, the colonists pushed back against the taxation and monopolist policies imposed from England. With this push back the English parliament controlled by George III either enacted and/or enforced more rigorous legislation. The colonists' resentment grew as they were influenced by ideas of the Enlightenment, such as the theory of natural rights promoted by John Locke. His natural rights theory provided a philosophical basis for the American Revolution. The colonists organized to discuss their grievances, and in 1774 they met as the Continental Congress and agreed to petition the king to have their grievances addressed. Before they could meet again, shots were fired at Lexington and Concord and the revolution began.

During the revolution, they were drawn towards France, a natural enemy of Britain. This increased the exposure to the French Enlightenment, which taught that people should be able to gain material well being, social justice and happiness in this life, not just the next. The ideas of the Enlightenment left their mark in America following the American Revolution. The United States Constitution and Bill of Rights hold many of the ideas of the Enlightenment. Most importantly, the Enlightenment included the ideas of inherent freedoms and self-determination that defines part of what the USA *is* today, and without the ideas of the Age of Enlightenment, America would not have the form of government that it *has* today.

12

Counter-revolution and Existentialism

Counter-revolution

In 1792, the monarchy was abolished and the French republic established. The French Convention declared that France would support all peoples seeking to overthrow their monarchy, and even before it made good on that promise, France's revolutionary principles stirred challenges to monarchial regimes throughout Europe. In Austria, Prussia and Russia, fears of the spreading influence of the French revolution put an end to the "enlightened absolutism" of Joseph II, Frederick II and Catherine II and inaugurated a prolonged era of conservative reaction. In Europe, the defeat of Napoleon and the arrangement of the victorious allied powers of the Congress of Vienna, in 1815, ushered in a period with the kings, nobles and priests in control, again.[188]

The Enlightenment had been about the messages of Spinoza and Locke. Baruch Spinoza's (1632-1677) message was that an individual had the right to liberty of thought and belief without interference from a sovereign power's (church's) determination of the truth or falsity of one's ideas. John Locke (1632-1704) championed the liberty of the individual conscience as justified in the case of most Christian rites. The role of the magistrate should be confined to the maintenance of public tranquility and the defense of individual rights rather than the soul. One's religious confession is a matter of individual choice rather than institutional imposition.

Natural law evolved into natural rights. Locke was the champion of natural rights, which existed independently of political recognition granted from the state, existed irrespective of the existing political system or government, and were possessed independently of, and prior to, the formation of any political community. When people entered society, they surrendered only such rights as were necessary for their security and for the common good. Each individual retained fundamental prerogatives drawn from natural law relating to the integrity of person and property (natural rights). Locke declared when a society unduly interfered with the property interests of the citizens, they were bound to protect themselves by withdrawing their consent. Only the people could decide whether great mistakes have been made in governance. In Locke's view then, the possibility of revolution was a permanent feature of any properly formed society.[189]

Under the influence of ideas from the French Revolution, various forms of socialism appeared. Henri de Saint – Simon (1760-1825) was the champion of Christian socialism, and the French Revolution influenced his ideas. His belief included the idea that the brotherhood of man must accompany the scientific organization of industry and society. Christian activists, who demanded social programs for all individuals irrespective of being rich or poor, adopted his philosophy. Robert Owen was a Welsh social reformer and one of the founders of socialism and the co-operative movement. He believed people were a product of their environment, championed better education and labor reform, and tried the great social experiment of New Harmony – the model community in Posey County, Indiana. From 1825-29 this community tried to live on communal principles with such innovations as banning money and other commodities. It failed. The Owenites in the 1830s used individualism as a pejorative term with reference to the utopian socialist philosophy of Robert Owen.[190]

The nineteenth century saw the appearance of Christian existentialism. Soren Kierkegaard (1813-1855), born in Copenhagen, the father of Christian existentialism, was concerned about conformity and assimilation into a crowd. However, he supported the community where individuals kept their diversity and uniqueness. Each individual made independent choices that then composed their existence. There was no mediation between self and a priest, but there was a need to repeatedly renewed faith. Individuals made choices to please God. He believed we exist in one of three spheres:(1) aesthetic – appearances, pleasures, follow happiness and social conventions; (2) ethical – do the best to do the right thing and see past the shallow pleasantries and ideas; (3) religious – give oneself entirely to God.

For Kierkegaard, the highest good for any individual was to find his or her own unique vocation against the traditional view that moral choice involved an objective judgment of right and wrong; existentialists have argued that no objective rational basis can be found for moral decisions. While objective facts are important, the more crucial element of truth involves how one relates to those matters of fact. Since how one acts is, from the ethical perspective, more important than any matter of fact, truth is to be found in subjectivity rather than objectivity. One must be constantly conscious of the potential consequences of one's actions and continually hold oneself up to divine scrutiny. He was concerned about the depersonalization of society and the mediocrity that the new social order generated. His main message was for each individual to make as fully conscious as possible choices among the alternatives that life offered became the fundamental of all existential writing and thought.[191]

The French Revolution and its excesses were attributed to the teachings of the Enlightenment. All who had been frightened by the violence of the movement were inclined to blame it on rationalism, materialism and individualism. Immediately following the revolution, thinkers attacked the ideas of the Enlightenment. Joseph de Maistre (1753-1821), uprooted by the French Revolution in 1789, became an influential spokesman for a counter-revolutionary and authoritarian conservatism in the period immediately following the French Revolution. His writings offered conservative ideas to support established authority and the church. He defended the principle of established authority which the French Revolution sought to destroy. In his writings he attacked the ideas of the Enlightenment and supported the principles that turned humanity back to God. According to de Maistre, only governments founded on the Christian constitution, implicit in the customs and institutions of all European societies, but especially that of Catholic European monarchies, could avoid the disorder and blood letting that followed the implementation of rationalist political programs such as those of the 1789 revolution. He became the publicist of the reaction. He equated "individualism" with the "infinite fragmentation of all doctrines."[192] Pat Buchanan, a voice of the religious right, praised de Maistre, calling him a "great conservative" in his 2006 book *State of Emergency*.[193]

De Maistre thought the revolution and the republic it created in the name of reason and individual rights had failed. He was one of the ablest of the neo-Catholic and anti-revolutionary movement after the French revolution who believed in the principle of established authority. He taught that social order had been "shattered to its foundation because there was too much liberty in Europe and not enough Religion."[194] He championed society the way the philosophers of the Enlightenment had championed the individual during the previous century.

The Industrial Revolution replaced feudalism. The two classes, landlords and peasants, were replaced by owners of capital and workers, or proletariat. It started in England as the large cloth industry was mechanized and organized into factories, and quickly spread to other manufacturing areas. During the Industrial Revolution, much of Europe underwent a thorough economic transformation associated with the rise of market capitalism, and levels of wealth and economic output in the West rose dramatically. Capitalism, or free market, was born out of the Industrial Revolution, as a defining characteristic of capitalism was individualism and the flood of inventions. This brought people into the cities and created unprecedented access to education. These events heralded a new era of power in the world for Europe and the United States of America in the 19th century.[195]

Jean-Paul Sartre

Jean-Paul Sartre (1905-1980) was a French philosopher known for existentialism and his social conscience. Existentialism is a movement that stresses individual freedom. He challenged the cultural and social assumptions and expectations of his upbringing. In 1932 his studies in Berlin exposed him to Hussel's idea of free, fully intentional consciousness and Heidegger's existentialism. His ideas revolved around the notion of human freedom and a concomitant sense of responsibility. He turned from Christianity, a system built around death, into an atheist who promoted a system of making conscious choices with life's alternatives in the here and now. His focus was on the profound nothingness of death – the human experience that each person necessarily experiences uniquely and individually. Posting the non-existence of God, each individual must create meaning in his or her life through acts of personal will. Depending on other people, government or religion leads to inauthentic forms of existence. The answer to the question: 'Why do I exist?' was clear – by deeds one freely performs does the authentic answer arise. In 1948, the Roman Catholic Church placed his complete works on the Index of prohibited books.

Sartre believed in an "authentic self" in which one lives without an ego. He felt people were responsible for their egos as for any object of consciousness. For authenticity, one was never identical with one's current state, but remained responsible sustaining it. In this situation one rejects the statement "that's just the way I am" and challenges oneself for failures to take responsibility for 'choosing' to remain that way. Authenticity excludes choices that oppress or consciously exploit others. For Sartre, freedom was the implicit object of any choice. He proposed ethics of authenticity through personal integrity rather than the ethics of worrying about keeping one's promises, paying one's debts and avoiding scandals.

The later part of his career concentrated on the socioeconomic and historical conditions that limited and modified that freedom (what you have been made into). After the war, he was attracted to Marxism as it supported his ideas that mankind live in a society of oppression and exploitation. He proceeded to reconcile existentialist ideas with Marxism. Marxist ideas are based on socio-economic forces beyond man's immediate control, which played a critical role in shaping his life. After the failure of the 1968 uprising in France, Sartre abandoned the Marxists and identified with the ideas of the Maoists.

For Sartre, freedom was more than the definition of a man, but includes the possibility of genuine options in concrete situations. His public debates explored the exploitive "systems" such as capitalism, colonialism and racism at work in society and the oppressive practices of individuals who sustained them. He was the social conscience of France.

Throughout his career Sartre was criticized for changing his mind on various previous ideas. His existentialist themes of alienation and commitment remained unique. A person had freedom from all authority and needed to commit himself/herself to a role in this world. The individualism of Sartre and the suspicion it stirred up towards authority made it a very attractive philosophy during the turbulent 1960s. In *Notebooks for an Ethics* (unpublished until after his death in 1980), Sartre attempted to develop an ethics consistent with the profound individualism of his existential philosophy. He became one of the most popular philosophers of the 20th century.[196]

Ayn Rand and Objectivism

Ayn Rand (1905-1982) emigrated from Russia to America in 1926. Much of her writing opposed communism that she knew first hand, and supported capitalism. Her ideas involved rejection of moral codes that condemn selfishness as the ultimate evil and held up self-sacrifice as the ultimate good. She applauded American values of rational egoism and individualism. The only moral social system was laissez-faire capitalism. Her philosophy declared that one's life and happiness were one's highest value. One did not exist as a servant or slave to others.

It was about self-responsibility – it's up to each one of us to determine what values our lives require, how best to achieve those values. In this system, governments should be limited to protecting each individual's freedom to do so. A free market system supports such interests – the free individual uses their time, money, property, as they see fit. She commented: "...the only valid justification of a government and... its only proper purpose: to protect man's rights by protecting him from physical violence."[197]

Traditional ethics has always been suspicious of self-interest, praising acts that are selfless in intent and calling amoral or immoral acts that are motivated by self-interest. Ayn Rand's view was that the exact opposite was true; self-interest, properly understood, is the standard of morality and selflessness is the deepest immorality. Rand brought together reason and ethics. Self-interest rightly understood also entails self-responsibility: one's own life is one's own and so is the responsibility for sustaining and enhancing it. Rational self-interests are not whatever one happens to feel like; reason takes into account all factors one can identify, projects consequences of potential causes of action, and adopts principles, and policies of action. The principled policies a person should adopt are called virtues. Virtues include rationality, productiveness, honesty, independence and integrity. One would judge people based on their value.

Ayn Rand opposed the traditional ideas of traditional European philosophy from the Enlightenment. The dilemma of her philosophy is it pits self-interest against morality. It appears that acting with the interests of others would be sacrificing one's self interest. As conflicts of interest are fundamental to the human condition, it takes ethics to be the solution. Rand believed that everyone was born as a blank slate; some people had mistakes in their development and other acquired bad habits. Her answer to most questions relied on humans being rational and producing ever-abundant food and alternate resources to answer challenges. She made a moral case for individualism and liberty through her novels.

The Cold War represented an intense rivalry between two great power blocks and ideologies; they represented democracy and capitalism in the case of the United States and its allies, and Communism in the case of the Soviet bloc. From Ayn Rand, western economists found a philosophy they could apply to 'the free market' system during the Cold War. Her writings support the capitalist system while attacking the socialist model under communism. In her philosophy, self-interest trumped altruism.

Conservatives liked her philosophy as it supported capitalism and free enterprise. She was an influence on Friedrich Hayek and Milton Freidman. She had a close inner group that included Alan Greenspan and Nathaniel Branden. A young Alan Greenspan defended her policies and, as Chairman of the Board of Governors of the Federal Reserve (1987-2006), was associated with a decade of deregulation and adjusting interest rates to historic lows that contributed to the housing bubble and subprime mortgage and credit crisis in 2007. Nathaniel Branden went from a strong proponent of objectivism to having considerable influence on the self-esteem movement. In his 1969 publication of *The Psychology of Self-Esteem,* he promoted self-esteem as the single most important facet of a person.[198] The belief that one must do whatever he can to achieve positive self-esteem has become a movement with broad societal effects. This self-esteem movement has had a significant impact on the school system – in order to ensure positive self-esteem educational standards were lowered, creating a milieu for extreme individualism. Rand's atheism tended to alienate the right, while her support of capitalism alienated support from the left. Rand espoused objectivism, the blending of free markets, reason and individualism. Her summary of objectivism: "My philosophy, in essence, is the concept of man as a heroic being, with his own happiness as the moral purpose of his life, with productive achievement as his noblest activity, and reason as his only absolute."[199]

Ayn Rand was a successful and widely read author who introduced the idea of individual liberty and free markets. In a 1991 survey of more than 2000 Book-of-the-Month Club members about books that made a difference in their lives, Rand's magnum opus, Atlas Shrugged written in 1957, came in a distant second to the Bible.[200] Ayn Rand, along with Friedrich Hayek and Milton Freidman, was highly instrumental in attracting generations of individuals to libertarian ideas, a collection of political philosophies possessing the common theme of limited government and strong individual liberty.

The counter-revolutionists and the existentialists both opposed ideas from the Enlightenment of the late 18th century. The French Revolution adopted ideas from the Enlightenment and opposed a system founded on the foundation of property, Christianity, and social distinction. The counter-revolutionary movement supported established authority and the church. Existentialism was largely a revolt against traditional European philosophy, which reached its climax during the late 1700s and early 1800s. They argued that objective, universal, and certain knowledge was an unattainable ideal. These feelings led to the idea that people had to create their own values in a world in which traditional values no longer govern. Existentialism insisted that choices had to be made arbitrarily by individuals; ideally an individual developed without hindrance. This freedom supported American individualism, allowing Americans to constantly reinvent themselves.[201]

13

Christian Fundamentalism

During the Age of Enlightenment, many thought science and reason were going to lead to progressive improvement of people's lives. On a personal level, it was the idea that every individual had the right to determine for him or herself how to live and what to live for; a person's own reason and conscience was the ultimate arbiter of right and wrong. This commitment to human self-determination had a profound effect on the religious life of the West. The Enlightenment thinkers reduced the role of God in the explanation of things and the influence of religion in public life as much as possible. There was some skepticism even then. Rousseau, although an Enlightenment thinker who criticized the French Enlightenment, was fundamentally hostile toward the scientific-rationalistic spirit of the Enlightenment. In Rousseau's mind the state is a construct of the rich to manipulate the poor. Some men are able in some way or other to aggrandize more property that others.

The inequalities of property then produce tensions between the rich and poor. As a consequence of the threat, the rich seek to use their reason to think up a way of protecting the property they have accumulated at the expense of the envious poor. The state, says Rousseau, was not established as Locke had said, to defend the natural rights of man. Rather, the establishment of the state was trickery played by the rich on the poor. This allows them to be kept in poverty, while they believe they have liberty. Objectively the state is created for the express purpose of enslaving the poor; only subjectively is it formed to protect their liberty. He sounded an early, much needed warning that material progress does not necessarily bring moral progress. He helped to keep alive the classical insight that good government requires moral foundations.[202]

Romanticism was a revolt against the political ideas of the Enlightenment and Industrial Revolution. It was a reaction against the intellectualism of the 18th century, including the scientific rationalization of nature. Romanticism became a significant force in the early 19th century and radically changed the way people perceived themselves and the state of nature around them. A person listens more intently to the individual conscience than to the demands of society, and prefers rebellion to acceptance. Romanticism allowed people to get away from the constricted, rational views of life and concentrate on an emotional and sentimental side of humanity. Romanticism was more appealing to less-educated common folk and pulled them away from the empirical, scientific ideas of earlier Enlightenment philosophers. The romantic era would be defined by an emphasis on emotion and instinct, instead of reason. This not only influenced political doctrines and ideology, but was also a sharp contrast from ideas and harmony featured during the Enlightenment. The Enlightenment attacked the church because it blocked human reason. The Romantics attacked the

Enlightenment because it blocked free play of the emotions and creativity.[203]

Richard Tarnas described the evolution of thinking in the 19th century;

> "A new awareness of the Renaissance now emerged, followed in subsequent years by a new consciousness of the age of Romanticism itself. By contrast such matters concerned the scientific mind not out of empathetic appreciation, but by the virtue of their historical and anthropological interest. In the Enlightenment –scientific vision, modern civilization and its values stood unequivocally above all it predecessors, while Romanticism maintained a profound ambilivance toward modernity in its many expressions. As time passed, ambivalence turned into antagonism as Romantics radically questioned the West's belief in its own "progress," in its civilization's innate superiority, in rational man's inevitable fulfillment." [204]

Existentialism was a 19th century reaction against "impersonal" rationalism of the Enlightenment and a wish to abandon a civilization grounded in reason. Søren Kierkegaard stressed the need for faith, only by an unjustified "leap into faith" could certainty be found – which would then be entirely subjective rather than objective. He described a moral individualism based on subjectivity, individual freedom and choice. Most philosophers since Plato have held that the highest ethical good is the same for everyone, insofar as one approaches moral perfection. For Kierkegaard the highest good for the individual is to find his or her own unique vocation. For existentialists, one must choose one's own way without the aide of universal objective standards. Against the traditional view that moral choice involves an objective judgment of right and wrong, existentialists have argued that moral choice involves subjective judgment of right and wrong. This subjectivity involves passionate individual action in deciding questions of both morality and truth that includes personal experience and acting on one's own convictions is essential for arriving at the truth.[205]

This atmosphere created the arch dissenter of the age, Fredrick Wilhelm Nietzsche (1844-1900), a German philosopher, who challenged the foundations of traditional morality and Christianity. Nietzsche shared Kierkegaard's convictions that philosophy should deeply reflect the personal concerns of individual human beings. Reason can distort our perception of the world; reason can falsify the evidence of our senses. The only real world is the world apparent to our senses. Genuine autonomy means freedom from all external restraints on one's behavior. In this state of existence each individual human being lives a life without the artificial limits of moral obligation. For Nietzsche this entailed rejection of traditional values, including the Christian religion. His existentialist call, "God is dead", aimed his message at redirecting people's attention to their inherent freedom, the presently existing world, and away from all escapist, pain relieving other worlds. His message was to become who you are following instinct not reason, and that there should be freedom from all external constraints including rejection of traditional values, in particular, the Christian religion.[206]

Modernism appeared during the late 19th century. It was a mind-set that considered traditional forms of art, architecture, literature, religious faith, social organization outdated in the emerging fully industrialized world. Modernism rejects the lingering certainty of Enlightenment thinking and the existence of a compassionate all-powerful Creator. With scientific discoveries and industrial civilization there is the realization of "the loss of certainty, and the realization that certainty can never be established, once and for all."[207] The modernists felt a growing alienation incompatible with Victorian morality, optimism and convention. This was associated with rapid social changes and advances in science such as Darwin's theories of evolution. There was a departure from tradition and religion toward individualism, rational or scientific organization, and egalitarianism.[208]

Christian fundamentalism arose in the early 20th century as a reaction to modernism. This could also be interpreted as a reaction to the increasing individualism appearing in society. For the Christian fundamentalist, Biblical readings were considered a literal historical record, stressing the Bible is literally inerrant in matters of faith and morals. Conservative Presbyterian academics at Princeton wrote twelve volumes between 1910 -1915 called *The Fundamentals* reaffirming orthodox Protestant Christianity. The books commented on such topics as liberal theology of the German scholars whose studies identified discrepancies between events in history and their record in the Bible. The writings of Darwin published in 1859 immediately called into question whether the world was only 10,000 years old as determined by literal interpretation of the Scriptures. Battles ensued within the churches. By the 1930s, they began to set up their own churches as they failed to move the moderates. In the 1940s, another group appeared, opposed to the separation that was occurring and the nature of the message that evolved. The new group, called Evangelicals, wanted to develop a less antagonistic message. Some had a role in the anti-communist agenda of denouncing the Soviet Union for its suppression of religion. However, during the first half of the 20th century, they were considered on the periphery of religious activities in America.[209]

In 1949 William Franklin Graham (1918-) organized an evangelical campaign in Los Angeles, which was noticed by the national press. At this time, the mainline Protestant churches controlled America's religious public square. The California revivals were followed with a series of preaching tours or crusades across the US and then the world. Billy Graham's group became known for its organizational skills. The Billy Graham Evangelical Association (BGEA) organized on several fronts: (1) the radio show 'The Hour of Decision', (2) televising crusades, (3) the "My Answer" international newspaper column, (4) publishing *Decision Magazine* (the official BGEA publication) and (5) World Wide Pictures, a company that produces evangelical films.

Billy Graham was the first popular fundamental evangelical in the last half of the 20th century. He built his success on charisma and organizational skills. He is known for his simple homespun message with the basic advice: "anyone who repents of sins and accepts Jesus Christ will be saved."[210] He abandoned the divisiveness of previous fundamentalists and welcomed Catholics, rejected segregation and removed suspicions of higher education. He did not endorse any particular political group.[211]

Other evangelical fundamentalists followed, but not necessarily down the middle of the road. This coincided with the rise of the religious right. In 1979, Rev Jerry Falwell (1933-2007) helped organize a group called the Moral Majority devoted to re-establishing traditional religious values in national consciousness. Issues around abortion and homosexuality which conflicted with fundamentalists' beliefs were soon on the agenda. However, the organization was wound down in 1986, while Falwell focused on developing new networks and a new university in Lynchburg.

When the presidential campaign of Pat Robertson, a socially conservative evangelical failed, reorganized the network that had been built-up to found the Christian Coalition.

Initially, the Christian Coalition focused on abortion and same sex marriage. With the recruitment of Ralph Reed, the Christian Coalition focused to fight for home and family, while recruiting a grassroots constituency. Ralph Reed was a more moderate evangelical, and attracted much support and turned it into an important Republican grassroots constituency. They were part of the Contract with America in 1994. The Contract with America was a document developed by the Republican Party that represented the view of many conservative Republicans on such areas as shrinking the size of government and lowering taxes. It became popular when the Republicans gained the majority of seats in the 104th Congress.[212]

The fundamentalist dogma is based on the inerrancy of the Bible and an adherence to the dogma of their individualism. This creates a culture of rigidity, male domination and exclusion, and a clash with intellectual freedom. This group was paranoid and ready to strike back at anything modern, such as evolutionism and rational criticism of any kind. Fundamentalists reject modern science because they take the word of the Bible as literally true. This created the climate for anti-intellectualism. The intelligent and informed are labeled as elite. Anti-intellectuals often perceive themselves as champions of the ordinary people and fighters for egalitarianism against elitism. Those who mistrust intellectuals will represent them as a danger to normality, suggesting they are outsiders with little empathy for the common people. Sakharov observes, "Intellectual freedom is essential to human society... Freedom of thought is the only guarantee against an infection of people by mass myths, which, in the hands of treacherous hypocrites and demagogues, can be transformed into bloody dictatorships." [213]

The fastest growing churches in North America are the mega churches. The mega church is a significant development in Protestant Christianity that began in the 1950's. They tend to have congregations of 2000 plus and use modern upbeat music rather than traditional hymns. The main criticism of these churches is that they draw members away from smaller churches. The majority of North America churchgoers attend small churches of fewer than 200 members. The mega churches are more concerned with entertainment than religion, non-challenging and present a comfortable environment. Some say they look after the wants of the self-centered person rather than his/her needs. The proponents say these members will not respond unless they have their personal needs met. The pastor employs extensive use of entertainment and performance and preaches a positive message. The focus of the message is to save one from life's problems, instead of his sins. This is part of making people feel comfortable. To their detractors who say they are missing the main message of salvation, once a person becomes interested in the church, they will congregate in smaller groups and have an opportunity to learn the essential truths of Christianity.[214]

The Christian right is known for its support for divisive issues and exclusion of those who do not agree. A Minnesota pastor, Greg Boyd, found himself labeled a heretic on Internet blogs because he supports separation of church and state, teaches his church members to focus on a personal relation with Jesus, and he supports separation of conservative Christianity from right-wing politics. Other churches have become concerned about the divisive messages from the Christian right and are now exploring community-building issues such as poverty and the environment.[215]

In his book, *God and Gold,* Walter Russell Meade asks how England and America were able to prevail over the last three centuries in military, economic and political contests to shape the emerging world order? He describes two centuries of power of the Anglo-Saxon free market system supported by "the invisible hand" first described as the force behind the free market by Adam Smith. This has blended into the Anglo-American acceptance of "unfettered operation of the free market in recent centuries."[216] Meade suggests that this is linked to a Protestant religion that can adapt quickly to the times. In America this allows those with a transcended faith in God a personal belief that their country has a covenanted relationship with the power or person who directs historical process. Meades observes, "American ... thoughts about the historical process and America's place in it are shaped by a sense of purpose and destiny rooted in the same cultural and religious complex that made the Anglo-American world such a seedbed for capitalism."[217] This supports the vision of the city on a hill that many Americans see as driving the role of their nation in the world.

The fundamentalist Christian movement appeared at the turn of the 20th century as a response to modernity. Their concern with culture would include the new personal freedoms and equality of the sexes in politics and economics. Christian Conservatives demand that Americans meet family obligations even if it infringes upon individual freedom. For fundamentalism, the Bible is at the centre of faith. They believe that alcoholism, abortion, homosexuality, feminism and martial infidelity are social ills derived from the rampant growth of individualism. In their eyes, individualism of the liberal left is destroying family values in America.[218] At the turn of the 21st century, Christian fundamentalists continue to have influence in America because of their organizing skills in elections.

14

Islamic Fundamentalism

In 1979-80, with the Ayatollah Khomeini and the Iranian Revolution, a new term appeared. An Islamic theocracy was established in Iran, as the revolution galvanized militant Muslims around the world and introduced the concept of Islamic Fundamentalism. While previous governments' Islamic teachings gave structure to almost every facet of society, this new government and the religious authorities made the final decisions in many areas. The Western media characterized the group running Iran as Islamic Fundamentalists. This definition developed in the West saw them as a group advocating a return to the "fundamentals" of Islam. Fundamentalist Muslims oppose modernity and have a vision of the old Islamic civilization.[219] Much of what they oppose is captured by extreme individualism of the West.

One of the early modern Islamic reformists of the 20th century was Hassan al-Banna (1906-1948). He rejected accommodation of positive elements of secular model from the West. His ideas are summarized in the statement "...the civilization of the West, which was brilliant by virtue of its scientific perfection for a long time, and which subjugated the whole world with the products of this science to its states and nations, is now bankrupt and in decline."[220] He created Jamat al-Ikhwan al-Muslimun (Society of Muslim Brotherhood) in 1928. The objective was to establish a government in Egypt that ruled on *the basis of Muslim values and norms.* [221]

Mawlana Abu'l – A'lu Mawadi, (1903-1979) the founder of the fundamentalist Jama' at-I Islami in India and Pakistan, attacked modernity but was also militantly opposed to individualism. In an Islamic state, he wrote: "no one can regard any field of his affairs as personal and private."[222] He became concerned with the drift in understanding of Arabic over the centuries, and he critically reviewed the Qur'an, the hadith and writings of ancient and medieval scholars, in minute detail, building his own reinterpretation of their original meanings. He developed the concept of "new jahiliyya" based on the writings of medieval radical scholar Ibn Taymiyya who concluded Muslims could attack Mongols even though they had converted because they continued to implement Yasa code of law and not strict Sharia.[223]

Sayyid Qutb (1906-1966) as a member of the Board of Education from Egypt, visited New York in 1948. His ideas were formed during the two years he spent in the United States, which seemed to him "a disastrous combination of avid materialism and egotistic individualism."[224] On his return to Egypt in 1951, he joined Hassan al-Banna's Ikhwan al-Muslinin (Muslim Brotherhood). He studied Abdul Ala Maududi's work, but recognized the importance of science and technology and believed technology could only be harnessed by Islamic methods. He believed the Qur'an and Sunnah provide a guide to all aspects of life, including government. He wrote of the belief that "An all out offensive, a jihad, should be waged against modernity so that ... moral rearmament could take place. The ultimate objective is to re-establish the Kingdom of Allah on earth."[225] He was rejecting modernity of the West and wanting a Muslim civilization back.

With over 200 years of decline of the Moslem civilization, Muslims have looked to the past for inspiration. Ibn Taymiyy, who wrote in the 14th century expounding a philosophy of Orthodox Islam, has become an inspiration to a wide range of Muslim scholars such as Syed Qutb. The Moslem heartland was under attack by Mogul invasions from the East and the associated uncertainty and violence influence Taymiyya's thinking. Ibn Taymiyya rejected fatalism and passivity in the face of injustice. He emphasized personal responsibility for one's own life. He wrote of the need to keep Islamic law as flexible as possible within the concept of itihad (independent reasoning based on the Qur'an or scholarly texts). Islamic law should be open to reinterpretation and needs to take into account the context in which society functions. He taught that Muslims in every generation must constantly revert to the original seventh century sources rather than mindlessly apply the teachings of the scholars.[226]

In 1988, al-Qaeda was founded in Afghanistan by Osama bin Laden (1957-2011). It was initially set up to fight the Soviet occupation of Afghanistan and was part of the US backed Mujihdeen movement. When the Soviets left Afghanistan, they looked for new jihads. A jihad is a holy struggle or striving by a Muslim for a moral, spiritual or political goal. The Gulf War in 1990 outraged bin Laden because US troops were in the country with the two holiest cities. He came under the influence of militant Muslims from Egypt who harnessed his anger. For bin Laden, the message was reduced to two precepts: (1) the need to actively defend Islam, (2) strive to recreate the purity of early Moslem society.

In October 1993, eighteen US servicemen involved in a UN peacekeeping mission were killed in Somalia when Somali militia shot down two Black Hawk helicopters. It is believed Al-Qaeda fighters helped train those responsible. In 1996, bin Laden left Sudan and returned to Afghanistan. In June 1996, the US military base in Saudi Arabia was bombed and nineteen US servicemen died. In February 1998, Bin Laden issued a "fatwa" calling for attacks on US citizens. In August 1998, at the US embassies in Kenya and Tanzania, 220 people were killed when trucks loaded with bombs drove into the embassies. The USA retaliated with air strikes in Sudan and Afghanistan. In 2000 the warship USS Cole was attacked in Yemen and seventeen sailors killed. On September 11, 2001, over 3000 people died when four airplanes were hijacked, two flown into the World Trade Centre, one into the Pentagon and one into a field in Pennsylvania. The symbols of capitalism and power in the US came under attack.

While some have called the recent attacks by al-Qaeda a clash of civilizations, it is clearly not. It is an attack on the economics of globalization associated with the spread of the culture of individualism. Some liken the response from the West to a crusade. However, the friction was not created by the Christian Church, but rather by capitalists and the oil companies with interests in the Middle East. Christianity and Islam are too similar in basic teachings to justify a religious war. Even though their religions stress non-violence, al-Qaeda demonize their alleged enemies like the Medieval Christian Church did. Christianity is non-violent scripture; the Medieval Church turned to the writings of Augustine to justify war in the name of religion. Similarly, fundamentalist Muslims use the writings of medieval radical scholars like Ibn Taymiyy to justify killing even their own people. Al-Qaeda has helped themselves to various teachings of the Islamic reformers to help justify their actions.

Many in the West believe that the problems with terrorism and al-Qaeda exist because Islam is a violent religion. The treatment of heretics by the Christian Church throughout history tells a story with about as much violence as there is in Islam, if not more. The Muslim Brotherhood became established in Europe in the 1950s when they were expelled from Egypt and Syria. A beacon of Islamic identity to many Muslims, the Muslim Brotherhood encourages assertive action in defending, preserving and transmitting Islamic tradition and identity. There is the question of how moderate have the Muslims of Western Europe become? The closest answer is that they are a modifying effect rather than a moderating trend. In 1990, Yusuf al-Qaradawi, a Sunni scholar, published a book, *Priorities of the Islamic Movement in the Coming Phases*, to describe the agenda for the "Islamic Movement" in its goal "to restore Islam to its leadership of society." This includes a middle way between violent extremism and secularism. He is concerned that "expatriates not be swept up by the whirlpool of materialistic trends that prevail in the West."[227] However, materialism is the symptom, not the disease. The disease is extreme individualism. Qaradawi calls for Muslim communities in Europe to be set off by themselves with religious, recreational and educational establishments within a "Muslim ghetto." [228]

Secularism is the belief that certain practices or institutions should exist separately from religion or religious belief. It can work in reverse to protect religion from government interference. Secularism in the West guarantees the rituals, worship and spirituality of the Sharia. However, the Muslim Brotherhood marches onward with plans for " implementation of Islamic law for Europe's Muslim population."[229] An area of friction between moderate thinkers and conservatives is the argument for the greater jihad of self-introspection and improvement being more fundamental for Muslims than the lesser jihad of war and violence. The conservative forces within Islam promote the lesser jihad as being more significant. Muslims remain committed to their faith and when faced by an external threat, all will defend it. Islamic fundamentalists applauded President George Bush, the champion of the invasions of Afghanistan and Iraq, as an important force in attracting youth to their cause. Organizations like al-Qaeda help themselves to various teachings of the Islamic reformers that help justify their actions. Their fatwa to kill American citizens will not affect the cult of individualism. Their attacks are crimes that need to be addressed by police action. Through cognitive dissonance, their actions make many in the West see them as different and actually increase resolve to hunt them down.

Islam has a system of support from intellectuals and scholars. Christianity mainly has a system of ministers and priests to provide religious interpretations. The Christian Church lost the support of philosophers when Newton's Law of Gravity, which the final piece of the puzzle for the Copernican Heliocentric Theory, challenged key teachings. The church had built dogma around Earth as the centre of the universe to help people understand interpretations of the scriptures. On the other hand, conservative Muslim thinkers today use scholarship to support religious dogma and suppress ideas from the Enlightenment that are accepted in the West. The fundamentalists are trying to retain their power and control of people much like the 16th century Catholic Church.

Important hegemonic bonds, while not originally part of Islam, have become integrated in many jurisdictions with Islamic culture. Islam developed in many jurisdictions where tribal customs and the rule of honour were, and continue to be, an important aspect of the community. Islamic tribes are large, powerful, fully developed societies. The removal of a powerful political group, such as the Taliban in Afghanistan tribal society, does not necessarily open the way for new ideas from the outside, like democracy. Cultural tradition is a strong force. The tribal system does not acknowledge the individualist. The development of individualism is brought to a halt at the point where it threatens the authority of a leader. The concepts of male honour and female subservience are deeply ingrained in these jurisdictions.[230] The Islamic fundamentalists and 9/11 created the Western image of Islam as a feared religion that supports terrorism and suppresses women. Islam provides an ideal to live up to in society, but tribal customs and traditions challenge, engage and sometimes overlap with these ideals.

15

Economic Fundamentalism

E mil Brunner's definition of theology is "the study of the development of dogma. Dogma is a belief or doctrine held by any kind of organization, thought to be authoritative and not to be disputed or doubted."[231] Like the early church, economists use a language that only they understand. Like the early church that used mathematic formulae to support an earth-centered cosmology, they have tried to use mathematics to support theories at play in the free market and, like the early church, their mathematics also failed. Economics is not an exact science, nor a form of reasoning; faith appears to be a principle driver.

The "Father of Economics", Adam Smith, used the metaphor of the "invisible hand" to describe forces at play in the free market place. Under this system the self-interest of the capitalist, an individual pursuing his own good, tends also to promote the good of the community. The free competitive market ensures that those goods and services, perceived as most beneficial, efficient or of the highest quality, will naturally be those that are most profitable. In a free price system, prices are not set by government or a central planning committee but by the interchange of supply and demand.[232] Proponents of the free enterprise system turn to the philosophy of Ayn Rand to support their system. Her writings support the capitalist system while attacking the socialist model under communism. Ayn Rand used Aristolean logic to explain the "new" theology, economics, much as Thomas Aquinas applied Aristolean logic to explain medieval church theology.[233]

John Stuart Mill (1806-1873) was an influential contributor to 19th century British thought and political discourse. Mill's writing supported the principles of free market and the equality of taxation. His philosophy was utilitarianism with a main thrust to act to create the greatest happiness for the greatest number of people. He challenged existing thinkers of the immutable laws of wages, rents and profit. He did so, believing that they were not tied that tightly together. He acknowledged that material wealth was created by industrialization, and was concerned that the division of labor with the increasing simplicity and repeatedness of work, and the growing size of factories and businesses, led to a spiritual and moral deadening.[234]

Friedrich Hayek admired Adam Smith and built upon the ideas of his teacher, von Miser. Hayek had a major influence on market liberalization strategies, which included discrediting government economic planning. In the 1930s, he studied at the London School of Economics debating John Maynard Keynes' theories on the correct response to the Great Depression. In 1950, he moved to the University of Chicago and became a colleague of Milton Friedman. His polemic against socialism and communism supported the rapidly growing anti-communism that dominated the Cold War. He founded the Mount Perlin

Society in 1947 to bring together like-minded economists. The goal of these meetings was to develop theories to turn back Keynesian thinking on government involvement in the market, support laissez-faire markets, and oppose government intervention. He declared, "The most significant fact about this (price) system is the economy of knowledge with which it operates, or how little the individual participants need to know in order to be able to take the right action." [235] This is captured by Adam Ferguson (1723-1816) who described the economy as a "product of human action, not human design." [236] In 1974, Hayek received the Nobel Prize for his economic work on the theory of money and economic fluctuations and interdisciplinary analysis of economic, social and institutional phenomena. His work influenced the Regan revolution in the USA and the Thatcher administration in Great Britain. In his writings, he developed an intellectual system covering economics, law and politics, ideas that were developed from the first principles that supported liberty, which gave these ideas an attractive element of coherence. With a foundation developed from simple first principles, his students took it all the way to Fundamentalism.

William Foster Lloyd (1795-1852) was a professor of political economy at Oxford who published a book on population in 1833. This publication included the parable of *The Tragedy of the Commons*. This story describes that when pastureland was available to all the "the commons", cattle owners have short-term interest in increasing the size of their herds. If unchecked, the size of the herds on the commons would lead to overgrazing and failure of the pastureland. The argument was used by Lloyd to dispute Adam Smith's invisible hand.[237]

Garret Hardin, in his 1968 essay *The Tragedy of the Commons* builds on the parable published by William Foster Lloyd. Hardin describes "commons" as including atmosphere, oceans, rivers, fish stocks, national parks and advertising. In his essay,

Hardin notes that reliance on conscience as a means of policing commons favours selfish individuals over those more far-sighted.[238] On the same theme, the Global Commons Institute an independent group concerned with the protection of the global commons or common heritage of all humanity, such as forests, biodiversity oceans and global atmosphere, was founded in 1990. Their main focus has been on global carbon dioxide reduction strategies.[239]

Global capitalism has extended to individualism. In Santa Clara County vs. South Pacific Railway, by invoking the 14th amendment, this court case defined corporations as "persons." This ruling meant that California could not tax corporations differently than individuals. Now, as a legal 'person', corporations had First Amendment rights.[240] While courts now permit government regulation of business, corporations still retain "free speech first-amendment rights" from earlier decisions. From the 1970s on, there have been creeping rights of individuals (corporations) versus community. This activity was initially funded by the Tobacco industry and continues as corporations speak out on controversial issues. In America, an economic entity is now equated with an individual.

During the Cold War, theories of capitalism continued to develop and be elaborated in order to explain, justify, or counter the criticism of private ownership of capital, to explain the operation of capitalist markets, and guide the reduction of government spending and government regulation of property and markets. In the 1980s, the International Money Fund, World Bank and US Treasury Department embraced free market economy as a universal recipe for economically wrecked countries as expressed in the *Washington Consensus*. John Williamson, an economist at the Institute for International Economics coined the phrase in 1989 in reference to the policies necessary for recovery of Latin America from financial crises of the 1980's. Naomi Klein describes these activities in her book, *The Shock Doctrine: The Rise of Disaster Capitalism* as "Friedman's neo-liberal triumvirate of privatization, deregulation/ free trade and drastic cuts to government spending."[241] These activities actually led to increased financial speculation and market volatility in the countries in which the policies were implemented.

The September 2008 issue of *Infectious Disease Alert* reports that the rate of tuberculosis (TB) in Central and Eastern Europe is linked to International Money Fund (IMF) loans. The IMF loans to countries are often pegged to a reduction in government spending, which all too often results in reductions in health care dollars. The IMF specifically grants loans in stages based on spending performance targets, putting pressure on governments to comply. Investigators examined TB data from twenty-one countries in Central and Eastern Europe from 1989 forward and found increased rates of TB and increased rates of death from TB in countries which received funding from the IMF. Despite declining rates of TB in several of these countries prior to receiving loans, cases of TB increased 13% and death rates from TB rose by 16% in countries receiving IMF loans, compared with countries not participating in IMF programs. Increased rates were associated with larger loans and a longer duration of participation in the loan program; for every year the country participated, death rates rose by another 4%. Specifically, the timing of the IMF program was associated with lower government spending on TB programs, and fewer persons receiving targeted therapy. This is an example of how the policies of economic fundamentalism can have serious and unintended consequences for health care.[242]

Economic fundamentalists declared their victory over the Keynesian Economic Theory as Reagan and Thatcher's policies took their dogma mainstream. Hayek's pupils continue defending this theology, and many people who became rich and powerful through the unregulated free market system resist any modifications or challenges to it. They develop arguments defending the dogma of economic fundamentalism much as those who enjoyed power and wealth defended the Medieval Church. This activity laid the groundwork for globalization. There is a communication strategy to advance the corporate agenda behind globalization, and these communications are designed to reduce resistance to the process by making it seem both highly beneficent, and unstoppable. The alleged inability of governments to halt the "progress" of globalization is widely perceived as beyond human control, which further weakens resistance.[243]

Globalization has been associated with manufacturers moving operations to areas of low wages and the internationalization of finance; banks and financiers have accompanied this with concentration or oligopolistic holdings. Authoritarian regimes have shown they can manage economic growth without making concessions to greater political freedom. Detractors of the global marketing system have significant criticisms, associated with unfair and inefficient distribution of wealth. There is a tendency towards market monopoly or oligopoly and market instability. In the first decade of the 21st century globalization has seen work moved off shore from the United States and Canada and be replaced by low paying service jobs for many and higher pay for a minority. These service jobs are promoted as entry jobs for young people to get experience, but unfortunately, the workers in these jobs are aging and false hope will breed resentment and anger. The widening income gap between rich and poor is not explained by the economic fundamentalist theory.

The personal self-regulation proposed by Ayn Rand's supporters does not take into account the irreversible ecological changes that remain even after the competition self-regulates by driving the people misusing the system out of business. Capitalist individualism militates against fully realized individuality for all. In his book, *Adam's Fallacy: a Guide to Economic Theology*, Duncan K. Foley describes Adam Smith's fallacy as the idea in the economics of the free enterprise system in which "the pursuit of self-interest is guided by objective laws to a socially beneficent outcome", but in the rest of social life, "the pursuit of self-interest is morally problematic and has to be weighed against other ends." He states that economics is a speculative philosophical discourse and not a deductive or inductive science.[244] This is consistent with the free market capitalist system as a successful, resilient and adaptive system for creating material wealth, but is not a stable self-regulating one. There are a few voices in the wilderness. Douglass North calls for new institutional economics for the development of a legal framework to facilitate the market operating optimally. North notes:

"We are still a long way from completely understanding how the mind processes information. Individuals possess mental models to interpret the world around them. These are, in part, culturally derived – that is, produced by intergenerational transfer of knowledge values, and norms which vary radically among different ethnic groups and societies. There is immense variation...as a result different perception of the world and the way it 'works'. And even the formal learning that individuals acquire frequently consists of conflicting models by which we interpret the world around us. Individuals make choices on the basis of their mental modes."[245]

While North focused on political processes, his system has the potential to incorporate the effects of the extreme individualism belief system. For the neo-classical system, institutions, ideas and ideologies do not matter, and efficient markets – both economical and political –characterize economics. The new institutional economics "extends economic theory by incorporating ideas and ideologies into the analysis, modeling the political process as a critical factor in the performance of economies."[246] He promotes:

> "Institutions are not necessarily or even usually created to be socially efficient, rather they, or at least the formal rules are created to serve the interests of those with bargaining power to create new rules. Institutions are formed to reduce the uncertainty of human exchange. They are composed of formal rules (statute law, common law, regulations) informal constraints (norm of behavior) and the enforcement characteristics of both."[247]

The economic fundamentalists see the unfettered market operating efficiently on its own. The neo-classical model assumes that all information for market decisions is freely available to all the players. The market instability in 2007 triggered by problems with US subprime mortgages is an example of inefficiency in the market due to the lack of information to some players. Innovative financial structures assembled by various companies were sold as packages of debt with varying amount of US subprime mortgages. Due to the lack of transparency no one knew who held the subprime mortgages. Under Douglas North's definition, this setting is an inefficient market and doesn't work on the principles of the neo-classical efficient market. Where is the lack of transparency? Students with degrees in mathematics and physics who had just been hired out of graduate school designed products that were opaque and hard to value. They eventually linked them to mortgages and other products.[248] Out of sight of investors, analysts and regulators is a shadow market of complex investment instruments. These are the product of over a decade of deregulation of one of Wall Street's biggest profit engines.

The market problems that surfaced in 2007 represented failure at many levels. In spite of a lack of transparency, credit rating agencies, which banks paid to grade some of the new products, provided high ratings to many of them despite the fact that many investors on Wall Street did not understand what they were buying and selling. The consensus is that the ability of mortgage lenders to package their loans as securities that were then sold to other parties, played a key role in allowing borrowing standards to plummet. Terrible risk was created when pieces of junk were underwritten and simply passed along to someone else. Advocates of derivates say they were unfairly being made scapegoats. Apologists suggest that the problem was bad investment decisions. However, these instruments allowed commercial banks to keep billions and billions of dollars in potential liability off their balance sheets and become so vulnerable. In the two decades before 2008 the shadow banking system expanded rapidly and surpassed the conventional investment banks in importance. The people who should have been watching were singing praises of 'financial innovation.' [249]

George Soros, an American investor, was an exceedingly successful speculator who made a huge fortune from his hedge fund speculating on currencies around the world. Soros, now a philanthropist supporting education initiatives around the world, pointed out "The salient feature of the current financial crisis is that it was not caused by some external shock like OPEC raising the price of oil...The crisis was created by the financial system itself." [250] The new institutional economics could be applied to the market systems, such as those that led to the housing bubble. The bad behavior of bosses at Merrell Lynch, Citigroup and Bear Stearns led to discredibility of the US mortgage credit creation process. North's observation that an individual's belief system has an effect on the market appears to support the action of these bosses. There was a lack of accountability, and decision-making as a risk was being passed on to others.

Economic fundamentalism evolved following Ronald Reagan's embracement of Hayek's ideas that became mainstream and was followed by progressive deregulation. With the simultaneous rise of the cult of individualism, this economic belief system has become part of the hegemony of the majority. The recent economic crisis in the banking system created a climate for change. These changes need to take into account the costs to the environment of capitalist production, including debating the trade offs in such areas as the widening wage gap between rich and poor, and degradation of the environment. For example, Douglass North's system that included the "political process" of incorporating ideas and ideologies into the analysis could serve as the foundation upon which to build the institutional regulations that the present economic situation dictates. Economic fundamentalism can no longer be allowed to justify simplistic government policies.

16
Evangelists for Atheism

Where are the heretics of the 21st century? Heresy is the rejection of a particular religious authority in favor of some other religious authority - an unorthodox one, to be specific. An atheist is an individual who does not believe in faith or God. The evangelist atheist includes such individuals as Richard Dawkins and Christopher Hitchins. Their theories support the concept that all evils of war and tyranny are the result of concepts from religion. They believe that in order to take control of the destiny of the human species, it is necessary to undo the ideas of religion. Religion is a relic of the past and stands in the way of progress.[251] One of their supporters, Richard Dawkins, an evolutionary biologist, in his book *The God Delusion*, criticizes religion for its intolerance. He argues that the potential dangers of religion can be responsible for closing people's minds to scientific truths, oppressing women and threatening people with eternal damnation. Religion creates a group of individuals who are vulnerable to recruitment by fundamentalists.[252]

Religion in the West has been associated with a great deal of violence and wars over the past ten centuries. Once Christianity became the state religion of the Roman Empire, the church was able to systematically persecute heretics. As the Medieval Church became rich and powerful, it was necessary to persecute heretics to protect the wealth and prestige of church officials. The Medieval Church was involved in secular activities of the feudal states, including war. However, the church also took steps to reduce the amount of fighting within Christian states. Part of the plan of the First Crusade in the 11th century was to have Christian states in Europe stop fighting amongst themselves and join forces under the pope's direction to help the Byzantine Empire recover territories recently lost to the Muslims.

A very significant theme in Dawkins book, *The God Delusion*, is that the power of religion, even moderate religion in which individuals accept information without question, is still a problem as it creates a pool of individuals with a belief system who are vulnerable to fundamentalists, both Muslim and Christian, who recruit them into their social networks. Such individuals, who accept information without question, are recruited and manipulated for such things as murdering abortionists and suicide bomb attacks. Dawkins identifies the violence in the world that has been associated with religion: the Crusades against Muslims and Christian heretics, fighting during the Reformation between Catholics and Protestants, the recent animosity between Catholics and Protestants in Northern Ireland, and the recent bombings in New York, Spain and London. He points to two events - distinguished author Salmon Rushdie was given a death sentence for writing a novel, and protests against cartoons in the Danish newspaper,

Jyllands-Posten that show the power of religion to suppress ideas not seen since the Middle Ages.[253] No one argues these points.

In *God and Gold, Britain, America, and the Making of the Modern World,* Walter Russell Meade describes an Anglo-American liberal democratic system that has been challenged repeatedly and prevailed with the fall of Napoleon, the fall of the Kaiser, the fall of Hitler and the fall of the Soviet Union. This creates faith in the system that the historical process is carrying forward some great, if unknown purpose.[254] There exists in America a culture of importance toward the idea of a covenant with God or at least history. Many see the claims to a special place in God's plan as the swaggering arrogance of a rich bully.[255] On the other hand, the USA does not look to others nor expect to find moral leadership from Europe or China. To his credit, Meade cautions the need in the 21st century to better understand the forces in the Middle East to ensure this process will continue.

The debate between seeking knowledge from either science or faith is not new. During the 12th century, Averroës, (also known as Ibn Rushd), wrote that there was no incompatibility between religion and philosophy based on his interpretation of Aristotle, when both were properly understood. Averroës believed that there is one truth, but there are (at least) two ways to reach it, through philosophy and through religion. European philosophers, labeled Averroists, applied these ideas to Aristotle's writings and Christian theology. The basic emphasis of Latin Averroism was the superiority of reason and philosophy over faith and knowledge founded on faith, and the independent use of reason. These ideas lead to great controversy within the church.

Thomas Aquinas sought to resolve the dispute between the Averroists and the Augustians by granting reason its own integrity. He used Aristotelian arguments to 'prove' God's existence and the truth of Christian beliefs, but held that some doctrinal truths are revealed only by faith. This was part of the scholastic tradition of applying Aristotle's ideas to support the teachings of the church. As previously discussed, William Ockham was a critic of the scholastic position used to defend theological positions, as they grew more and more elaborate without a corresponding increase in predictive power. He applied his principle of parsimony "entities are not to be multiplied beyond necessity", to the scholastics of the 14th century defending the church dogma. The humanism of the Renaissance brought in new thinking that no religious doctrine can be supported by philosophical arguments, challenged the legitimacy of the institutional church as an intermediary between God, and eroded old alliances between reason and faith laid out by Thomas Aquinas.[256] Martin Luther's teaching that man can be saved by the Grace of God alone, undermined the legitimacy of the rigid institutions of the church meant to provide a channel for man to do good works and get into heaven. The desire of the educated burghers (middle class) of northern Europe to run their new businesses free of institutional barriers or outmoded cultural practices, contributed to the humanist individualism. Luther borrowed from the humanists the sense of individualism, that each man can be his own priest and that the only true authority is the Bible.

The ideas of the Age of Enlightenment included the premise that science could explain everything, where previously God had controlled the universe. The philosophers thought they had discovered a simple formula for perpetual human happiness. They sought to deliver individuals from restraints so that they could act freely in accordance with their nature. On the one hand, the formula promised that the pursuit of self-interest would benefit society; on the other, it promised that free human reason would produce sound moral judgments. In other words, individual freedom permitted the operation of natural laws. People believed this would lead to the disappearance of the fanatical and bloody wars fought in the name of religion, the dogged adherence to opinions and customs, and the persecution of so-called heretics. The Age of Enlightenment coincided with the American Revolution that embodied many of these new ideas. Religion became merely a personal and private affair - the separation of state and church an accepted principle in the new nation that rose from the revolution.

The 19th century challenge to religion came from two areas. Charles Darwin's Theory of Evolution provided a logical explanation for the origin of the world and the species. This challenged the ideas of those following the literal interpretation of the Bible such as the world being 10,000 years old. The second challenge came from German theologists who documented that many things in the Bible could not be proven to have happened in history. There was a reaction to this in the United States. To counter the modernist movement and promote the infallibility of the Scriptures, the Princeton scholars published *The Fundamentals* and distributed them at the turn of the 20th century. These were meant to counter Darwinism, and the writings of German scholars whose studies identified discrepancies between events in history and their record in the Bible. The movement started amongst Presbyterian academics and theologians and spread to conservative Baptists after the First World War.[257] The Scopes Monkey Trial in the 1920s emphasized the debate over creationism. For fundamentalists, the Holy Scripture became the object of their faith, a most tangible form of connection with the past. Fundamentalists claim to be guardians of ancient truths and moral commandments and they demand that Americans meet family obligations, even if it infringes upon individual freedom.[258]

Atheists often write of their concern of the control that religion has over the individual. For Nietzsche and Sartre, their philosophy was to see life without a God as key to providing freedom for the individual in this world. Nietzsche sought freedom from all external constraints on one's behavior, especially the control of religion over people. His message was to become whom you are, following instinct, not reason.[259] Sartre's idea of freedom — it is entirely up to us to become who we are, there are no constraints. Ayn Rand was an atheist who believed reason was the only guide to action. Rand taught that "mysticism" is man's chief enemy. She emphasized the irrationality in the belief of God and lack of proof in the existence of God. Dawkins expresses his concern over the power of religion in which individuals accept information without question.

In *The God Delusion*, Richard Dawkins identified the debate over creationism and its dressed up version, intelligent design as an attack on science that needed to be challenged. Intelligent design was developed by creationists in the USA in order to use the court system to force schools to provide an alternate to the teaching of Darwin's Theory of Evolution. Dawkins illustrated how organized religion can get individuals to accept information without question and push aside science such as Darwin's Theory of Natural Selection.[260] With his powerful arguments that religion stands in the way of progress in the world, Dawkins shares Nietzsche's call to reject traditions and opinions that are not one's own and think for one's self.

In the 21st century, many are desperately searching for individualism. This includes consumerism and virtual reality narcissism, the bubble in which the narcissist lives. The self-esteem movement has created a population with an exaggerated sense of entitlement. The world viewed from an emotional rather than a rational perspective allows personal feelings to override the distinction between right and wrong. Another aspect of self-centeredness is self-tolerance. Such individuals learn to tolerate their errors and personal flaws and come to accept themselves as okay. They feel justified in asserting themselves and defending their perceived rights.[261] Dawkins speaks out elegantly against the influence of organized religion in society, in particular the promotion of creationism and intelligent design. Dawkins writes logically and rationally and many see his writing as a source of reason and scientific truth. In the culture of extreme individualism, such an individual does not find a way of life based on reason. These people cannot hear Dawkins' message based on rigor and logic.

The *Manhattan Declaration*, the 4,700 word declaration signed by 152 Christian leaders defends three truths that include the justice of sanctity of human life, the dignity of marriage as the union of husband and wife, and religious liberty and freedom of conscience. It is called the *Manhattan Declaration* because an early meeting included Eastern Orthodox, Catholic, Anglican, and Evangelical religious leaders in Manhattan in the fall of 2009. It calls for civil disobedience if the signer is pressed to comply with any action that violates any part of these three issues. It minimizes reference to Scriptures and turns to natural law for support. The lead authors are Chuck Colson and Robert George. George has parlayed a 13th-century Catholic philosophy into an intellectual framework to attack such emotional issues as abortion and same sex marriage. This group cultivates emotions and anger to recruit people into a social network; an example of how a small group whose ideas that are otherwise based on dogma, is able to influence individuals and decisions in the 21st century, through emotional appeal of the argument.[262]

The evangelist for atheism attacks religion as the main obstacle to the progress of humanity, which is based on such issues as individuals recruited to religious social networks accepting information without question. Any success that the atheist has using logical debates to affect the thinking of the cult of individualism will consequently be minimal. The crusade of evangelists for atheism will do little to counter extreme individualism. On the other hand, under the cult of self-esteem, people make decisions based on emotions and desires. This creates a pool of individuals with a belief system who respond to emotional debates.

17

Individualism vs. The Community

The Industrial Age ended and the Information Age began with the fall of the Berlin Wall in 1989. We are consumers with a need to be satisfied. There is a contest between individualism and a sense of belonging to the community. TV screens and computer monitors present much information with very little that ties us together as a community. Community today is found in religion, work based professional societies, recovery rehabilitation centres or political activism. Business strategists observe that people are increasingly seeking emotional fulfillment through their work. The weakening of a sense of belonging to a community could account for this observation.

Alexis de Tocqueville (1805-59) toured the United States in 1831 officially to review the penal system. During this time, he documented many activities in America. While admiring the energy and versatility of the Americans, he also thought they were too intent on making money, and would be condemned to a commercial culture. In de Toqueville's opinion, an American's notion of equality was derived from their "general quality of condition," [263] rather from moral condition. In his study of America de Tocqueville observed:

> "...men are forever rising and sinking upon the ladder of society...there are ...a large number of men whose fortune is upon the increase, but whose desires grow much faster than their fortunes... Such men eager to find some short cut to these gratifications, already almost within their reach...there are always a multitude of individuals whose wants are above their means."[264]

De Tocqueville commented that private interest and personal gain motivated the actions of most Americans, which in turn cultivated a strong sense of individualism (the ethos which emphasizes the autonomy of the individual against the community or the group). His definition of individualism was withdrawal from society at large, a spiritual isolationism. Tocqueville supported a liberal view toward freedom of the press at a time when most governments feared it. In his view, newspapers guarded against the evils which many leaders of the day felt newspapers created. Equality, while bringing great benefit to the world, tends to isolate men from each other and has the potential to create problems. He noted, "It tends to isolate them from one another, to concentrate every man's attention upon himself; and it lays open the soul to an inordinate love of material gratification." The advantage of religion is "to impose on man some duties towards his kind and draw him from the contemplation of himself."[265] He saw individualism and market capitalism as a significant force in America. To keep individualism from slipping out of control, he recommended that there should be participation in public affairs, growth of associations and newspapers, ensuring that the principle of self-interest was properly understood and creating a support system from religion.[266]

John Stuart Mill (1806-1873), one of the most influential English-speaking philosophers of the 19th century, wrote on individual liberties. He believed that democracy was the best form to foster self-development and individualism, and it leads people to take a more active intelligent participation in society. He wrote on the extent of power that can be legitimately exercised by society over the individual. Free discourse was necessary for intellectual and social discourse, creating the debate so one understands why an idea is true. He introduced the 'harm principle' in which each individual has the right to act as long as they do no harm to others. The harm may include acts of omission such as failing to save a drowning child or failing to pay taxes. He also wrote on freeing people from the tyranny of custom. He likened the 19th century removal of medieval apprenticeship laws to woman's suffrage. Society was educating women to be meek and submissive and resigning their will into the hands of a man. The key to countering this is the ballot for women. Mill was concerned with de Tocqueville's observations of developments in the US and promoted the idea of community. In his ideal community, one does not lose their personal identity. It is not necessary to neither look alike nor be reduced to some least common denominator.[267]

Mill did not apply his ideas of individualism equally. Mill wrote Britain was doing non-European countries a favour by maintaining them as colonies because the duty of Britain was bringing 'freedom' to these societies. Such 'improvement' of colonized populations wasn't the main point of foreign intervention but rather a euphemism for incorporating these non-Western societies into Britain's capitalist mode of production.

'Bringing freedom' to these populations simply gives a moral veneer to what was essentially an economic mission in the 19th century. A hundred and fifty years later, the US promotes bringing democracy to the Middle East as an important feature of their foreign policy, while the economics of oil dependence sits not far below the surface. For 19th century thinkers, individualism did not have a role for colonized non-European people.[268]

Kierkegaard believes "genuine community emerges only when the egoism of individuals has been transformed into unselfish benevolence."[269] Ferdinand Tonnies (1855-1936) documented a change from "a older spontaneous community based on mutual aide and trust to a modern society in which self-interest predominates." He noted there is a distinction between society and community.[270] Ayn Rand insisted there was no such entity as "society", as only individuals exist. Prime Minister Margaret Thatcher commented on October 31, 1987 to *Women's Own Magazine*:

> "I think we've been through a period where too many people have been given to understand that if they have a problem, it's the government's job to cope with it. 'I have a problem, I'll get a grant.' 'I'm homeless, the government must house me.' They're casting their problem on society. And, you know, there is no such thing as society. There are individual men and women, and there are families. And no government can do anything except through people, and people must look to themselves first. It's our duty to look after ourselves and then, also to look after our neighbour. People have got the entitlements too much in mind, without the obligations. There's no such thing as entitlement, unless someone has first met an obligation."[271]

Every right implies a responsibility, every opportunity an obligation, every possession, a duty claimed John D. Rockefeller.[272] Obligation is defined as a commitment; something one is bound to do, such as responsibilities. Responsibility and accountability are essentially synonymous. Accountability is the awareness and acceptance of positive and negative consequences of our behaviour. In modern life, the art of fan dancing is in better shape than the ability to demand accountability. Hardly anyone tells anyone else to shape the hell up, and then takes the trouble to make sure they do.[273]

Maureen Stout in the *Feel Good Curriculum* observes "the current definition of self-esteem used by education and psychologists seems to be … feeling good about oneself irrespective of individual or social attributes or characteristics."[274] We may choose to booster our self-worth by refusing to judge ourselves by external standards. Accepting ourselves without regard to external criteria is a dangerous aspect of false self-esteem. Now educators voice concern that feelings have been given greater weight than competence and character.

During the 20th century, the influence of economic thought followed the same path as individualism. Economists, such as Friedrich Hayek, described a system limiting the power of the state and permitting a broad scope of individual choices in all spheres. This work supported individualism in the marketplace. By embodying corporate identities that are radically individualistic and perpetually new, the brand attempt to inoculate themselves against accusations that, in fact, they are selling sameness. Under branding, brand X is not a product but a way of life, an attribute, a set of values, a look, an idea.[275] Conservatives championed those individual freedoms associated with the free market, while deriding the hedonism associated with the counter culture. This supports materialism as a means of expressing yourself. Calvinism identified thrift, industry and hard work as forms of moral virtue, but this supported production, not consumption.

The difference between ancient and modern personalities is illustrated by a quote from Malina and Neyrey's *Portrait of Paul,* "...ancient Mediterranean people identified themselves as situated and imbedded in various other persons with whom they formed a unity of sorts ... the individual person shares a virtual identity with the group as a whole and with other members."[276] The opposite is self-centeredness, believing one is more important than others. One aspect of self-centeredness is self-tolerance. Self-tolerance leads to a sense of entitlement and a belief that the world owes them something. With the cult of entitlement many social problems seem to be a result of "what's missing." The world of community history has become so eroded that people have only the inner world in which to search for meaning. The subsequent narcissism leaves the individual being preoccupied with mundane aspects of their private life. As Freud succinctly put it, "A good part of the struggles of mankind centre around the task of finding an expedient accommodation – one, that is, that will bring happiness between the claims of the individual and the cultural claim of the group."[277]

Countering Individualism

Individualism has evolved over time and its characteristics are well established in America, in parallel with growing secularization. Christian fundamentalists demand that Americans meet family obligations even if it infringes upon individual freedom. The Christian fundamentalist blames abortion, homosexuality, feminism and infidelity as the result of the rampant growth of individualism. Islamic fundamentalists denounce the West as a disastrous combination of materialism and egotistic individualism while sharia law is used to regulate their societal and personal affairs. What is the best approach to counter extreme individualism in the community? Individualism did not appear over night. Many have commented on it throughout history.

One who has commented is the French aristocrat, Alexis de Tocqueville, who made many insights during his 1831 tour of the USA. De Tocqueville observed that private interest and personal gain motivated the actions of most Americans, which in turn cultivated a strong sense of individualism. To keep individualism from slipping out of control he recommended that there should be participation in public affairs, growth of associations and newspapers, support from religion, as well as the principle of self-interest properly understood.[278]

De Tocqueville spoke of the importance of the growth of newspapers and associations. Today volunteer associations and independent newspapers are in decline. If the news media had not been concentrated into the hands of a few, a process that started in the 1920s, then de Tocqueville's statement would still be valid. The greater problem lies in the fact that the news media is concentrated in a handful of players. In the Information Age, cultural hegemony is created by the mass media that promotes individualism and consumerism. John Stuart Mill wrote that the tyranny of the majority was a greater problem than the tyranny of government. It is much harder to be protected against the "tyranny of the prevailing opinion and feeling."[279] A considerable price is extracted for the concentration of newspapers, radio and television and their control of public opinion and marketing.

In the West, the court systems corrected many historical problems of hegemonic bond such as the rights for minorities and women. Other decisions addressed various levels of discrimination. However, the consequence of some court decisions involving individual rights leave communities divided at the very time when communities need to be strengthened in order to counter individualism. This can be tracked throughout history.

The Scottish Reformation began with a national revolution in 1559 led by Protestant churchmen and their lay supporters. Initially the Scottish church officially disapproved of the non-scriptural feast of Christmas. It took another thirty years before the Scottish parliament agreed with this decision. James I did a balancing act with respect to religious affairs in Britain, while religious violence gripped much of the continent. King James moved to bring the three national churches of Britain together. This included encouraging the Scottish church to follow the English example of observing Christmas and Easter as festivals. Both continued to develop as community celebrations. Later the same century Oliver Cromwell's government closed the theatres, took down the maypoles and ordered shopkeepers to stay open on the superstitious feast of Christmas Day.[280] These activities of the Cromwell government decisions were very unpopular with the public and consequently increased support for the return of the monarchy. The old Christmas celebrations brought the community together. These activities were subsequently incorporated into Christian Christmas celebrations, an important tradition that strengthened the community. Similarly, the Christmas tree came to North America with the Hessian troops stationed in New York and Quebec City during the American Revolution. This was another community celebration associated with Christmas. Communities no longer place Christmas trees in public places because of the threat of court action - a mind set created by court challenges.

In the 19th century, Romanticism was a reaction against the intellectualism of the 18th century, against the social structures protecting privilege and against the materialism of the Industrial Revolution. As time passed, sophisticated writers and artists were less and less likely to be conventionally pious; but during the Romantic era, many of them were drawn to religious imagery. Religion was idealized, and writers felt free to draw on Biblical themes with the same freedom their predecessors had drawn on classical mythology, and with as little reverence.

Also appearing at this time was the romantic celebration of the individual at the expense of society and tradition.[281] Christianity was part of the dominant class of the West in the 19th century, however, Christianity is no longer a significant influence of the dominant class in North America in the 21st century. Court actions are over 100 years behind. They need to focus on rulings that strengthen the community, not divide it. They need to realign themselves against the true dominant culture today (big media and advertisers) with its cultural hegemony. Strong communities counter extreme individualism.

De Tocqueville spoke of a role for religion and a need for education on the principle of self-interest. Today, religion can serve two roles: the small community that provides support for the individual, and to counter the messaging from the media and pop culture by incorporating messages on the problems of individualism by building it into self-esteem messages of the church. In addition, schools require focused messages on self-esteem. To control self-esteem from becoming the self centeredness of "I have high self-esteem, I will be successful", to "self-esteem is of two kinds: earned and unearned. Only earned self-esteem is healthy and satisfying and doesn't precede achievement, but follows it." [282]

Since the free market revolution of the 1980s, a huge amount of emphasis has been placed on people's right to choose for themselves. The cult of individualism has created the culture of entitlement to consume. The individualistic consumer society creates a strong focus on rights. Materialism, consumerism and advertising have joined together to create individuals with high expectations.[283] Re-education using messages on proper self-esteem will have a significant role in countering such a culture.

Opportunities exist in Islam. Moderate thinkers can promote arguments for the 'greater jihad' of self-introspection and improvement being more fundamental for Muslims than the 'lesser jihad' of war and violence. The 'greater jihad,' involving self-introspection, offers a powerful tool for education on the effects of individualism throughout the community. Akbar Ahmed, Islamic scholar at the American University in Washington, suggests that the best interface with the West is the Sufi sect of Islam, which emphasizes compassion and love for all mankind, and would provide the best opportunities to build bridges between Islam and the West. This would help each side understand the other. A view of common humanity and inclusiveness could also help reduce cognitive dissonance and make Muslims more comfortable in discussing the various aspects of individualism within the community.[284]

Pope Benedict XVI triggered an opportunity as a consequence of a lecture on September 12, 2006 at the University of Regensburg in Germany. During the lecture he quoted a 14th century Byzantine emperor's description of Islam "Show me just what Muhammad brought that was new and there you will find things only bad and inhuman, such as his command to spread by the sword the faith he preached." [285] Islamic politicians and religious leaders vigorously protested against what they believed was an insulting mischaracterization of Islam. A month and a day later, thirty-eight religious and Islamic scholars sent an *Open Letter to the Pope* with their observations. Their main observation was "What the emperor failed to realize – aside from the fact…no such command has ever existed in Islam – is that the Prophet never claimed to be bringing anything fundamentally new." On October 13, 2007, 138 Islamic scholars and multiple Christian leaders around the world sent an open letter to many Christian leaders around the world. This letter was titled, *A Common Word Between You and Us*, and identified that Jews, Christians and Muslims have the love of God and one's neighbour as the heart of their faith, and common ground between Christianity and Islam for future dialogue and understanding between the faiths. This, in turn, opens the door to opportunities for future dialogue and the understanding of each others' value systems.[286]

The West believes it has successfully come to terms with and has balanced faith and reason, whereas Islam has not. It is necessary to consider the complexity of Muslim society. In the first part of the 20th century, Muslim establishment figures were unable to provide meaningful direction that would allow Muslims to adapt to changing times, while still maintaining the integrity of their faith. Muslims are committed to their faith and all will defend it against real or perceived threats. An Islamic Renaissance is best directed at reducing the influence of tribal customs and traditions and encouraging an understanding of the expectations of democracy and good government.[287]

The mega church, as discussed before, has a role in countering individualism with a marketing strategy that brings many new people into the church. This provides an opportunity to communicate both sense of community and messages for handling the following problems of the week in the church messages. These messages can counter the problems of the cult of individualism. All churches have a role in such a ministry. The problems of individualism could be incorporated into messages on self-esteem that churches have in place. This provides another opportunity to shift culture from the individual to the community.

It is possible for a Christian to counter individualism outside the structure of an organized church by living certain messages from the Scriptures. For this discussion, a Christian is anyone who consciously chooses to become a follower of Jesus, that is, as far as it is within him or her to decide to use Jesus' life and teachings as a model for his or her life. One message that can be used for guidance and the right self-esteem is the Golden Rule, "Do unto others as you would have them do unto you."[288] The "self esteem movement" has led to the enshrining of the self, which obstructs one's vision of right self-esteem and its foundation. This leads to a change from self-control to self-indulgence. People no longer take responsibility for their actions. The Golden Rule counters these aspects of the cult of self-esteem. Another message from the Scriptures to counter this extreme individualism is the second commandment of Jesus, "You shall love your neighbour as yourself."[289] This is the outward love that will counter the self-love of extreme individualism. This is the love of the true concerns of the well being of others – this love is the core of the healthy esteem. Here exists the force to counter the modern world's inward focus that promotes self-tolerance, entitlement, victimhood and narcissism.

With the self-esteem movement embedded in child development programs, young adults are encouraged to develop image rather than character. "When success is more important than self respect, the culture itself overvalues image and is narcissistic."[290] With narcissism, the greatest problem is profound disconnection from reality. This in turn promotes extreme responses to needs and desires that are perfectly normal, and includes requiring constant attention and admiration, believing that one is entitled to special favours, without the need to reciprocate. These people believe they are always right and that there is nothing that they cannot achieve. They tend to exploit others. In this system of self-tolerance, their sense of entitlement leads to victimhood – placing the blame for personal inadequacies elsewhere. They lack respect for authority and habitually lie to people. Students demand better grades than they earn. Corporate executives award themselves exorbitant salaries.

Countering the effects of the emphasis of individualism and the subsequent narcissism requires a two-pronged approach: the analysis of self, looking within, and through advocacy. Looking inward can be achieved by analyzing self-esteem. The popular psychology of Western culture has firmly established a connection between happiness and self-esteem. Everyone wants to enjoy a healthy level of self-esteem, which is defined by how much value people place on themselves. Self-esteem is a perception rather than a reality. It refers to a person's belief about whether he or she is intelligent and attractive, for example, and it does not necessarily say anything about whether the person actually is intelligent and attractive.

In the heady days of the 1970s, it was suggested that self-esteem has a casual effect on every aspect of human life. The self-esteem movement appeared as a relatively new development of Western individualistic cultures. In science, the proof that one can improve performance by enhancing self-esteem is weak. The costs of high self-esteem were described by Roy Baumiester, Jennifer Campbell et al as:

> "There appear to be relatively few personal costs to high self-esteem. If anything the cost of high self-esteem.... such as narcissism are born by other people. People high in self-esteem or narcissism are prone to bully others, to retaliate aggressively, and to be prejudiced against out-group members. Self-enhancers are sometimes annoying or obnoxious to others. They may be willing to cheat and perform other antisocial self-serving acts."[291]

Self-esteem has many definitions, but all address aspects of how we view and value ourselves. While self-esteem confers some benefits on the self, such as happiness, its costs accrue to others. A better investment would be cultivating accurate understanding of self. Cultivating accurate understanding of self or self-knowledge (knowledge of one's own character, powers and limitations, that allows one to predict and control their own behaviour), would pay off better dividends than just enhancing self-esteem. For example, accurate self-knowledge would help one to know which course or what occupation to choose, avoiding ones that are too difficult (which would produce failure) and those that would be too easy (and hence would be unrewarding).

The second prong to counter extreme individualism involves advocacy. Advocacy would include processes to educate others of the problems of extreme individualism and the dysfunction it creates in daily activities in schools and the work place. This could be modeled after the policies that are presently in place for bullying in the work place. This includes a tool to check for the traits that would raise a flag to trigger closer monitoring or investigation by a supervisor or teacher to determine whether events may be the consequences of excessive individualism.

Damon describes in *Hands On Parenting* that "self esteem is a perfectly good thing for people to have, but it should be the result of good behaviour. In other words, you should feel good about yourself because you have done something right…We want to promote self esteem that comes from achievement and from service to others."[292] Schools need to adjust the self-esteem message that they provide students, and to continue to promote volunteer activities in the community. Self-esteem should be used as a reward rather than an entitlement. It is necessary to provide school systems and work places with tool kits and processes to identify the signs of excessive individualism.

Advocacy needs to include resources for early childhood literacy programs. Children with preschool experience develop motivation to achieve. A good public policy to provide print rich environment will facilitate all children starting school with similar cognitive scores.[293] This would replace the mantra that no child should fail as they progress through school because of the effect on self-esteem, with a child commencing school ready to succeed because they possess the necessary cognitive and non-cognitive tools. It is vital to understand how the culture of self-centeredness and entitlement can affect the home, the work place, the community and country. The future requires a process for ongoing evaluation and validation of information. There is a need for greater understanding of the consequences of individualism, and evaluating its effect on one's life.

18

Ready to Succeed

The Student

The development of extreme individualism was supported by the culture of the school system in the 1980s, when it became necessary to do whatever was possible to achieve positive self-esteem. This ushered in the cult of self-esteem; the world was to be saved from crime, drug abuse and under achievement through boosting self-esteem. School systems lowered educational standards to protect children from failure. Students soon had the attitude "I have a right to my opinion, so my opinions are right." [294] From this assumption one has no need to consider other viewpoints before selecting one. These decisions were made with the good intentions of making everyone feel they were all equal. With focus on self, a sense of entitlement and its negative consequences appeared.

The problems start before a child reaches the school system. Before entering school the average cognitive scores of pre-school age children are 60% above the scores of children in the lowest socioeconomic group. Poverty and low level of literacy tend to co-occur. Children living below the poverty line at age four are eighteen months below the normal in literacy skills for their age group, and, by age ten, the gap is still present. Early literacy programs can address this gap. Early literacy includes everything children know about reading and writing before they can actually read and write. It involves a set of skills that children will need to read, write, calculate and communicate. This is the story of the toddler who wants his or her favourite book read over and over, or preschooler who wants to 'read' the story to you from memory.[295] The consequence of not investing in early literacy is a child who enters the school system 'not ready to succeed'.

What helps young low-income children catch-up is early intervention with intentional curriculum. There is a need for interventions to narrow the literacy gaps. There is a need to introduce literacy skills at ages three to five so that all children enter the school system with equivalent skills. For low-income preschoolers, increasing early literacy and math skills are critical to success in school and vital to closing the achievement gap. The challenges to obtaining early literacy skills include (1) lack of adequate exposure to appropriate instruction and (2) the stable individual characteristics required in early literacy instruction, as children acquire early literacy skills at different rates.

Generally, there is fundamental optimism about the possibility of human change. There was a time when we looked to schools to reduce skill gaps across socioeconomic groups. The Coleman Report and others show that families, and not schools, are the major sources of inequality in student performance. Cognitive skills are important, but non-cognitive skills such as motivation, perseverance and tenacity are also important for success in life. In preschool systems, besides accessing cognitive test scores, there is a need to follow achievement test scores that are a measure of the motivation to learn. By the third grade, gaps in test scores across socioeconomic groups are stable by age, suggesting that later schooling and variations in schooling quality have little effect in reducing or widening the gaps that appear before children enter school. Studies from MIT show that the best return in human capital investment in education is achieved in preschool programs. In regular school and job training programs, the return on investment is significantly less.[296]

Economists offer considerable support for early literacy programs. People with low literacy skills are twice as likely to be unemployed, and up to 50% of adults with low literacy levels live in low-income households. A 2004 Statistics Canada report states that a 1% rise in literacy scores relative to the international average would be associated with an eventual 2.5% relative rise in labour productivity and a 1.5% rise in gross domestic product per person. Programs that produce substantial improvements in the cognitive development and school success of children in poverty can be expected to produce substantial direct benefits through educational cost savings and substantial indirect benefits as the result of increased productivity and social responsibility. Investing in disadvantaged children promotes the correct self-esteem and, at the same time, productivity in the economy and in society at large. This leaves no room for an exaggerated sense of entitlement.[297]

There are various levels of support for early literacy. There is a need to encourage the distribution of information packages through physician's offices. Libraries need support to develop and deliver information sessions for parents and to provide a good selection of books for a preschool literacy program. Dissemination of information on the use of community libraries and encouraging families to get a library card and visit the library is required. These would be oriented to provide a print rich environment for the kindergarten child and involve the parents in the child's education. Children who enter school with strong literacy skills are more likely to become strong readers.[298]

Preschool child development programs rich in cognitive interactions between teacher and children, would be an expansion and enrichment of present day-care services. These programs need standards and an inspection system to ensure minimal requirements are met, funded through tax deductions similar to present childcare and targeted funds for the working poor. When children arrive in the public school system ready to succeed, there is little opportunity for the appearance of the entitlement of extreme individualism. The definition of self-esteem that goes with entitlement: "I have high self-esteem, I will be successful." is replaced with "I achieve, and therefore I am good." In addition, schools can focus their message: "Self-esteem is of two kinds: earned and unearned. Only earned self-esteem is healthy and satisfying and doesn't precede achievement, but follows it."[299]

Early literacy programs will lay a foundation to address the cult of individualism in the future. What about the present? Is there a personal formula to address extreme individualism and its consequences? As Margaret Thatcher noted in 1987, there is "no such thing as society", but "...individuals must look after affairs."[300] Every individual needs to recognize the persistent messages on individualism and consumerism coming from the media and recognize its effects on themselves and the world around them. M. Scott Peck observes, "The whole course of human history may depend on a change of heart in one solitary and even humble individual – for it is in the solitary mind and soul of the individual that the battle between good and evil is waged and ultimately won or lost." [301]

The Individual

Individualism is a balance between self-reliance and personal responsibility and egotism. The rise of individualism is about people living and acting as individuals rather than as members of a larger group. On the other hand, the Internet is redefining individualism as part of experiencing who we are; a person in the privacy of their home is never alone, without contact, without means to acquire new friendships, information or goods. Culture can now be tailored to our requirements, and the choices available adapted to fit our desires.

The 1980s was the decade when making money was important. In the 1990s, people began to focus on lifestyle – and were driven by independence that a higher disposable income allows. This money provided more freedom and choices. Communities changed: from communities of geography to communities of interest, i.e. school and church. More and more people now define themselves by their pastime, and interests, rather than birthplaces or family networks.

There has been a change from communities of necessity to communities of choice. People now mix with people they have chosen, in locations they prefer and under circumstances that suit them. There is a shift from permanent communities to transient communities. Communities of interest and choice are less likely to be permanent affairs, as personal tastes and ambitions change with time and fashion. However, there are consequences to the rise of individualism. There is decreased membership in volunteer organizations and groups. Gym membership has risen while political activism has fallen. People have more money but less time to spend it. Some find themselves in a 'time squeeze' of busy lifestyle, now too tired to get everything done.

For a long time, people have welcomed the chance to express their individuality through exercising choice. The ultimate goal of this individualism and personalization is commonly known as self-actualization: seeking personal growth and fulfillment, to realize personal potential. People take time and resources to invest in themselves. This includes using personal trainers and life coaches to help 'live an ideal life.' Such people want more from their lives, or want to break a pattern. The coaches provide the tools, support and structures to accomplish more. This includes helping the client set clear goals and achieve them. For some, this means developing specific habits for versatility and personal effectiveness to advance their career, while others seek growth for internal reasons.

To many the world seems to have more and more controversial ideas around. Such ideas appear on television and computer monitors. Challenges to belief systems present an immense cognitive dissonance. The social group is a source of cognitive dissonance as well as a vehicle for reducing it. Disagreement from others in a group generates dissonance, and subsequent movement towards group consensus reduces this negative tension. Cognitive dissonance is central to many forms of persuasion. It is part of the process in changing beliefs, values attitudes and behaviours. The tension can be injected suddenly or allowed to build up over time. People can be moved in many small jumps or one large one. When you start to feel uncomfortable, stop and see if you can find the inner conflict. Then notice how that came about. If it was somebody else who put that conflict there, you can decide not to pay any more attention to him or her.

Over 1800 years ago, Epictetus noted: "Men are disturbed not by things that happen, but by their opinions of the things that happen." Epictetus observed that it is our opinions of things and not things themselves that cause the disturbances of our lives, for "what disturbs men's minds are not events, but their judgment on events."[302] From this, one can extrapolate that nothing out there can make us miserable, that we control how we feel by how we process things, events and other people and their opinions. Stoics support a rational approach to life. For stoics, the good life is living in agreement with nature, and consists of a system of checks and balances. Virtue is the only real good- a virtuous life is free of all passions, which are intrinsically disturbing and harmful to the soul. Stoics advise control only things over which there is power: attitudes, beliefs, desires, judgments. Attitude recognizes there are things within one's power and there are things beyond that power. Many things in life are controlled by nature over which we have no control. This means taking a rational approach to a changing world.

Within the desires of the stoic is a need to search for an ideal life in a world where forces mold a person's environment beyond his greatest understanding. While encouraging one to strive to be free of passion, it is not necessary to extinguish all emotions. What distinguishes normal impulses or desires from passions is the idea that the latter are excessive and irrational. There is a need for balance; recognizing that some things are within our grasp and others not, and disappointment and frustration occur only when we don't get what we desire. Stoic ethics says, 'follow where reason leads.' While one can't control events one can control his/her reactions to events. The message is to take control of how someone controls their judgment. The modern Stoic makes proper use of impressions, with the appropriate emotive response conditioned by rational understanding. Do not allow oneself to be carried away by intensity or emotions. It involves waiting a bit and testing one's impression. Often that first impression of disaster, and the emotional energy that this consumes, can be replaced with a judgment that is more pragmatic and driven less by the panic of the moment. This leads to the appropriate emotional responses conditioned by rational understanding and fulfillment of one's personal, social, professional and civic responsibilities.[303]

The cult of individualism makes us particularly prone to cognitive dissonance because our personal identity is very important. We see ourselves as stable self-contained beings. The media create cognitive dissonance. For example, advertising that we may be missing something, or not fitting in, creates anxiety. Increased cognitive dissonance is a source of psychological suffering and the vast amounts of stress we see today. Do not withdraw.

Studies show that social contact improves health and promotes longer life. Reports in neuro-endocrinology suggest that good feelings from doing good deeds may lower the output of stress hormones.[304] Be aware of the cognitive dissonance from co-workers, from advertisers and the mass media as they affect your opinion of your self-image. It is important not to be caught up in a pathological envy driven by a belief in a lack, deficiency or inadequacy in oneself. Marketing can create a sense that we need something, especially for identity.

The secret is to understand the difference between self-centered and self-care. Self-centered is limited to caring about oneself and one's own needs. In this instance, the individual is concerned solely with his or her own desires, needs, or interests. A consequence of the cult of individualism is that everyone strives to be different, to be original, or stand out from the vast crowd. In the extreme, this means feeding their narcissism. Self-care refers to the decisions and actions taken by people to maintain and improve their health (Health Canada, 1997). Self-care in the 18th century referred to the condition of acquiring scientific information.[305] This concept started in the 1970's as an effort to reduce dependency on professional health care services and institutions by providing individuals with the tools to undertake their own self-care. By the 1980s, in parallel with the rapid expansion of the self-help section of bookstores, self-care was labeled as egotism and individualism.

It has continued to evolve. With self-care, the emphasis is on the individual becoming involved in all aspects of their life and includes a wide range of actives such as eating habits, relationships and exercise. Concrete examples include such things as sunscreens, vitamins and toothpaste.

Self-care decision-making has an important role in reducing the burden of illness and strain on the health services system. Each individual needs a process to identify the appropriateness, relevance and usefulness of health information. The key to self-care decisions is to find and access reliable, relevant and understandable information. This would be part of a "warm" self-care promotion described by Christopher Ziguras in *Self-Care: Embodiment, Autonomy and the Shaping of Health Consciousness,* which actually encourages mutual support and counters individualistic tendencies.[306] Such self-care promotion could be one way of shaping an individual's personal negotiation of the tension between selfishness and cooperation, desires and dissatisfaction and perceived freedom and actual limitations.

In the 21st century, self-care is the myriad of practices that individuals engage in to maintain and improve their health. Optimal health is achieved by managing one's life in such a way that one consistently maintains a balance of physical, emotional, intellectual and spiritual well-being This means taking care of oneself in all areas of his life. Much of the information that is available through the media is under the influence of industry. There is a role for public health departments to promote peer-reviewed information for self-care. The pandemic influenza plans developed for the general public provides good evidence-based models to follow in developing messages to cover other situations. This includes messages to provide insight into the role of self-care and discussions on the challenges an individual can face with the behaviour change that is often required in self-care. Self-awareness has an important role to play in decision-making with respect to the health of the individual.

The communication processes within organizations must include discussions of extreme individualism and the effects such a belief system has on personal interactions and perception of the world. This messaging can become part of self-esteem messages provided in schools, churches and work places. Nina H. Shokraii noted that self-esteem is not based on actual accomplishments and "threatens to deny children the tools they will need in order to experience true success."[307] There are investments that can be made in early childhood education to create the culture in which public schools are able to promote the self-esteem that is earned and follows achievement, not precedes it. These systems are necessary to counter the self-esteem binge and sense of entitlement that have crept into people's expectations. Such long-term investments will counter extreme individualism and create a culture that supports strong communities that are necessary for good government.

John Stuart Mill described two criteria that ensured the quality of good government, consisting of bureaucracy and elected officials. In this system, there must be individuals of superior virtue and intellect available. Mill's first criteria, "The first element of good government, therefore, being the virtue and intelligence of the human beings composing the community, the most important point of excellence which any form of government can possess is to promote the virtue and intelligence of the people themselves." He believed that the functioning of a government depended on the intellectual qualities of the people, fostering learning or education ensured a government that was best at everything. The corollary is good governments look after the welfare of the community by supporting educational institutions. Mill's second criteria of good government, "A representative constitution is a means of bringing the general standard of intelligence and honesty existing in the community, and the individual intellect and virtue of its wisest members, more directly to bear upon the government, and investing them with greater influence in it than they would have under any other mode of organization..." Organizations need to ensure the participation of all people, especially educated members of the community. A good democratic government is the consequence of participation of educated members of the community, and "the greater the amount of these good qualities," Mill claimed "the better will be the government." He believed that education, and not the intrinsic nature of the educated, qualified individuals to have more influence in government. Ideally, a good government taps into the good qualities of individuals who exist in the community.[308]

19

Good Government

Two thousand years ago, good government was associated with providing money, roads and laws for commerce in the Roman Empire. With the fall of the Roman government, the Catholic Church became the only organized force in Western Europe. The Pope concentrated power in Rome and was able to be a force in church affairs as well as secular affairs. By the 14th century, the Roman Catholic Church had become very rich and powerful. The church owned large tracts of land in Medieval England, the peasants had to work on church land for free, pay ten percent tithes, pay for baptisms, and pay for burials. Failure to meet any of these obligations would prevent their soul getting to heaven, and these payments all contributed to the wealth of the church.[309] A corrupt and extravagant papacy had significant detractors by the 14th century, who challenged the wealth and secular activities of the church.

During the 14th century the power of the church diminished considerably, with the Avignon, followed closely by the Western Schism, with two popes vying for power. In the 15th century it was the humanism of the Renaissance that challenged the church. Milton Viorst observed, "The seminal notion that the Renaissance introduced to the West was that mankind, not God, is the hub of the social universe." [310] It was the humanist outlook that placed man and human achievement at the centre of all things. Renaissance scholars celebrated the works of the ancient Greeks and Romans for their own sake, rather than for their relevance to church doctrine.

The Renaissance helped learning spread through Europe and provided support for the ideas of the Reformation. Martin Luther's premise that anyone can read the Bible and find salvation by faith alone was a revolutionary idea. Luther's concept that individuals were justified, and made able to meet God's justice, by faith alone removed the need for a priestly hierarchy to mediate between God and the individual. He advocated a "priesthood of all believers."[311] By removing the power of the priest and the coercive power of the Catholic Church, it made Christianity a deeply personal religion, emphasizing the faith of the individual over formal rituals and social practices.

The Catholic Church Counter-Reformation denotes the period of Catholic revival from the pontificate of Pius IV in 1560 until the end of the Thirty Years War in 1648. It had a two-fold purpose: to eliminate the abuses within the church, and gain back Protestant jurisdictions. The subsequent religious intolerance of the 17th century led to violence on the continent. Following the Glorious Revolution, the British Parliament put even more limits on the power of the monarchy in order to ensure separation of church from government. With foreign kings, the British parliament became more powerful.

The evolution of democracy in Britain includes separation of the church from the state.

During the reign of Charles I, William Laud activities upset many in England, subsequently, 20,000 Protestants left Britain and immigrated to New England. They used covenants when they established congregations in the Old World. Many of these new religious groups moved to America to escape prosecution as heretics. The Presbyterian assemblies that organized the new congregations that left the Old World to escape persecution facilitated the development of democracy in America. The principles of democracy developed in the American colonies based on the principles of the Presbyterian Assemblies that had been established during the Reformation.[312] The American Revolution embodied many of the new ideas from the Age of Enlightenment. These thinkers and writers believed that human reason could be used to combat ignorance, superstition, and tyranny and to build a better world.

No one church predominated in the American colonies. There was no Catholic counter reformation. The Protestant Reformation continued longer in America than Europe. Alexis de Tocqueville, observed that private interest and personal gain motivated the actions of most Americans, which in turn cultivated a strong sense of individualism.

The influence of religion on government decreased throughout the 19th century with the appearance of new ideas. These ideas included the liberal theology of the German scholars whose studies identified discrepancies between events in history and their record in the Bible, and the writings of Darwin that called into question whether the world was only 10,000 years old as determined by literal interpretation of the Scriptures. In response to the weakening of traditional values in the community, the ideas of German scholars and the writings of Darwin on evolution, Christian fundamentalist theology developed in the early 20th century. The Christian Right organized into a political force, but only existed as a like-minded group. It became a significant grassroots constituency in the last decade of the 20th century. There is little role for literal interpretation of the Bible in developing good government, however, the Christian Right influences the agenda of political parties in North America through effective use of the media and advertising.

Adam Smith described the basis for classical economics. His theories supported the flow of capital in the Industrial Age. Economic theories of free markets evolved over the last fifty years of the 20th century, and played an important part in the Cold War in pushing back communist ideas. They are associated with respected writers such as Friedrich Hayek and Ayn Rand. Hayek developed an intellectual system covering economics, law and politics while supporting the free enterprise system. Ayn Rand's writings described the process of self-responsibility – it is up to each one of us to determine what values our lives require, how best to achieve those values. Times change, and the individualism of objectivism has been replaced by the individualism of entitlement. The definition of self-esteem that goes with entitlement: 'I have high self-esteem, I will be successful.' The cult of individualism appeared at the same time as Milton Freidman's liberal economics of privatization, deregulation/free trade and reduction in government spending became mainstream economic thought in North America. When there is too much self-esteem, there are problems of self-tolerance, entitlement and narcissism. In the Age of Entitlement there is an entitlement to consume. In the individualist's consumer society there is a strong focus on rights. Rights imply an entitlement to goods and services.[313] The extreme individualist manipulates the market with high expectations and little concern for consequences to others.

How does the Age of Entitlement affect the economic system? Douglass North notes "Individuals possess mental models to interpret the world around them. There is immense variation ... as a result different perceptions of the world and the way it works."[314] Different belief systems affect how the free market functions. To counter this North has proposed a framework called 'economic institutions' that would be composed of formal rules and informal constraints to reduce the uncertainty of human exchange, and developed to function with inefficient markets. Inefficient markets occur when there is "incomplete information and limited mental capacity by which to process information. It is exceptional to find economic markets that approximate the conditions necessary for efficiency."[315]

The asset-backed commercial paper led to market instability in 2007, as various companies produced rather opaque financial structures. With a downturn in the US housing market, no one knew who held the subprime mortgages and this created collateral damage to parties not particularly exposed to the debt. This is an example of where the new economic institution with some rules could have a role in controlling those promoting debt packages to unsuspecting customers. What is their belief system? It is important to be aware of the culture of the individuals that one interacts with in business. The cult of individualism affects how an individual interprets events and reacts to other people. The decline in the stock market from the fiasco of asset-backed commercial paper is a consequence of a culture that peddles entitlement, greed and self-centeredness.[316]

Ethics does not come from religious, moral, political or social sources. Ethics are personal. Everyone has a different foundation on which they build their moral code. People are involved and they come to the system or organization with personal motives. The cult of self-esteem and the cult of self-centeredness reinforce this. The rugged individualism of the

19th century has been replaced by a narcissistic form of individualism, that celebrates self-expression and self-gratification.[317] This challenge to governments has been described by Richard Sennett in *The Fall of the Public Man* (1974), who describes a process in which people turn to private lives for authenticity and meaning. This creates confusion between the boundary between self and the external world, as emotion becomes involved in decisions.[318] Narcissism creates a threat to democracy, as the individual is unable to think beyond his/her own self-interest. The consequence is a system where the community is a distant second behind the person.

Ethics is about social conscience; what is absolutely just and required when dealing with other human beings. It is the discipline of dealing with what is good and bad and with moral duty and obligations, and can begin with humility and extend to empathy. Morality is conduct that conforms to an accepted standard of right and wrong, and includes decency and goodness. The opposite of morality is judgment, self-congratulatory, self-righteousness, underhandedness, meanness and unscrupulousness. Such action meets Kant's categorical imperative: what if everyone did this and people are treated as an ends rather than a means?[319] In the 21st century where is the best-established information for developing good government? Where is the science? In the 14th century, Ockham deduced that theology was not an exact science and religion had a role limited to spiritual affairs. When Adam Smith laid out the basics of classical economics, religion still played an important part in how one made decisions. His work was popular because it provided an 'ethical' rational for the capitalist system that explained how one acted in their own interest, actually helped someone unknown to you. Throughout the 20th century, secularism became the major force. Economics is not an absolute science; decisions are based on observational data. That the free market system works there is no doubt. However, it remains an unregulated system. There are no mathematical formulas to support the predictability. As religion, and in particular ethical thinking in religion, is removed from the work force in the Western world, there need to be processes to keep ethics in the playing field. Ayn Rand's objectivism requires a rational mind to operate without Christian (religious) ethics. The culture of self-centeredness does not support the rationalization of objectivism.

The political economist, Friedrich Hayek was a champion of the free market economy and an outspoken critic of market socialism. He is famous for describing the price system as a communication network, the price system value to social well-being is the system's capacity to transmit information from one part of the market to another. As a social philosopher, Hayek's main task was the finding of rules that enable men with different values and convictions to live together. These rules were established so as to permit each individual to fulfill his aims and to limit government action. He was more than a simplistic supporter of laissez-faire; he was concerned to explore the necessary framework of government and the rule of law in which freedom and commerce could prosper. Hayek wrote that government is "necessary" to fulfill the following tasks: "law enforcement, defense against external enemies" and in advanced society, government ought to use its power of raising funds by taxation to provide a minimum of services which for various reasons cannot be provided adequately, by the market. Besides relief from various natural disasters, this included such things as most roads and certification of goods and services offered by the market. To Hayek, it was irrelevant how big government was and how fast it grew. What was important was that government actions fulfilled certain formal requirements. It was the character rather than the volume of government activity that was important.[320]

Individualism, which is a positive force behind the development of democracy and free enterprise, has continued to evolve. Good government consists of checks and balances to cover the many interests that exist. In extreme individualism, the sense of entitlement gives them the perceived high ground at the same time they experience a declining sense of personal responsibility.[321] Individuals using these belief systems can affect good government. For this reason, there is a need to define the attributes of good government. A good government requires good governance. Governance is the process of decision making and the process by which decisions are implemented (or not implemented). Eight characteristics of good governance were defined by the United Nations' paper published in December 2006, *What is good governance?* The eight characteristics of good governance are accountability, consensus-oriented processes, effectiveness and efficiency, equity and inclusiveness, participation, responsiveness, rule of law and transparency.[322]

"Accountability is the key requirement of good governance." [323] Accountability is about obligation to answer for one's actions. In addition to being responsible for one's actions, one may be required to explain them to others. A government is accountable to those who will be affected by its decisions or actions. Central to the principle of accountability is information sharing and transparency, which should be promoted by governance structures. Accountability cannot be enforced without transparency and the rule of law.

"Consensus orientation is part of good governance of mediating differing interests to reach a broad consensus on what is in the best interest of the community and, where possible, on policies and procedures." [324] Consensus decision-making involves identifying and addressing concerns, generating new alternatives and checking that people understand a proposal or argument. This includes how it happens, intent and direction, and the process. How it happens includes the need for clear definition of the problem to be addressed, and a provision of opportunities for interested stakeholders to present their views. The process must identify the benefits and costs of the proposed action.

"Processes and institutions produce results that meet needs while making the best use of resources." [325] This is effectiveness and efficiency of good governance, which requires honesty, integrity and fairness. Honesty is communicating and acting truthful and with fairness as best one is able. It is related to truth as a value. All relationships are built on this basis. The opposite is falsehoods, manipulation and exploitive actions. Integrity is conduct that conforms to an accepted standard of right and wrong, faithfulness to high moral standards. The opposite is sense of entitlement, discredit and corruption. Fairness competes with self-centeredness, and is the ability to make judgments free from discrimination or dishonesty. Being fair-minded includes intellectual humility, intellectual empathy and intellectual integrity; basically, treat people the way one wants to be treated. Efficiency includes sustainable use of natural resources and the protection of the environment. Unique requirements in this area include having environmental protection laws align with economic analysis. Beware of regulations as these can get in the way of companies using efficient ways to reduce their emissions and actually increase costs to society. Innovation would include greater use of taxes to encourage expenditures on infrastructure that helps in reducing pollution.

"Equity and inclusiveness requires all men and women have opportunities to improve or maintain their well being."[326] The well being of a community depends on ensuring that all its members feel that they have a stake in it and do not feel excluded from the mainstream of society. This requires that all groups, but particularly the most vulnerable, have opportunities to improve or maintain their well being. Unique requirements include such items as the need for the health care policy to effectively cover the population. Public spaces need to be regulated as they have an effect on global warming and recreation spaces. There is a need for transparency in subsidy policies. Subsidies are a blunt tool and can have harmful effects on the environment and people's health.

"Participation by both men and women is a cornerstone of good governance." [327] Participation is built around three pillars: public access to information, public participation in decision-making processes, public access to judicial and administrative redress, often termed "access to justice."[328] There is a need to use clear comprehensive language in communication and legislation and for the resulting rules to be accessible. The system needs to have appropriate complaint-resolution processes in place.

"Good governance includes responsiveness. Institutions and processes try to serve all stakeholders within a reasonable time frame."[329] The availability of manpower is an important aspect of the process of a government providing responsiveness. There is a need to predict the labor requirements in a global economy. An example of failed government policy was the incredible health care policy implemented during the 1990s in Canada. Canada's health ministers, (federal, provincial, territorial), commissioned two veteran health economists, Morris Barer and Greg Stoddart, to provide "a review of issues and policy options for assuring an adequate supply of medical services for Canadians."[330] The Barer-Stoddart Report, *Toward Integrated Medical Resource Policies for Canada*, made over fifty recommendations that included cutting medical school enrollment by 10%. Enrolment in medical schools across the Canada was religiously reduced, believing by limiting the number of doctors practicing, the costs to the system could be controlled. The medical community point to this action as aggravating the physician shortage in Canada.

Apologists (i.e. other health care researchers) defend the study claiming policy-makers cherry picked the easiest recommendations to save money. However, at the same time two other independent events were occurring: more and more graduates sought out specialties other than family practice, and the family practice program increased the length of their training program. The apologists note the number of physicians per hundred thousand in Canada remained remarkably stable in the ensuing two decades following implementation of the policy.[331] What eludes these data crunchers is the fact that Canada had been raiding Third World countries for family doctors during this time. Now the debate has correctly switched to 'supply of services' from the number of doctors. With the graying of the work force and the desire of young doctors for a better family-work balance, doctors are working fewer hours. When medical schools in Canada expanded in the first decade of the 21st century, not all the training slots in family medicine were filled – students fed by stories of the strain on family doctors over the past two decades continued to choose other specialties. Today many families in Canada cannot find a family doctor due to shortages in both urban and rural areas. Doing nothing also costs money. The uncontrolled development of the oil sands in Alberta in the early 21st century has led to a shortage of workers in many areas in Canada – from affecting the ability to fill potholes in Nova Scotia to limiting the development of the economy of the province of Saskatchewan. While the emigration policy can be part of the solution, it is prone to political manipulation for the emigrant vote.

"Good governance requires fair legal frameworks that are enforced impartially; and is known as rule of law."[332] There is a need to use clear comprehensive language in communications and legislation, and for the resulting rules to be accessible. It is necessary to implement effective compliance and enforcement strategies, and allocate adequate resources to support the regulations. It is important to provide the necessary resources to support legislation to enforce laws to protect workers in the workplace. Protection in the workplace includes policies to deal with both harassment and the dysfunction created by those living a narcissist's vocation. This will reduce the stress due to the cult of self-esteem.

The availability of information is critical to good governance of the rule of law. Computer systems need to be able to talk to each other and exchange data. There is a need to collect comparable data, across all jurisdictions in order to measure the effects of interventions. This would provide much of the factual data used for measuring benchmarks to create the framework where accountability and improved delivery could enhance change. Legislation must be in place to protect the privacy of the individual in the era of digital data storage.

In the physical world a transparent object or issue is one that is seen clearly, and readily understood. In good governance "Transparency means that decisions made and their enforcement are achieved in a manner that follows rules and regulations. It also means that information is freely available and directly accessible to those who will be affected by such decisions and their enforcement. It also means that enough information is provided, and that it is provided in easily understandable forms and media." [333]

A good government creates the milieu for good governance. The eight characteristics of good governance are an exercise of economic, political and administrative authority to manage a country's affairs at all levels. It ensures that political, social, and economic priorities are based on a broad consensus in society and that in decision-making the voices of the most vulnerable in society are heard. What is the answer to the culture of self-centeredness in which too many people are out for themselves? Accountability is required. Accountability is the obligation or willingness to accept responsibility for one's actions. Accountability is a key requirement of good governance. Narcissism and the emotions that accompany the feeling of entitlement will interfere with any obligation to bear the consequences for failure. The characteristics needed for responsibility, or accountability, include self-criticism, self-denial, self-discipline, and self-control. Self-centeredness of extreme individualism supports governments having but a little role in the affairs of individuals. Small government thinking (of less regulation and oversight of the financial institutions) is something that could influence the chance of another economic crisis. The fact that the elected government allows multinational corporations more power is the consequence of participating in corporate dominant globalization of the market place. Corporations have been quietly usurping political power, and as political systems give legislative power to the corporations, accountability has been transferred to the corporations.

Where has accountability found support in the past? The ancient writings include the Golden Rule and have a role in countering the self-centeredness of extreme individualism. The Golden Rule supports the correct self-esteem in which one is accountable and behaves responsibly and ethically, and is found throughout ancient writings including the Koran, the writings of Confucius and the Scriptures, Jesus in the Sermon on the Mount. Sir John Templeton notes the Golden Rule "...is found in every major religion and regarded as one of the basic spiritual principles of life."[334] Among the earliest appearances in English is Earl Rivers' translation of a saying of Socrates in *Dictes and Sayenges of the Philosophirs*, published in 1477. "Do to others as thou wouldst they should do to thee, and do to none other but as thou wouldst be done to." [335] Over time it has been shortened to "Do unto others as you would have them do unto you" or treat others the way you would want to be treated. In 1809 Thomas Jefferson declared, "I never did, or countenanced, in public life, a single act inconsistent with the strictest good faith; having never believed there was one code of morality for a public, and another for a private man." [336] Today, the norm is to leave ethics at home when the individual goes to work.

In the late 17th century, John Locke popularized the idea of natural rights. Natural rights (also called moral rights or inalienable rights) are the rights that are not contingent upon the laws, customs, or beliefs of a particular society or polity. During the Age of Enlightenment natural law theory challenged the divine rights of kings, and became an alternative justification for the establishment of a social contract or government. Locke believed when securing social order through government the will expressed by the majority must be accepted. There is an implicit agreement that when an individual chooses to live in a society, they consent to submit themselves and their property to its governance. Through legislative power is found the ability to provide for social order and the common good by setting standing laws over the acquisition, preservation, and transfer of property. These services are provided for in ways to which everyone consents. Locke had specific ideas on the abuse of power. He declared when a society unduly interfered with the property interests of the citizens, they were bound to protect themselves by withdrawing their consent. Only the people can decide whether great mistakes have been made in governance. In Locke's view then, the possibility of revolution was a permanent feature of any properly formed society. These ideas made Locke the most quoted Enlightenment philosopher leading up to and during the American Revolution.[337]

20

Conclusion

Reforming the financial services industry requires dedicated input from government. Today, various forces compete to influence government decision-making. These forces include the media (newspapers, TV, Internet), supporters of economic fundamentalism, and the culture of extreme individualism. These forces create three major spheres that affect the decision-making in government in the first decade of the 21st century. The first sphere of influence is the cultural hegemony in the West, propagated by the mass media and advertisers supporting the free market system. This system of control is built around the concentration of the news media and large advertising budgets. This ensures ongoing support for globalization. Globalization is associated with efforts to maximize consumption and minimize production costs. Large budgets for advertising are part of this system. The advertisers focus a great deal of resources on branding. Products are made in a factory; a brand is something bought by a customer. Branding is about imprinting a feel good feeling – called brand recognition.[338] Media and advertisers work by giving brand meaning, which feeds the cult of individualism and influences our self-esteem and decision-making.

Mass media and advertisers are part of the dominant culture in the West. This drives an individualistic consumer society. The hegemony is strengthened as fewer and fewer corporations control the media. Information in the media is open to the practice of manipulation (i.e. amount of airtime given an event), and it is easy for a powerful group to manipulate the media through various means, to magnify the effect of a story. There is a need for accountability. Accountability is a promise and an obligation, to both one's self, and the people around one, to deliver specific defined results. Accountability is the foundation for an ethical business practice.[339]

In the 21st century, control of people's thinking through the mass media is well established. Messaging uses cognitive dissonance to market messages that support their cause. Cognitive dissonance is achieved by the pairing of unrelated facts to create correlation. The close proximity of mentions is designed to create a correlation in people's minds even when the reality is different. By insinuation, people subconsciously take the idea and turn it to a possibility, and through repetition, the correlation becomes fact based upon misinformation. The media also controls the perception of events. It labels destructive actions of Cho (who killed 32 and wounded many others at Virginia Tech) a case of extreme narcissism, while managers in the financial services (who destroyed millions of citizens' dreams and standard of living) are portrayed as innocent bystanders of the effects of globalization.

On November 5, 2009 Rep. John Boehner of Ohio, the House minority leader, took the podium at a Republican rally, waved a document defiantly and declared: "This is my copy of the Constitution, and I'm going to stand here with the Founding Fathers who wrote in the Preamble, 'We hold these truths to be self-evident, that all men are created equal, that they are endowed with the unalienable rights of life, liberty, and the pursuit of happiness'..." Mr. Boehner was encouraging participants to protest the pending House vote for health care reform by insinuating their constitutional right to make medical decisions will be violated.[340] Boehmer was creating cognitive dissonance by linking the proposed legislation on health reform in the USA with the violation of constitutional rights and freedom to make choices. The media enabled this activity. John Kenneth Galbraith (1908-2006) noted "Television newsmen are breathless on how the game is being played, largely silent on what the game is all about."[341]

In the first decade of the 21st century, the second sphere of influence in the West that affected decision-making was the dogma of economic fundamentalism. Economic fundamentalism supports an unfettered free market system. Economic fundamentalism was embraced during the Reagan and Thatcher administrations, and simultaneously, Milton Friedman's teachings of privatization/deregulation/free trade and reduced government spending went mainstream. This had significant effect on the world economy. These processes laid the groundwork for globalization: world trade increased significantly and was associated with increased wealth in the world; a new growing middle class appeared in India and China. However the picture of increased wealth in the West is more complex.

The last two decades of globalization jobs in Western economies have moved off shore and a supply of inexpensive consumer goods stream from China (which has become the factory of the world). The consequent consumer price drop allows Friedman's students to point to a corresponding increase in purchasing power in the West. However, the greatest numbers of new jobs that appear in the West are now low paying positions in the service industry. The consequence of this shift is the widening of the income gap between rich and poor in the West, and the standard of living for the middle class fell during the last three decades, when market downturn is factored in.[342]

Rand and Hayek have woven individualism into the fabric of economics. People need to understand that economic decisions will not escape the cult of individualism. Materialism, consumerism and advertising have joined to create very high expectations.[343] Consumers consume to feed images of themselves, and individuals are consumers driving financial speculation and volatility in the market. The scope of the financial fallout from the US housing collapse around subprime mortgages challenges the dogma that the free market system is self-regulating. Extreme individualism affects an individual's decision-making, and perception of the world. This mind set will influence government efforts to ensure there is structure in place, with respect to economic policies, to prevent a repeat of the events driven by greed and pursuit of narcissistic gratification that triggered the market instability in 2007.

The third sphere of influence that can affect good decision-making in government is the mindset that supports extreme individualism. Since the 1970s, extreme individualism found a favourable milieu in school systems. Rights replaced responsibilities. The world would be saved from crime, drug abuse and under achieving through boosting self-esteem. School systems lowered standards, with less emphasis on tests, to create feel-good education. This led down the path of extreme individualism and problems of self-tolerance. In the cult of self-esteem, individuals tolerate errors and flaws in their actions, which lead to a sense of entitlement. Entitlement is the feeling that we deserve something, whatever it may be, regardless of what we may or may not have done to earn it. The mind-set that they want it when they want it, no matter if it damages others, is characteristic of greed. There is a preoccupation with self at the expense of community living for oneself in the here and now, without any accountability. Helen Coale notes "The only threads that seem to weave us together are the dream of personal achievement and success, the expression of vivid personal feeling about our situations, and a consumer market that offers us pleasure."[344] In a culture of self-centeredness and entitlement, the world is viewed from an emotional rather than a rational perspective. This allows personal feelings to override the distinction between right and wrong.[345] Besides affecting the decision making of individuals, this belief system also affects organizations such as corporations and governments.

Too much self-esteem, problems of self-tolerance, entitlement and narcissism, resulted in the self-esteem movement creating a significant population of adults in the 21st century, with an exaggerated sense of entitlement, and the belief the world owed them something. Such individuals learn to tolerate their errors and personal flaws and come to accept themselves as okay. They feel justified in asserting themselves, defending their perceived rights. With narcissism, the greatest problem is profound disconnection from reality. The person living the narcissist's vocation has many tools to manipulate those around him. This person rarely admits to ignorance and regards his intuition and knowledge as superior to objective data. Part of the bubble universe in which they recruit others involves 'groupthink'.[346] Groupthink is a pattern of thought characterized by self-deception, created by a faulty group decision-making process, which is not critical of each other's ideas. Groups experiencing groupthink do not consider all the alternatives, and they desire unanimity at the expense of quality decisions.

The group is highly cohesive, isolated from contrary opinions, and is ruled by a directive leader who makes his wishes known.

The individualism of the 21st century favours 'checkbook' organizations. This creates, for the political consumer, a system with people distrustful of political institutions, but more trusting of citizens. It is unusual for members to meet face to face; all they need to do is write a check once a year. This creates a type of self-absorbed, self-congratulatory, socially inept people.[347] One such protest group, called the Tea Party, appeared in early 2009. The Tea Party movement began in the USA as protests against government bailouts and healthcare legislation. The protest movement is named after the Boston Tea Party of the pre-revolution years that became a symbol of tax revolt. The coalition was tagged as extremist because of disruptions during health care town hall meetings during the summer of 2009. They believed that the purpose of American independence is to throw off not just the British government, but any big government. In Tea Party recruiting, emotions rule, and the organizers try to channel anger to help attract conservative candidates. Organized into groups all across the USA, they believe they are giving 'the little person' a voice in government.[348] Such organizations are free to follow their own inclinations. These protest groups, tapping anger in the community, tend not to be specific to financial reform.

Some groups have come together for social marketing in which branding is important. Branding is often a subliminal process by which a business employs marketing strategies to get people to remember their products and services over a competitor. Social marketing applies the same principles that are used to sell products to consumers to 'sell' ideas, attitudes and behaviors. The goal is to influence social behavior. Social marketing involves the media, including the Internet. Part of the Tea Party movement has set up a website, the 'Tea Party

Nation,' to serve as a source of information for sharing and networking. The use of Twitter and Facebook makes presence known within social media networks. This increases brand visibility and creates awareness. They are able to recruit friends who join the conversation in the media, on the Internet, on what their product is. This is an opportunity to personalize the brand and helps spread the message in a relaxed and conversational way. This creates personality behind the brand and makes the ideas visible to people who do not know the movement.[349] The present protest groups do not lend support to financial reform. For example, the financial services industry is out of direct reach of reformers protected by the umbrella of the principle of limited government and free market. While there is a need to introduce regulation of financial institutions to prevent abuses of the system, it will be difficult, over time, for regulations to stay ahead of evolving financial services. No matter how hard regulators try and how smart they are, they often cannot keep on top of the risk.[350]

John Locke considered people to be naturally independent and equal which, to him, meant that nobody had the right to harm another person's "life, health, liberty, or possessions."[351] Possessions had a wide definition of material things that included money. Each individual in the state of nature has the right to enforce the natural law in the defense of property interests. Locke viewed property as a natural right, and he contended that it was derived from labor. Thus labour was naturally owned by the person; consequently, anything that labour was applied to was similarly owned by the labourer. He observed that money allowed a person to retain possession of the value of their labour without wasting it. There was agreement among individuals to the value assigned to coins to create a monetary system. This need for agreement, in turn, gave rise to social order. The formation of a civil society required all individuals to voluntarily surrender this right to the community at large. Locke declared that the fundamental purpose of government was the maintenance of basic security and public order. He maintained that government rested on popular consent and rebellion was permissible when government subverted the ends – the protection of life liberty and property for which it was established.[352]

Corporations and the Medieval Church share similarities. The Medieval Church had popes and priests who discerned the will of God, and directed the congregations; the modern corporation has CEOs and managers who discern the will of the market and direct the employees. The Medieval Church was a monopoly. Individuals were forced to conform to the institutions. There was variation in the ancient world, but it was squelched. The use of force to protect dogma was facilitated by the Inquisition, which was established to impose conformity of thought and crush heresy.

As markets mature, they become dominated by a few major corporations, who collude and exhibit cartel-like behaviour. Generally they have been incapable of developing new ideas and rely on buying up under-capitalized start-ups to keep up. Today, the corporate strangleholds on information and communication guarantees ongoing support for marketing messages supporting globalization. Economic dogmas are characteristic of a single belief, attribute or statement. Dogma is not good or bad. The problem with dogma is that it is the enemy of critical thinking and requires the suspension of normal faculties of questioning and skepticism that are essential for intellectual progress. On the other hand, the Medieval Church believed any challenge to its dogma was evil and justified suppression of variation and oppressing the individual.[353] Both corporations and the Medieval Church were ways of organizing human activity in the West. The church participated in collecting rents, negotiating trade deals, waging wars and maintained armies. In the 14th century, the church owned one-third of the land in England and paid no taxes. The upper echelons of the church considered the accumulation of wealth important to support the growth of the church. Both modern corporations and the Medieval Church developed processes to make money from the system; the church introduced new offices to sell to generate cash flow, while the financial services industry introduced new instruments like derivatives. Derivatives were developed for risk management, have no intrinsic value, but rely on something else for their value. Banks collect many billions of dollars annually in undisclosed fees associated with such financial instruments. The big banks influence the rules governing derivatives and this ensures a healthy profit margin.[354] Corporations have grown in size and numbers all over the world because of their ability to mobilize productive resources and create new wealth. The greatest advantage of a corporation is the ability to avoid paying taxes. 'Lean and mean' corporations focus on the bottom line. A recognized procedure is to fire experienced full time staff and replace them by a combination of junior and part time staff to improve the quarterly report.[355]

In *Passion of the Western Mind*, Richard Tarnas identifies the change from medieval era to the modern character, the modern mind required a systematically critical independence of judgment. Tarnas described the process as: "The modern emergence of autonomous personal judgment, prototypically incarnated in Luther, Galileo and Descartes, made increasingly impossible any continuation of the medieval era's virtually universal intellectual deference to external authorities, such as the Church and Aristotle, that had been culturally empowered by tradition."[356]

In *The Ascent of Money*, Niall Ferguson matter-of-factly describes the cyclic nature of the investment markets:

"In the four hundred years since shares were first bought and sold, there has been a succession of financial bubbles. Time and time again, share prices have soared to unsustainable heights only to crash downward again. Time and time again, this process has been accompanied by skullduggery, as unscrupulous insiders have sought to profit at the expense of the naïve neophytes. … asymmetries always exist in business, of course, but in a bubble the insiders exploit them fraudulently…. The seasoned speculator, based in a major financial centre, may lack the inside knowledge of the true insider. But he is much more likely to get his timing right – buying early and selling before the bubble bursts - than the naïve first time investor. …without easy credit creation a true bubble cannot occur. That is why so many bubbles have their origins in the sins of omission or commission of central banks." [357]

The repetitive history of stock market bubbles and the actions of unscrupulous insiders have become part of corporate globalization. The Wall Street debate in response to the economic debacle of 2008 has been 'culturally empowered' since the 1980s by intellectual deference to external authorities such as Friedrich Hayek and Milton Friedman. This is the foundation of the polarized debates on financial reform in the first decade of the 21st century. There is a need to introduce critical thinking into the debate to address the asymmetry in the financial services industry that is repeatedly exploited by insiders.

There is one major difference between the Medieval Church and corporations. The Medieval Church had a soul or conscience, especially the lower rung dedicated to the problems of the common people. In contrast, the corporation does not have a conscience, but has a personality much like a person. Capitalism supports individualism. Extreme individualism leads to narcissism. Narcissism makes individuals and corporations dangerous because it deprives them of the empathy or restraint that result in respect for the other. Narcissism creates selective blindness; the narcissist may not "see" others at all. While a narcissist can lead a large corporation successfully, if the leadership surround themselves with a bubble of like-thinkers, they will meet the same fate as the Enron management. The Medieval Church engaged change. The Protestant Revolution and Reformation created new rules, ones that offered individual opportunities never before given to the common man. The basis of the Protestant revolution was Luther's claim that individual revelation and conviction ought to be the root of religious belief. In this system there is a shift of authority to the individual; the church either meets the needs of the congregation or the congregation goes elsewhere (or nowhere). Over 450 years later this principle still functions.

Organizations like the IMF, World Bank and World Trade Organization do not have the teeth to ensure the accountability in corporations needed to avert the next financial crisis. The influence of corporations has spread worldwide and affects a far greater per centage of the population than the Medieval Church did. Corporations are centres of power to be accommodated within the legal and political structures. When interacting with corporations, their narcissistic traits must be taken into consideration. This means specific boundaries must be developed in well constructed regulations. Behind their corporate economic dogma they believe they are right, and resist challenges to their beliefs. Capitalism encourages a focus on gratification and social approval and hence encourages more open narcissism. Manufacturers doing the advertizing are selfish and, drawing on emotion; can manipulate the consumer into wanting just about anything. Narcissism thrives in this culture.

"Narcissism sets up the illusion that once one has feeling, it must be manifest – because after all, "inside" is an absolute reality," Richard Sennett noted.[358] Narcissism involves self-deception; the greatest weapon against narcissism is reality and critical thinking. A new culture to counter the forces that peddle greed, entitlement and self-centeredness is required. This new culture must include introducing proper self-esteem – "self-esteem is of two kinds: earned and unearned. Only earned self-esteem is healthy and satisfying and doesn't pre-cede achievement, but follows it."[359] One goal is to introduce the proper self-esteem into the school system, but it will take time to spread through the school system into the workplace. In time, this new way of thinking will allow for less regulation and interventions by regulators; but this change is a long-term objective.

The foundation for a new model for globalization is to rec-ognize the need for a new corporate culture. It is necessary that individuals recognize the need for corporate power to be exer-cised to benefit the community at large. Daniel Boorstin (1914-2004), American historian, observed, "The greatest obstacle to discovery is not ignorance, it is the illusion of knowledge."[360] In *Free Will and Illusion*, Saul Smilansky explains: "Much of the story of the growth of human knowledge, and possibly human progress, can be told in terms of overcoming of comfortable illusions – from Copernicus to Darwin and to Freud, many of our pleasant illusions about ourselves and the world have been realized as such."[361] Dogma supports the illusion of knowl-edge, and it is necessary to confront dogma. This is apparent in medicine today; dogmatic ideas on treatment are chased by evidence-based medicine. Also, dogma in the church had noth-ing to do with spirituality and everything to do with main-taining social and political control. One counters dogma with critical thinking.

Copernicus did not publish the book, *De revolutionbus orbium coelestrum (On the Revolution of the Celestial Spheres)*, putting forward that the Earth and the other planets instead revolved around the sun until 1543 (the same year as his death). It wasn't until the first decade of the 17th century that thinkers such as Galileo brought attention to the heliocentric hypothesis of *De Revolutionibus*. It was then that the Catholic Church condemned and placed it on the *Index of Forbidden Books* because the theory conflicted with parts of the Bible. It was associated with a shift from an earth-centered to a sun-centered universe – weakening the power of the established church. By 1630, most astronomers and philosophers accepted the heliocentric hypothesis. In 1687, Isaac Newton devised his law of universal gravitation, which introduced gravitation as the force that both kept the Earth and planets moving through the heavens and also kept the air from flying away, allowing scientists to quickly construct a plausible heliocentric model for the solar system.[362] During the Age of Enlightenment the ideas of the Renaissance continued to grow and become more widespread.

Charles Darwin's book, *On the Origin of Species,* published in 1859, explained the process of natural selection that populations evolved over the course of generations, which supported the process of evolution. While similar theories circulated earlier in the 19th century, they did not gain acceptance as the English scientific establishment was closely tied to the Church of England. Darwin's book was written for the non-specialist reader and its popularity generated widespread discussion. The book was extremely controversial as it suggested that human beings may be descended from the apes. It took two decades after the publication of *On the Origin of Species* before there was widespread scientific agreement in evolution.[363] In 1900, Sigmund Freud published his book *Interpretation of Dreams*, introducing to the world psychoanalytical theories representing a radical change in conceptions of the nature and constitution of the human psyche. His new concepts were initially met with scorn and open hostility. Subsequently, a group of Vienna's brightest minds gathered at Freud's home in Vienna for conversation and debate. This inner circle included Adler and Carl Jung, well-known names in the history of psychoanalysis. Freud launched a revolution that shaped modern psychology. And while Adler and Jung each eventually put forth deeply differing views of psychological development, it was Freud's theories of the id, the ego and the superego that underlay them all.[364]

Paul Volcker, the previous Fed Chairman known for keeping inflation under control, was fired because the Reagan administration didn't believe he was up to the task of implementing deregulation. Since early 2009 he has worked as a financial advisor to President Obama. In the July 11, 2010 Sunday Times Volcker commented, "You had an intellectual conviction that you did not need much regulation – that the market could take care of itself. I am happy to say that that illusion has been shattered."[365] His advice on the proposed legislation for regulation of the financial services industry is to prevent commercial banks from owning and investing in hedge funds and private equity. Legislators have ignored this advice and allowed commercial banks limited exposure. The regulatory council charged with enforcing the legislation will have its work cut with this type of regulation that lacks clear boundaries for commercial banks. This will ensure that lawyers are fully employed.[366] It will take years to get this activity focused.

By the end of the first decade of 21st century, two former directors of the Federal Reserve had signaled a warning. Alan Greenspan's admission, as Chairman of the Federal Reserve, in the autumn of 2008 that the regimen of deregulation he oversaw was based on a "flaw"; he had overestimated the ability of the free market to self-correct, and had missed the self-destructive power of deregulated mortgage lending.[367] In the second case, as previously mentioned, Paul Volcker observed, that the market was unable to take care of itself. When two distinguished long-term players in monitoring the economy suggest problems with the existing system, one is foolish not to consider the need for change. Machiavelli commented on the challenges to new ideas over 400 years ago:

> "We must bear in mind, then, that there is nothing more difficult and dangerous, or more doubtful of success, than an attempt to introduce a new order of things in any state. The innovator has for enemies all those who derived advantages from the old order of things, whilst those who expect to be benefited by the new institutions, will be but lukewarm defenders. This indifference arises in part from fear of their adversaries who were favoured by the existing laws, and partly from the incredulity of men who have no faith in anything new that is not the result of well-established experience. Hence it is that, whenever the opponents of a new order of things have the opportunity to attack it, they will do it with the zeal of partisans, whilst the others defend it but feebly, so it is dangerous to rely on the latter." [368]

To avoid cognitive dissonance, many accept the status quo. We need to bring forward the best arguments to carry the day for change. The writing of John Locke on the defense of property, and also the non-interference in the value of money and work provides the opportunity to drive critical thinking. In today's case it is not a decision made by the state interfering with individual choice; it is the financial services industry decision-making that interfered with a social contract of voluntary participation.

Globalization exerts effects over great distances, and people's lives can be fundamentally changed as a result of decisions made only days or moments earlier, thousands of miles away. Many had nothing invested with asset-backed mortgages, but unintended consequences of decisions by financial institutions created an economic meltdown affecting the value of homes and pension funds. The market cycle affected individuals who had nothing to do with the speculation. We must overcome 'pleasant illusions.' The present system failed the middle class dream of providing their children better lives than they have. The present system of small government and less taxes is not delivering the results delivered by capitalism in the past, and consequently has failed them. Secrecy is the key factor enabling banks to make large profits from financial instruments like derivatives. They have become one of the most profitable businesses in finance and are responsible for increased business costs across America.[369]

Kant had studied theology, mathematics and physics, but after reading the philosophy of David Hume, woke from his 'dogmatic slumbers', spending twelve years looking for answers to the questions posed by Hume's skepticism, resulting in Kant's writings combining elements from the rival schools of rationalism and empiricism which he found to be true.[370] Winston Churchill, England's great war time prime minister, complained in disgust, trying desperately to get his people to prepare for the attack by Adolf Hitler's Germany: "The average man simply cannot tolerate the truth. And should he inadvertently stumble over it, he immediately hurries away lest it force him to discard the delusions with which he comforts himself." [371]

The Narcissist's Vocation and the Economic Debacle is a wake up call to the middle class that, even with the proposed reforms to the financial services industry on the way, for real change to occur to reduce the risk for further economic turmoil, there needs to be sustained effort to drive change at two levels, the corporate buy-in for need for regulations, and the need to change the narcissism that influences thinking today.

In 2003, in *Understanding the Process of Economic Change*, Douglass C. North observed, that with the present size of the market with globalization, reputation no longer serves as "an effective vehicle in constraining human behaviour" and there is need for "third-party enforcement, and that means government and the state." [372] There is a success story that does not follow all the economic fundamentalist rules, such as secure property rights, that have underpinned the development in the US and the western world. This success story is China. A central political dictatorship has provided various levels of autonomy to local governments. This autonomy has facilitated the flow of capital from overseas creating a system with the highest growth of any economy in the world. China manages to structure their system to provide the correct incentives to do the right thing for growth. North points out:

> "...there is no way to make intelligent predictions of long-range change. And that is because we cannot know today what we will learn tomorrow and believe tomorrow. ...there is no such thing as laissez-faire... Any market that is going to work well is structured, it is structured by deliberate efforts to make the players compete by price and quality rather than compete by killing each other or other means." [373]

The present system in the West is the consequence of three decades of deregulation. Changes or structures are needed to address the action of the unscrupulous insiders who take advantage of the asymmetries that exist. The less tax and less government solutions do not deal with the asymmetrical market manipulated by the insider during the bubble. This is only addressed by a system that allows critical thinking and judgment to be applied. Regulation would put accountability back within a government jurisdiction; however, full acceptance and application may take twenty years to implement, and ensure competition by price and quality.

In the short term, corporations must be effectively regulated to ensure accountability. A watered down definition of accountability to be simply a reaction to a scandal is unsatisfactory. The core values of a targeted economic individualism must champion good governance that includes accountability and transparency, to counter the manipulation of the system that presently occurs. However, a communication process is required to start the shift in thinking. There is a need to use language familiar to the group caught up by the dogma of small government and few regulations and taxes. Unfamiliar language may create cognitive dissonance so strong that people will react to the discomforting evidence by strengthening their original beliefs and creating rationalizations to dismiss the discomforting evidence. In explaining the need for change to the corporations, it is necessary to illustrate that the status quo is bad for them, not that it is something immoral or unethical. Taking a page from the writings of John Locke, whose ideas are well known to the advocates of small government and low taxes, the natural rights of individuals as defined by Locke should be applied. One challenges the jurisdiction which, in this case, is the corporation not the government. The financial institutions interfered with our choices and must be held accountable. This action is modeled as targeted economic individualism with the development of social networks to pressure economic concerns with a vengeance, to support the government action for the necessary rules and enforcement structures. Over time, as the cult of extreme individualism is reduced, less regulation will be required. The long-term goal is not to replace capitalism, but rather the culture that supports corporations.

Works cited:

Ahmed, Akbar. *Journey Into Islam The Crisis of Globalization*. Washington: Brookings Institute Press, 2007.

Alphern, Henry. *An Outline History of Philosophy Scholastics to Schopenhauer*. Toronto: Forum House, 1969.

Barnett, William Steven. "Long-Term Cognitive and Acedemic Effects of Early Childhood Education on Children in Poverty." *Preventative Medicine*. 27 (1998).

Baumeister, Roy F, et al. "Does High Self-esteem Cause Better Performance, Interpersonal Successs, Happiness, Or Healthier Life Styles?" *Psychological Science in the Public Interest*. 4.1 (2003).

Beattie, Alan. *False Economy A Surprising Economic History of the World*. Toronto: Penguin Books, 2009.

Burns, Edward McNall and Philip Lee Ralph. *World Civilizations There History and Their Culture*. 5th Edition. New York: Norton, 1974.

Burston, Daniel. *The Legacy of Eric Fromm*. Cambridge: Harvard University Press, 1991.

Cambridge. *Illustrated History Islamic World*. Ed. Francis Robinson. New York: Cambridge University Press, 1996.

Canadian Pediatric Society. "Read, Speak, Sing: Promoting Literacy in the Physician's Office." *Pediatric Child Health* 11.9 (2006).

Coale, Helen W. *The Vulnerable Therapist: Practicing Psychotherapy in an Age of Anxiety.* Binghampton: The Haworth Press, 1998.

Dawkins, Richard. *The God Delusion.* New York: First Mariner Books, 2008.

Deresinski, Stan ed. "TB Linked to IMF Loan Funding." *Infectious Disease Alert.* 27.12(2008).

Donaldson Thomas. *Corporations and Morality.* Englewood Cliff: Prentice Hall Inc, 1982.

Ehrman, Bart D. *Misquoting Jesus The Story Behind Who Changed the Bible and Why.* New York: Harper Collins, 2005.

Ferguson, Niall. *The Ascent of Money A Financial History of the World.* New York: Penguin Books, 2008.

Fegley, Randall. *The Golden Spurs of Kortrijk: How the Knights of France Fell to the Foot Soldiers of Flanders in 1302.* Jefferson: McFarland and Company, 2002.

Hannay, Alstair. *Kierkegaard.* Routledge and Kegan Paul Ltd: London, 1982.

Hayek, Friedrich. *The Road to Serfdom.* Phoenix Books: Chicago, 1944.

Heckman, James J. "Skill Formation and the Economics of Investing in Disadvantaged Children." *Science.* 312 (2006).

Kagan, Robert. *Dangerous Nation.* New York: Vintage Books, 2006.

Keay, Douglas. "Aids, Education and the Year 2000." *Woman's Own.* 31 October 1987.

Klatt, Bruce, Shaun Murphy and David Irvine. *Accountabilty Getting a Grip on Results.* 2nd Edition. Calgary: Bow River Publishing, 2003.

Klein, Naomi. *No Logo Taking Aim at the Brand Bullies.* Toronto: Vintage Canada Edition, 2000.

—. *The Shock Doctrine The Rise of Disaster Capitalism.* Toronto: Alfred A Knopf, 2007.

Krugman, Paul. *The Return of Depression Economics and the Crisis of 2008.* New York: Norton, 2009.

LaFeber, Walter. *The New Empire: An Interpretation of American Expansion, 1860-1898. Ithaca:* Cornell University Press, 1963.

MacCulloch, Diarmaid. *Reformation, Europe's House Divided 1490-1700.* London: Penguin Books, 2003.

Machiavelli, Niccolò. *The Prince.* Trans. C E Deymold. Ware: Wordsworth Editions Limited, 1997.

Mead, Walter Russell. *God and Gold Britain, America and the Making of the Modern World.* New York: Vintage Books, 2007.

North, Douglass C. "Institutions and Economic Theory." *American Economist.* (1992).

—. "Understanding the Process of Economic Change." *Forum Series on the Role of Institutions in Promoting Economic Growth.* Washington: Mercatus Center at George Mason University, 2003.

Rand, Ayn. *Capitalism: The Unknown Ideal.* Centennial Edition. New York: Penguin Group, 1967.

—. *The Virtue of Selfishness A New Concept of Egoism.* New York: Signet Books, 1964.

Sennett, Richard. *The Fall of Public Man.* London: Penguin Books, 1974.

Steckel, Richard H. "New Light on the 'Dark Ages:' The Remarkably Tall Stature of Northern European Men During the Medieval Era." *Social Science History.* 28.2 (2004).

Tarnas, Richard. *The Passion of the Western Mind Understanding the Ideas That Have Shaped Our World View.* New York: Ballantine Books, 1991.

Trevor-Roper, Hugh. *The Rise of Christian Europe.* Norwich: Thames and Hudson, 1966.

Wells, H. G. *The Outline of History.* I and II vols. New York: Garden City Books, 1949.

Williams, Roy. *Magical World of the Wizard of Ads.* Marietta: Bard Press, 2001.

Ziguras, Christopher. *Self-care: Embodiment, Personal Autonomy and the Shaping of Health Conciousness.* London: Routledge, 2004.

Endnotes

1 LaFeber, Walter. (66)

2 Cassidy, John, "Death Of The Middle Class." *New Internationalist Magazine*. 282, <http://www.newint.org/features/1996/07/05/death/>.

3 Wikipedia contributors. "Alan Greenspan." *Wikipedia, The Free Encyclopedia*. 6 Mar. 2011. Web. 9 Mar. 2011. <http://en.wikipedia.org/w/index.php?title=Alan_Greenspan&oldid=417425601>.

4 Wikipedia contributors. "Nathaniel Branden." *Wikipedia, The Free Encyclopedia*. 7 Mar. 2011. Web. 9 Mar. 2011. <http://en.wikipedia.org/w/index.php?title=Nathaniel_Branden&oldid=417576741>.

5 Orchard, Brian. "Changing the Self in Self-esteem." *Vision*. Spring 2004 issue, <http://www.vision.org/visionmedia/printerfriendly.aspx>.

6 Butler, Chris. (2007) "The Italian Renaissance." *Flow of History*. Web March 9, 2011 <http://www.flowofhistory.com/units/west/11/FC76>.

7 Beattie, Alan. (194-198)

8   Dwyer, John. "The Enlightenment and its Critics." <http://
    opencopy.org/lectures/intellectual-history/03-the-enlig-
    tenment-and-its-critics/>.

9   Agrawal, M. M. (1999) "Modernity and Individual
    Responsibility." Indira Gandhi National Ccntre for the
    Arts <http://www.ignca.nic.in /cd_09011.htm>.

10 Augsburg, Luther and the Fuggers. "History fused with theo-
    logical, political and economic implications." September 23,
    1999 from tthe Lutheran World Federation, Geneva <http://
    www.lutheranworld.org/News/LWI/EN/694.EN.html>.

11 Davidson, Ron. (30 Jan 2007) "The Corporation is Today's
    Dominant Institution." <http://www.the-next-transforma-
    tion.blogspot.com/2007/01/corporation-is-todays-domi-
    nant.html>.

12 Donaldson, Thomas. (78)

13 Scheuerman, William, "Globalization", *The Stanford Encyclo-
    pedia of Philosophy* (Summer 2010 Edition), Edward N. Zalta
    (ed.), URL = <http://plato.stanford.edu/archives/sum2010/
    entries/globalization/>

14 Maccus, Nick. "Globalization and the United States: Positive
    and Negative Impacts on American Domestic Policy." <http://
    www.hubpages.com/hub/Globalization-and-the-United-
    States-Positve-and-negative-Impacts-on-American-Domestic
    -Policy>.

15 Tabb, William. "Globalization Is An Issue, The Power
    of Capital Is The Issue." *The Monthly Review.* June 1997. Vol
    49 No. 2 <http://www.monthlyreview.org/697tabb.htm>.

16 Vidino, Lorenzo. (Nov 2006) "Aims and Methods of Europe's
    Muslim Brotherhood." *Current Trends in Islamist Ideology.*

vol. 4 <http://www.futureofmuslimworld.com/research/ pubID.55/pub_detail.asp>. Hudson Institute.

17 "Consumption Statistics." *Green Living Tips*. March 22, 2009 <http://www.greenlivingtips.com/articles/185/1/ Consumption-statistics.html>.

18 "The IMF and the World Trade Organization." 17 Sept 2010 <http://www.imf.org/external/np/exr/facts/imfwto.htm>.

19 "The Insider: Joseph Stiglitz, Ex-World Bank Chief Economist, Speaks Out Against The IMF." *The Ecologist*. Sept 2000 <http://findarticles.com/p/articles/mi_m2465/is_6_30/ ai_65653647/>. BNET

20 "Globalization." *Encyclopedia for Business*. 2ed. <http:// www.referenceforbusiness.com/small/Eq-Inc/Globalization. html#ixzz0olc1vWa>.

21 Buck, Adam. "Frederich Engels A Lifetimes Service." 17 May 2009 <http://socialismoryourmoneyback.blogspot. com/2009/05/frederick-engels-lifetimes-service.html>.

22 de Tocqueville, Alexis. translator Henry Reeve, The Project Gutenberg EBook of *Democracy In America*. Vol 2, Chapter IV <http://www.gutenberg.org/files/816/816-h/816-h.htm>.

23 Kaufmann, Walter. (384, 386)

24 Orchard, Brian. "Changing the Self in Self-esteem." *Vision*. Spring 2004 <http://www.vision.org/visionmedia/article. aspx?id=791>.

25 MacCullock, Diarmaid. (545-546)

26 Wikipedia contributors. "Austrian School." *Wikipedia, The Free Encyclopedia*. 24 Feb. 2011. Web. 10 Mar. 2011. <http://en.wikipedia.org/w/index.php?title=Austrian_ School&oldid=415655327>.

27 "Meaning of Adam's Fallacy: An Interview with Duncan K. Foley." 8 Feb 2007 <http://radicalnotes.com/content/view/33/30/>.

28 Rand, Ayn. 1964 (43-49)

29 Wikipedia contributors. "Nathaniel Branden." *Wikipedia, The Free Encyclopedia*. 7 Mar. 2011. Web. 10 Mar. 2011. <http://en.wikipedia.org/w/index.php?title=Nathaniel_Branden&oldid=417576741>.

30 Burke, B. (1999, 2005) "Antonio Gramsci, Schooling and Education." *The Encyclopedia of Informal Education*. <http://www.infed.org/thinkers/et-gram.htm>.

31 "Sharpton Urges Divestment to Clean Up Rap Lyrics." <http://www.reuters.com/article/idUSN0722977220070808>.

32 Horning, Rob. (2004) "The Barnum Affect." 25 October 2004 <http://marginal-utility.blogspot.com /2004_10_01_archive.html>.

33 Klein, Naomi. 2000 (23)

34 "Advertising and Identities." <http://www.sagepub.com/upm-data/9376_016783Part3.pdf>.

35 Noomii, Terrene. (2010) "Wellness Coaching Is it Effective?" <http://hubpages.com/hub/wellnes-coaching>.

36 McChesney, Robert. (Nov/Dec 1997) "The Global Media Giants We Are the World." <http://www.fair.org /index.php?page=1406>.

37 Klein, Naomi. 2000 (35)

38 Wolske, Martin. (2010) "The Bootstrap Myth." <http://mwolske.wordpress.com/2010/07/15/the-bootstrap-myth/>.

39   "The American Dream." <http://www.gotessays.com/essays/145/index.php>.

40   Barker, Phil. (Sept 2003) "Cognitive Dissonance." <http://www.beyondintractability.org/essay/cognitive_dissonance/>.

41   Bateman, Chris. (2006) "Only a Game." <http://onlya-game.typepad.com/only_a_game/2006/08/a_problem_in_mi.html>.

42   Meisenhelder, Helen. "Selective Perception: Turning Green into Blue." <http://pages.uoregon.edu/bfmalle/jdm/Helen3.html>.

43   Beatty, Jack. "Cognitive Dissonance." *The Atlantic.* <http://www.theatlantic.com/doc/200707u/beatty-bush>.

44   Klein, Naomi. 2000 (3)

45   Williams, Roy H. (44-51)

46   Wolfe, Karl R. (2010) "Narcissism & Envy." <http://karlrwolfe.com/narcissism-envy.html>.

47   Wikipedia contributors. "Nathaniel Branden." *Wikipedia, The Free Encyclopedia.* 7 Mar. 2011. Web. 10 Mar. 2011. <http://en.wikipedia.org/w/index.php?title=Nathaniel_Branden&oldid=417576741>.

48   "Maslow's Hierarchy of Needs." <http://en.wikipedia.org/wiki/Maslow's_hierarchy_of_needs>.

49   Shepard, Peter. "The Road to Self-actualization." <http://www.trans4mind.com /mind-development/maslow.html>.

50   "Self-esteem." <http://www.reference.com/browse/Self-esteem>.

51   Klein, Naomi. 2000 (374)

52 Wikipedia contributors. "Heinz Kohut." *Wikipedia, The Free Encyclopedia*. 27 Jan. 2011. Web. 10 Mar. 2011. <http://en.wikipedia.org/w/index.php?title=Heinz_ Kohut&oldid=410409448>.

53 "Attention Deficit Disorder ADD/ADHD." *Statement of Drug Enforcement Administration*. <http://www.add-adhd. org/ritalin.html>.

54 Von Drehle, David "It's All About Him." *Time Magazine*. 19 April 2007. <http://www.time.com/time/magazine/ article/0,9171,1612688,00.html>.

55 Brus, Michael. (June 2006) "Take the Shrink Challenge. Can a Psychiatrist really tell what's wrong with you?" *Slate*. <http://www.slate.com/id/2144123/>.

56 "Alienation – Bibliography." <http://science.jrank.org/ pages/7480/Alienation.html>.

57 Wikipedia contributors. "Vocation." *Wikipedia, The Free Encyclopedia*. 3 Mar. 2011. Web. 10 Mar. 2011. <http:// en.wikipedia.org/w/index.php?title=Vocation&oldid=416 891032Vocation http://en.wikipedia.org/wiki/Vocation>.

58 Wikipedia contributors. "Calling (religious)." *Wikipedia, The Free Encyclopedia*. 14 Oct. 2010. Web. 10 Mar. 2011. <http://en.wikipedia.org/w/index.php?title=Calling_ (religious)&oldid=390780152>.

59 Krajco, Kathleen. (2007) "What Makes Narcissist's Tick." <http://www.escapeabuse.com/npd.pdf>.

60 "Study: Narcissists Tend to Lead, But Not Better." (2008) <http://www.world-science.net/othernews/081008_narcis- sism.htm>.

61 Wilfelise, Rohiranna. "How Christianity Spread in the Roman Empire." <http://www.helium.com/items/551691-how-christianity-spread-in-the-roman-empire>.

62 Trevor-Roper, Hugh. (33-70)

63 Wikipedia contributors. "Battle of the Milvian Bridge." *Wikipedia, The Free Encyclopedia.* 7 Mar. 2011. Web. 10 Mar. 2011. <http://en.wikipedia.org/w/index.php?title=Battle_of_the_Milvian_Bridge&oldid=417531590>.

64 "Theodosuis I. Christian History." <http://www.christianitytoday.com/ch/131christians/rulers/theodosius.html>.

65 Tarnas, Richard. (143–150)

66 Tarnas, Richard. (37)

67 Wikipedia contributors. "Theodoric the Great." *Wikipedia, The Free Encyclopedia.* 25 Feb. 2011. Web. 10 Mar. 2011. <http://en.wikipedia.org/w/index.php?title=Theodoric_the_Great&oldid=415836689>.

68 "Geiseric." <http://www.economicexpert.com/a/Geiseric.htm>.

69 "Troubled Times. Tree Rings." <http://www.zetatalk.com/theword/tword27k.htm>.

70 Tarnas, Richard. (158-160)

71 Tarnas, Richard. (118)

72 Wells, H. G. Vol. 1, (556-557)

73 Wikipedia contributors. "Plague of Justinian." *Wikipedia, The Free Encyclopedia.* 3 Mar. 2011. Web. 10 Mar. 2011. <http://en.wikipedia.org/w/index.php?title=Plague_of_Justinian&oldid=416936064>.

74   Wikipedia contributors. "Battle of Tours." *Wikipedia, The Free Encyclopedia*. 1 Mar. 2011. Web. 10 Mar. 2011. <http://en.wikipedia.org/w/index.php?title=Battle_of_Tours&oldid=416598328>.

75   Trevor-Roper, Hugh. (33-70)

76   "Umayyads, the first Muslim dynasty (661-750)." <http://www.princeton.edu/~batke/itl/denise/umayyads.htmUmayyad Caliphate>.

77   Wikipedia contributors. "Charlemagne." *Wikipedia, The Free Encyclopedia*. 9 Mar. 2011. Web. 10 Mar. 2011. <http://en.wikipedia.org/w/index.php?title=Charlemagne&oldid=418042747>.

78   "Otto I, the Great Western and Central Europe Chronology." <http://www.thenagain.info/webchron/westeurope/OttoGreat.html>.

79   Robinson, Francis. (37)

80   Trevor-Roper, Hugh. (101-105)

81   Wikipedia contributors. "Sicily." *Wikipedia, The Free Encyclopedia*. 8 Mar. 2011. Web. 10 Mar. 2011. <http://en.wikipedia.org/w/index.php?title=Sicily&oldid=417763350>.

82   Wikipedia contributors. "Pope Gregory VII." *Wikipedia, The Free Encyclopedia*. 9 Mar. 2011. Web. 10 Mar. 2011. <http://en.wikipedia.org/w/index.php?title=Pope_Gregory_VII&oldid=41798742>.

83   "Filioque Controversy." <http://mb-soft.com/believe/txn/filioque.htm>.

84   Wikipedia contributors. "East–West Schism." *Wikipedia, The Free Encyclopedia*. 9 Mar. 2011. Web. 10 Mar. 2011. <http://en.wikipedia.org/w/index.php?title=East%E2%80%93West_Schism&oldid=417943587>.

85   Robinson, Francis. (42-45)

86   Trevor-Roper, Hugh. (106-130)

87   Wikipedia contributors. "Albigensian Crusade." *Wikipedia, The Free Encyclopedia.* 9 Mar. 2011. Web. 10 Mar. 2011. <http://en.wikipedia.org/w/index.php?title=Albigensian_ Crusade&oldid=418023542>.

88   Wikipedia contributors. "Waldensians." *Wikipedia, The Free Encyclopedia.* 2 Mar. 2011. Web. 10 Mar. 2011. <http://en.wikipedia.org/w/index.php?title=Waldensians &oldid=416787165>

89   "Chronology of the Crusades." <http://atheism.about.com/ library/FAQs/christian/blchron_xian_crusades10.htm>.

90   Wikipedia contributors. "Teutonic Knights." *Wikipedia, The Free Encyclopedia.* 9 Mar. 2011. Web. 10 Mar. 2011. <http://en.wikipedia.org/w/index.php?title=Teutonic_ Knights&oldid=417909821>.

91   "History of the Reformation." <http:www.historyworld. net/wrldhis/PlainTextHistories.asp?historyid=ad03>.

92   Trevor-Roper, Hugh. (101-130)

93   Wikipedia contributors. "History of the Knights Templar." *Wikipedia, The Free Encyclopedia.* 2 Mar. 2011. Web. 10 Mar. 2011. <http://en.wikipedia.org/w/index.php?title=History_ of_the_Knights_Templar&oldid=416816413>.

94   Burns and Ralph. (426-428)

95   Classic Encyclopedia. "Guillaume De Nogaret." <http:// www.1911encyclopedia.org/Guillaume_De_Nogaret>.

96   "Jacques de Molay.org." <http://www.jacquesdemolay.org/>.

97   Crusades-Encyclopedia. "Pope Innocent III." <http:// www.crusades-encyclopedia.com/innocentIII.html>.

98 "Christianity and its Persecutions of the Cathars." <http://www.heretication.info/_cathars.html>.

99 Wells, H. G. Vol. 2 (692)

100 Wikipedia contributors. "Unam sanctam." *Wikipedia, The Free Encyclopedia.* 20 Dec. 2010. Web. 10 Mar. 2011. <http://en.wikipedia.org/w/index.php?title=Unam_sanctam&oldid=403272550>.

101 "Avignon Papacy." <http://faculty.ucc.edu/egh-damerow/avignon_papacy.htm>.

102 "Books and Bookmaking." <http://www.skypoint.com/members/waltzmn/BookMaking.html>.

103 Famous Medieval People. "William Caxton." <http://www.medieval-life-and-times.info/famous-medieval-people/william-caxton.htm>.

104 Robinson, Francis. (26, 215, 229)

105 "Averroism." <http://www.muslimphilosophy.com/ip/rep/B012.htm>.

106 Wikipedia contributors. "Averroism." *Wikipedia, The Free Encyclopedia.* 5 Mar. 2011. Web. 10 Mar. 2011. <http://en.wikipedia.org/w/index.php?title=Averroism&oldid=417337014>.

107 Liukkonen, Petri, and Ari Pesonen. "Dante Alighieri (1265-1321)." <http://www.kirjasto.sci.fi/dante.htm>.

108 Baker, Alan, "Simplicity." *The Stanford Encyclopedia of Philosophy.* (Spring 2010 Edition), Edward N. Zalta (ed.), <http://plato.stanford.edu/archives/spr2010/entries/simplicity/>.

109 Spade, Paul Vincent, "William of Ockham." *The Stanford Encyclopedia of Philosophy.* (Fall 2008 Edition), Edward N.

Zalta (ed.), <http://plato.stanford.edu/archives/fall2008/entries/ockham/>.

[110] Kiefer, James E. "John Wyclif, Translator and Controversialist." <http://justus.anglican.org/resources/bio/27.html>.

[111] Wikipedia contributors. "Henry V of England." *Wikipedia, The Free Encyclopedia.* 9 Mar. 2011. Web. 10 Mar. 2011. <http://en.wikipedia.org/w/index.php?title=Henry_V_of_England&oldid=418001639>.

[112] "History of the Reformation." *History World.* <http://www.historyworld.net/wrldhis/PlainTextHistories.asp?historyid=ad03>.

[113] Gerrish, Chris. (March 1995) "Jan Hus." <http://www2.kenyon.edu/projects/margin/hus2.htm>.

[114] "Fifth Lateran Council (1512-17)." *Catholic Encyclopedia.* <http://www.newadvent.org/cathen/09018b.htm>.

[115] Wikipedia contributors. "Renaissance humanism." *Wikipedia, The Free Encyclopedia.* 4 Mar. 2011. Web. 11 Mar. 2011. <http://en.wikipedia.org/w/index.php?title=Renaissance_humanism&oldid=417125842>.

[116] "Petrarch." *New World Encyclopedia.* 29 Aug 2008, 15:11 UTC. 11 Mar 2011, 01:45 <http://www.newworldencyclopedia.org/entry/Petrarch?oldid=794994>.

[117] Fajardo-Acosta, Fidel. (2002) "Giovanni Boccaccio (1313-1375)." <http://fajardo-acosta.com/worldlit/boccaccio/>.

[118] Wikipedia contributors. "Chaucer coming in contact with Petrarch or Boccaccio." *Wikipedia, The Free Encyclopedia.* 3 Feb. 2011. Web. 11 Mar. 2011. <http://en.wikipedia.

org/w/index.php?title=Chaucer_coming_in_contact_with_Petrarch_or_Boccaccio&oldid=411805193>.

[119] Smith, Ray. "The Humanism of the Renaissance." <http://www.all-about-renaissance-faires.com/renaissance_info/renaissance_and_humanism.htm>.

[120] "The Protestant Reformation." <http://www.harvestlondon.ca/Content/10194/185919.pdf?site_id=10194>.

[121] Wikipedia contributors. "Nicolaus Copernicus." *Wikipedia, The Free Encyclopedia*. 8 Mar. 2011. Web. 11 Mar. 2011. <http://en.wikipedia.org/w/index.php?title=Nicolaus_Copernicus&oldid=417823753>.

[122] Wikipedia contributors. "Galileo Galilei." *Wikipedia, The Free Encyclopedia*. 9 Mar. 2011. Web. 11 Mar. 2011. <http://en.wikipedia.org/w/index.php?title=Galileo_Galilei&oldid=417880177>.

[123] Machamer, Peter, "Galileo Galilei." *The Stanford Encyclopedia of Philosophy*. (Spring 2010 Edition), Edward N. Zalta (ed.), <http://plato.stanford.edu/archives/spr2010/entries/galileo/>.

[124] Weisstein, Eric W. (1996-2007) "Kepler, Johannes." <http://scienceworld.wolfram.com/biography/Kepler.html>.

[125] Hall, Alfred Rupert. "Isaac Newton's Life." <http://www.newton.cam.ac.uk/newtlife.html>.

[126] Turner, Elizabeth. (2006) "History of the Decimal System." <http://e-articles.info/e/a/title/History-of-the-Decimal-System/>.

[127] "Italian State." <http://medievalcoins.ancients.info/Italy.htm>.

[128] Brotton, Jeremy. (2010) "The Myth of the Renaissance in Europe." <http://www.bbc.co.uk/history/british/tudors/renaissance_europe_03.shtml>.

[129] "The Black Death : Bubonic Plague." <http://www.the-middleages.net/plague.html>.

[130] Wikipedia contributors. "Medici Bank." *Wikipedia, The Free Encyclopedia*. 25 Jan. 2011. Web. 11 Mar. 2011. <http://en.wikipedia.org/w/index.php?title=Medici_Bank&oldid=409958738>.

[131] "1911 Encyclopædia Britannica/Bruges." Wikisource, The Free Library. 18 May 2008, 06:33 UTC. Wikimedia Foundation, Inc. 11 Mar 2011 <http://en.wikisource.org/w/index.php?title=1911_Encyclop%C3%A6dia_Britannica/Bruges&oldid=662882>.

[132] "The Hanseatic League." <http://members.bellatlantic.net/~baronfum/hansa.html>.

[133] Morin, Paul. "Bruges; fair city of Flanders; A Medieval Centre of Commerce." *UNESCO Courier.* June 1984. <http://findarticles.com/p/articles/mi_m1310/is_1984_June/ai_3289702>. BNET

[134] Fegley, Randall. (43-45)

[135] Information Bible. (16 March 2010) "Stock Exchange." <http://www.informationbible.com/article-stock-exchange-27.html>.

[136] Jewelry History. (2010) "History of Diamond Cutting in Bruges." <http://www.allaboutgemstones.com/history_gem_cutting_bruges.html>.

[137] Beattie, Alan. (194-198)

[138] Hooker, Richard. (1996) "Background to the Italian Renaissance." <http://wsu.edu/~dee/REN/BACK.HTM>.

[139] MacCullock, Diarmaid. (545-546)

[140] Orchard, Brian. "Changing the Self in Self-esteem." *Vision.* <http://www.vision.org/visionmedia/article.aspx?id=791>.

[141] Robinson, Francis. (134-137)

[142] Wikipedia contributors. "Treaty of Breda (1667)." *Wikipedia, The Free Encyclopedia.* 7 Jan. 2011. Web. 11 Mar. 2011. <http://en.wikipedia.org/w/index.php?title=Treaty_of_Breda_(1667)&oldid=406550957>.

[143] Ferguson, Niall. (129-137, 175)

[144] The Educational Legacy of Medieval and Renaissance Traditions. "Medieval Universities." <http://www.csupomona.edu/~plin/ls201/medieval2.html>.

[145] Mann, Michael E. *Medieval Climatic Optim.* 2002, (514-516) <http://www.meteo.psu.edu/~mann/shared/articles/medclimopt.pdf>.

[146] WordiQ. "Medieval University – Definition." <http://www.wordiq.com/definition/Medieval_university>.

[147] "History of Toledo." <http://www.t-descubre.com/en/toledo/historia.php>.

[148] Lay Dominicans. "St. Dominic." <http://www.3op.org/stdominic.php>.

[149] Wikipedia contributors. "Thomas Aquinas." *Wikipedia, The Free Encyclopedia*. 10 Mar. 2011. Web. 11 Mar. 2011. <http://en.wikipedia.org/w/index.php?title=Thomas_Aquinas&oldid=418098666>.

150 School of Mathematics and Statistics, University of St Andrews, Scotland. (Dec. 2003) "Roger Bacon." <http://www-groups.dcs.st-and.ac.uk/~history/Biographies/Bacon.html>.

151 Reference Answers. "Martin Luther." <http://www.answers.com/topic/martin-luther>.

152 NNDB. "Niccolò Machiavelli." <http://www.nndb.com/people/654/000034552/>.

153 Fletcher, Adrian. (2010) "Medici Popes Leo X and Clement VII." <http://www.paradoxplace.com/Perspectives/Italian%20Images/Montages/Firenze/Medici%20Popes.htm>.

154 Wikipedia contributors. "Pope Clement VII." *Wikipedia, The Free Encyclopedia*. 9 Mar. 2011. Web. 11 Mar. 2011. <http://en.wikipedia.org/w/index.php?title=Pope_Clement_VII&oldid=417877430>.

155 The Lutheran World Federation. (1999) "Augsburg, Luther and the Fuggers." <http://www.lutheranworld.org/News/LWI/EN/694.EN.html>.

156 Classic Encyclopedia. (Sept. 2006) "John Tetzel." <http://www.1911encyclopedia.org/Johann_Tetzel>.

157 Jeffcoat III, John L. (2002) "English Bible History." <http://www.greatsite.com/timeline-english-bible-history/>.

158 Greatsite Marketing. (1997-2003) "Thomas Linacre." <http://www.greatsite.com/timeline-english-bible-history/thomas-linacre.html>.

159 Ehrman, Bart D. (55)

[160] Nauert, Charles, "Desiderius Erasmus." *The Stanford Encyclopedia of Philosophy*. (Winter 2009 Edition), Edward N. Zalta (ed.), <http://plato.stanford.edu/archives/win2009/entries/erasmus/>.

[161] Wikipedia contributors. "Tyndale Bible." *Wikipedia, The Free Encyclopedia*. 5 Feb. 2011. Web. 11 Mar. 2011. <http://en.wikipedia.org/w/index.php?title=Tyndale_Bible&oldid=412161188>.

[162] Wikipedia contributors. "Geneva Bible." *Wikipedia, The Free Encyclopedia*. 9 Mar. 2011. Web. 11 Mar. 2011. <http://en.wikipedia.org/w/index.php?title=Geneva_Bible&oldid=418001148>.

[163] Arnold, Jack. "John Calvin: Second Reform in Geneva to Death (1541–1564)." *IIM Magazine* on line, Vol. 1 no. 8 April 1999 <http://thirdmill.org/newfiles/jac_arnold/CH.Arnold.RMT.8.html>.

[164] MacCulloch, Diarmaid. (176)

[165] "Holy Roman Empire." <http://www.fact-index.com/h/ho/holy_roman_empire.html>.

[166] The Free Dictionary. "Hapsburg." <http://encyclopedia2.thefreedictionary.com/Hapsburg>.

[167] Wikipedia contributors. "Henry VII, Holy Roman Emperor." *Wikipedia, The Free Encyclopedia*. 21 Feb. 2011. Web. 11 Mar. 2011. <http://en.wikipedia.org/w/index.php?title=Henry_VII,_Holy_Roman_Emperor&oldid=415133145>.

[168] Questia. "Louis IV, Holy Roman Emperor." *Columbia Encyclopedia*. (2004) 6th ed. <http://www.questia.com/library/encyclopedia/louis_iv_holy_roman_emperor.jsp>.

169 Reference Answers. "Hapsburg." *Columbia Encyclopedia*. <http://www.answers.com/topic/hapsburg>.

170 "The Eighty Years War." <http://www.cuci.nl/~pattie/HOL.htm>.

171 Burns and Ralph. (573)

172 Wikipedia contributors. "Fall of Antwerp." *Wikipedia, The Free Encyclopedia*. 26 Jan. 2011. Web. 11 Mar. 2011. <http://en.wikipedia.org/w/index.php?title=Fall_of_Antwerp&oldid=410148507>.

173 "Portuguese Empire." *New World Encyclopedia*. 10 Nov 2008. Web 12 Mar 2011. <http://www.newworldencyclopedia.org/entry/Portuguese_Empire?oldid=849061>.

174 Wapedia. "Bank of Amsterdam." <http://wapedia.mobi/en/Bank_of_Amsterdam>.

175 Wikipedia contributors. "Tulipmania." *Wikipedia, The Free Encyclopedia*. 24 Feb. 2011. Web. 13 Mar. 2011. <http://en.wikipedia.org/w/index.php?title=Tulip_mania&oldid=415699515>.

176 Shapin, Steven. "Floating Medicine Chests." *London Review of Books,* Vol. 30 No. 3 Feb 2008 <http://www.lrb.co.uk/v30/n03/steven-shapin/floating-medicine-chests>.

177 Burns and Ralph. (407-408)

178 "The British Monarchy." <http://www.royal.gov.uk/HistoryoftheMonarchy/KingsandQueensoftheUnitedKingdom/TheStuarts/CharlesII.aspx>.

179 Wikipedia contributors. "Glorious Revolution." *Wikipedia, The Free Encyclopedia*. 8 Mar. 2011. Web. 13 Mar. 2011. <http://en.wikipedia.org/w/index.php?title=Glorious_Revolution&oldid=417866298>.

180 Wikipedia contributors. "Age of Enlightenment." *Wikipedia, The Free Encyclopedia.* 10 Mar. 2011. Web. 13 Mar. 2011. <http://en.wikipedia.org/w/index.php?title=Age_of_Enlightenment&oldid=418163488>.

181 De Pierris, Graciela and Friedman, Michael, "Kant and Hume on Causality." *The Stanford Encyclopedia of Philosophy.* (Fall 2008 Edition), Edward N. Zalta (ed.), <http://plato.stanford.edu/archives/fall2008/entries/kant-hume-causality>.

182 Halsall, Paul. (1997) "Immanuel Kant: What is Enlightenment? 1784." *Modern History Sourcebook.* <http://www.fordham.edu/halsall/mod/kant-whatis.html>.

183 Alphern, Henry (140)

184 "Kant: Self-Determination in the Age of Reason." <http://faculty.frostburg.edu/phil/forum/Kant.htm>.

185 Hacket, Lewis. (1992) "The European Dream of Progress and Enlightenment." <http://history-world.org/age_of_enlightenment.htm>.

186 Wikipedia contributors. "American Revolution." *Wikipedia, The Free Encyclopedia.* 12 Mar. 2011. Web. 13 Mar. 2011. <http://en.wikipedia.org/w/index.php?title=American_Revolution&oldid=418446537>.

187 MacCulloch, Diarmaid. (543-544)

188 Kagan, Robert. (124)

189 Kemerling, Garth. (1999-2002) "Locke: Government." <http://www.philosophypages.com/hy/4n.htm>.

190 Wikipedia contributors. "New Harmony, Indiana." *Wikipedia, The Free Encyclopedia.* 26 Feb. 2011. Web. 13 Mar.

2011. <http://en.wikipedia.org/w/index.php?title=New_ Harmony,_Indiana&oldid=416064553>.

191 Wikipedia contributors. "Christian existentialism." *Wikipedia, The Free Encyclopedia.* 7 Mar. 2011. Web. 13 Mar. 2011. <http://en.wikipedia.org/w/index.php?title=Christian_exi stentialism&oldid=417643922>.

192 "Joseph de Maistre." *New World Encyclopedia.* 2 Apr 2008, 05:40 UTC. 13 Mar 2011. <http://www.new-worldencyclopedia.org/entry/Joseph_de_Maistre?oldid= 679149>.

193 ibid.

194 Classic Encyclopedia. "Joseph de Maistre." <http:// www.1911encyclopedia.org/Joseph_De_Maistre>.

195 Burns and Ralph. (777)

196 Flynn, Thomas, "Jean-Paul Sartre." *The Stanford Encyclopedia of Philosophy.* (Spring 2010 Edition), Edward N. Zalta (ed.), <http://plato.stanford.edu/archives/spr2010/entries/ sartre>.

197 Rand, Ayn 1967 (371)

198 Wikipedia contributors. "Nathaniel Branden." *Wikipedia, The Free Encyclopedia.* 7 Mar. 2011. Web. 13 Mar. 2011. <http://en.wikipedia.org/w/index.php?title=Nathaniel_ Branden&oldid=417576741>.

199 The Atlas Society. "What is Objectivism?" <http://www. atlassociety.org/what_is_objectivism>.

200 Young, Cathy. "Ayn Rand at 100." *Reason Magazine.* March 2005. <http://reason.com/archives/2005/03/01/ayn-rand-at-100>.

201 Gillespie, Nick. "Jean Paul Sartre." <http://www.sartre. org/Articles/strangerinastrangeland.htm>.

202 Glendon Mary Ann. (1999) "Rousseau and the Revolt Against Reason." *First Things* <http://www.leaderu.com/ ftissues/ft9910/articles/glendon.html>.

203 Wikipedia contributors. "Romanticism." *Wikipedia, The Free Encyclopedia*. 12 Mar. 2011. Web. 13 Mar. 2011. <http://en.wikipedia.org/w/index.php?title=Romanticism &oldid=418498229>.

204 Tarnas, Richard. (372)

205 Crowell, Steven, "Existentialism." *The Stanford Encyclopedia of Philosophy* (Winter 2010 Edition), Edward N. Zalta (ed.), <http://plato.stanford.edu/archives/win2010/entries/exis-tentialism/>.

206 Wicks, Robert, "Friedrich Nietzsche." *The Stanford Encyclope-dia of Philosophy*. (Summer 2010 Edition), Edward N. Zalta (ed.), <http://plato.stanford.edu/archives/sum2010/entries/ nietzsche/>.

207 Wikipedia contributors. "Modernity." *Wikipedia, The Free Encyclopedia*. 12 Feb. 2011. Web. 13 Mar. 2011. <http:// en.wikipedia.org/w/index.php?title=Modernity&ol did=413404324>.

208 ibid

209 Wikipedia contributors. "Fundamentalist Chris-tianity." *Wikipedia, The Free Encyclopedia*. 12 Feb. 2011. Web. 13 Mar. 2011. <http://en.wikipedia. org/w/index.php?title=Fundamentalist_ Christianity&oldid=413462740>.

210 Balmer, Randall. "Graham, Billy." <https://edit.britan-nica.com/getEditableToc?tocId=260469>.

211 ibid

212 Wikipedia contributors. "Contract with America." *Wikipedia, The Free Encyclopedia.* 27 Feb. 2011. Web. 13 Mar. 2011. <http://en.wikipedia.org/w/index.php?title=Contract_with_America&oldid=416280071>.

213 "Andrei Sakharov." *New World Encyclopedia.* 30 Aug 2008, 17:28 UTC. 13 Mar 2011. <http://www.newworldencyclo-pedia.org/entry/Andrei_Sakharov?oldid=795951>.

214 Church Bible "Church Growth." <http://church-bible.com/church-growth/>.

215 Wikipedia contributors. "Greg Boyd (theologian)." *Wikipedia, The Free Encyclopedia.* 20 Feb. 2011. Web. 13 Mar. 2011. <http://en.wikipedia.org/w/index.php?title=Greg_Boyd_(theologian)&oldid=414937577>.

216 Meade, Walter Russell (305)

217 Meade, Walter Russell (298)

218 Ault Jr, James and Alfred A. Knopf. (2005) "Spirit & the Flesh: Life in a Fundamentalist Baptists Church." <http://www.massbook.org/reading_guides/Spirit%20and%20Flesh%20discussion%20guide%20PDF.pdf>.

219 Palmowski, Jan. "Islamic fundamentalism." *A Dictionary of Contemporary World History.* 2004. Encyclopedia.com. (March 12, 2011). <http://www.encyclopedia.com/doc/1O46-Islamicfundamentalism.html>.

220 Stanley, Trevor. (2003-2004) "Hassan al-Banna." <www.pwhce.org/banna.html>.

[221] ibid

[222] Wikipedia contributors. "Abul Ala Maududi." *Wikipedia, The Free Encyclopedia.* 10 Mar. 2011. Web. 13 Mar. 2011. <http://en.wikipedia.org/w/index.php?title=Abul_Ala_Maududi&oldid=418140040>.

[223] ibid

[224] Liu, Henry C. K. (2003) "The Abduction of Modernity." <http://www.atimes.com/atimes/China/EG11Ad01.html>.

[225] ibid

[226] Wikipedia contributors. "Ibn Taymiyyah." *Wikipedia, The Free Encyclopedia.* 6 Mar. 2011. Web. 13 Mar. 2011. <http://en.wikipedia.org/w/index.php?title=Ibn_Taymiyyah&oldid=417447673>.

[227] Vidino, Lorenzo. (2006) "Aims and Methods of Europe's Muslim Brotherhood." <http://www.futureofmuslimworld.com/research/pubID.55/pub_detail.asp>.

[228] ibid

[229] ibid

[230] Akbar Ahmed. (83-96)

[231] Daniels, Mark. (2005) "What is Theology?" <http://jollyblogger.typepad.com/jollyblogger/2005/10/what_is_theolog.html>.

[232] Joyce, Helen. (2001) "Adam Smith and the Invisible Hand." <http://plus.maths.org/issue14/features/smith/>.

[233] Wikipedia contributors. "Ayn Rand." *Wikipedia, The Free Encyclopedia.* 4 Mar. 2011. Web. 13 Mar. 2011. <http://en.wikipedia.org/w/index.php?title=Ayn_Rand&oldid=417028174>.

234 Heydt, Colin. (2006) "John Stuart Mill." *Internet Encyclopedia of Philosophy.* <http://www.iep.utm.edu/m/milljs.htm>.

235 Wikipedia contributors. "Friedrich Hayek." *Wikipedia, The Free Encyclopedia.* 12 Mar. 2011. Web. 13 Mar. 2011. <http://en.wikipedia.org/w/index.php?title=Friedrich_Hayek&oldid=418485709>.

236 Horwitz, Steven. (2009) "Spontaneous Order Cooperation in the Market Place." <http://www.fraseramerica.org/commerce.web/product_files/KeyConcepts-SpontaneousOrder_US.pdf>.

237 Wikipedia contributors. "Tragedy of the commons." *Wikipedia, The Free Encyclopedia.* 1 Mar. 2011. Web. 13 Mar. 2011. <http://en.wikipedia.org/w/index.php?title=Tragedy_of_the_commons&oldid=416602621>.

238 Wikipedia contributors. "William Forster Lloyd." *Wikipedia, The Free Encyclopedia.* 22 Nov. 2010. Web. 13 Mar. 2011. <http://en.wikipedia.org/w/index.php?title=William_Forster_Lloyd&oldid=398283149>.

239 Wikipedia contributors. "Aubrey Meyer." *Wikipedia, The Free Encyclopedia.* 1 Mar. 2010. Web. 13 Mar. 2011. <http://en.wikipedia.org/w/index.php?title=Aubrey_Meyer&oldid=347069836>.

240 Wikipedia contributors. "Santa Clara County, California." *Wikipedia, The Free Encyclopedia.* 11 Mar. 2011. Web. 13 Mar. 2011. <http://en.wikipedia.org/w/index.php?title=Santa_Clara_County,_California&oldid=418214255>.

241 Klein, Naomi. 2007 (194-195)

242 Deresinski, Stan (144)

[243] Herman, Edward S. "The Threat of Globalization New Politics." Vol 7. No. 2, Winter 1999, last accessed Oct 23, 2010. <http://ww3.wpunj.edu/newpol/issue26/herman26.htm>.

[244] Chandra, Pratyush and Pattanayak. (2007) "The Meaning of Adam's Fallacy: An Interview with Duncan K. Foley." <http://radicalnotes.com/content/view/33/30/>.

[245] North, Douglass C. 1992 (4)

[246] North, Douglass C. 1992 (5)

[247] North, Douglass C. 1992 (6)

[248] Schmerken, Ivy. (2006) "Hiring the Next Generation of Quants." <http://www.advancedtrading.com/issues/200604/showArticle.jhtml?articleID=184417510>.

[249] Krugman, Paul (158-164)

[250] Soros, George. "The Crisis and What to Do about It." *New York Times on the Web.* December 14, 2008 <http://www.nybooks.com/articles/archives/2008/dec/04/the-crisis-what-to-do-about-it/>.

[251] Tauton, Larry. "Richard Dawkins: the Atheist Evangelist." *By Faith.* No. 18, Dec 2007. <http://byfaithonline.com/page/in-the-world/richard-dawkins-the-atheist-evangelist>.

[252] Dawkins, Richard. (320-323)

[253] Dawkins, Richard. (44-46, 344-348)

[254] Mead, Walter Russell. (78)

[255] Mead, Walter Russell. (310-313)

[256] Wikipedia contributors. "Thomas Aquinas." *Wikipedia, The Free Encyclopedia.* 10 Mar. 2011. Web. 13 Mar. 2011. <http://en.wikipedia.org/w/index.php?title=Thomas_Aquinas&oldid=418098666>.

257 Baset, Paul Merritt. "Christian Fundamentalism." <http://mb-soft.com/believe/text/fundamen.htm>.

258 Wikipedia contributors. "Scopes Trial." *Wikipedia, The Free Encyclopedia*. 7 Mar. 2011. Web. 13 Mar. 2011. <http://en.wikipedia.org/w/index.php?title=Scopes_Trial&oldid=417671572>.

259 Kemerling, Garth. (2001) "Nietzsche: Beyond Morality." <http://www.philosophypages.com/hy/5v.htm>.

260 Dawkins, Richard. (150-151, 157-161)

261 *Outlook Associates of New England Newsletter.* Vol. 3, No. 3. (Nov/Dec 2007) "Entitlement: A Road to Anger." <http://www.outlookassociates.com/newsletter/pdf/newsletter-200711.pdf>.

262 Wikipedia contributors. "Manhattan Declaration: A Call of Christian Conscience." *Wikipedia, The Free Encyclopedia.* 7 Mar. 2011. Web. 13 Mar. 2011. <http://en.wikipedia.org/w/index.php?title=Manhattan_Declaration:_A_Call_of_Christian_Conscience&oldid=417635297>.

263 de Tocqueville. *Democracy in America.* Vol 1 Intoductory Chapter <*http://www.gutenberg.org/files/816/816-h/816-h.htm*>.

264 de Tocqueville Vol II Section 1 Chapter XI

265 de Tocqueville Vol II Section 1 Chapter V

266 de Tocqueville Vol II Section 1 Chapter V

267 Wilson, Fred, "John Stuart Mill." *The Stanford Encyclopedia of Philosophy.* (Spring 2009 Edition), Edward N. Zalta (ed.), <http://plato.stanford.edu/archives/spr2009/entries/mill/>.

268 Galloway, Shirley. (1993) "John Stuart Mill's *On Liberty:* Only for the Exceptional Few." <http://www.cyberpat. com/shirlsite/essays/mill.html>.

269 Hannay, Alstair. (305)

270 Questia. "Ferdinand Tonnes." <http://www.questia.com/library/sociology-and-anthro-pology/ferdinand-tonnies.jsp>.

271 Keay, Douglas (8-10)

272 Quote. "John Davison Rockefeller, Sr." <http://www. quotes.net/quotations/duty>.

273 Klatt, Murphy and Irvine. (7-19)

274 Curtler, Hugh Mercer. "Making Kids Feel Good." <http:// www.mmisi.org/ma/46_03/curtler.pdf>.

275 Klein, Naomi. 2000 (118, 232)

276 Holding, James Patrick. "The Bible on Self-Esteem." <http://www.tektonics.org/qt/selfesteem.html>.

277 Burston, Daniel. (139)

278 de Tocqueville. *Democracy in America.* Vol 2 Section 1 Chapter VI <http://www.gutenberg.org/files/816/816-h/816-h. htm>.

279 "John Stuart Mill's Essay On Liberty." <http://www.seren-dipity.li/jsmill/jsmill.htm>.

280 MacCulloch, Diarmaid (379-380, 515)

281 Wikipedia contributors. "Romanticism." *Wikipedia, The Free Encyclopedia.* 12 Mar. 2011. Web. 13 Mar. 2011. <http://en.wikipedia.org/w/index.php?title=Romanticism &oldid=418498229>.

[282] Ruggiero, Vincent Ryan. (2000) "Bad Attitude Confronting the Views That Hinder Students Learning." <http://www.aft.org/pdfs/americaneducator/summer2000/Bad-Summer2000.pdf>.

[283] McGregor, Sue L. T. (2003) "Consumer Entitlement, Narcissism, and Immoral Consumption." <http://www.kon.org/hswp/archive/mcgregor_1.htm>.

[284] Akbar Ahmed. (33-34)

[285] Samir Khalil Samir. (2007) "The Letter of 138 Muslim Scholars to the Pope and Christian Leaders." <http://www.asianews.it/index.php?l=en&art=10577>.

[286] Wikipedia contributors. "A Common Word Between Us and You." *Wikipedia, The Free Encyclopedia*. 8 Mar. 2011. Web. 13 Mar. 2011. <http://en.wikipedia.org/w/index.php?title=A_Common_Word_Between_Us_and_You&oldid=417783800>.

[287] Akbar Ahmed. (143-144)

[288] WiseGeek. "What is the Golden Rule?" <http://www.wisegeek.com/what-is-the-golden-rule.htm>.

[289] Piper, John. (May 1995) "The Greatest of These Is Love." <www.soundofgrace.com/piper95/05-07-95.htm>.

[290] Orchard, Brian. "Changing the Self in Self-esteem." *Vision*. Spring 2004 issue, <http://www.vision.org/visionmedia/printerfriendly.aspx>.

[291] Roy F. Baumeister et al. (1-95)

[292] Sweat, Rebecca. "Hands on Parenting." *Vision*. Winter 2002 <http://www.vision.org/visionmedia/article.aspx?id=465>.

293 Heckman, James J. (1900-1902)

294 Ruggiero, Vincent Ryan. (June 2002) "Opinionated Students, Organization for Quality Education." <http://www.societyforqualityeducation.org/newsletter/archives/opinionated.pdf>.

295 Heckman, James J. (1900-1902)

296 Barnett, William Steven. (204-207)

297 Heckman, James J. (1900-1902)

298 Canadian Pediatric Society. (601-609)

299 Ruggiero, Vincent Ryan. (2000) "Bad Attitude: Confronting the Views That Hinder Students Learning." <http://www.aft.org/pdfs/americaneducator/summer2000/Bad-Summer2000.pdf>.

300 Keay, Douglas (8-10)

301 BrainyQuote. "M. Scott Peck." <http://www.brainyquote.com/quotes/authors/m/m_scott_peck.html>.

302 Christenbury, Shaun. "Epictetus." <http://personal.ecu.edu/mccartyr/ancient/athens/Epictetus.htm>.

303 Smith, Barry D. "Stoicism" <http://www.abu.nb.ca/Courses/GrPhil/Stoic.htm>.

304 Davis, Jean. "The Science of Good Deeds." <www.goodhousekeeping.com/health/emotional/science-good-deeds-1105>.

305 Wikipedia contributors. "Royal College of Physicians." *Wikipedia, The Free Encyclopedia*. 19 Feb. 2011. Web. 13 Mar. 2011. <http://en.wikipedia.org/w/index.php?title=Royal_College_of_Physicians&oldid=414808508>.

[306] Ziguras, Christopher (158,163)

[307] "Self-esteem." *New World Encyclopedia.* 4 Apr 2008, 01:03 UTC. 13 Mar 2011. <http://www.newworldencyclopedia. org/entry/Self-esteem?oldid=687694>.

[308] Mill, John Stuart. *Representative Government.* Chapter 2. 12 Jan 2011 <http://ebooks.adelaide.edu.au/m/mill/john_stu-art/m645r/chapter2.html>.

[309] Trueman, Chris. "The Medieval Church." <http://www. historylearningsite.co.uk/medieval_church.htm>.

[310] Orchard, Brian. "Changing the Self in Self-esteem." *Vision.* Spring 2004 <http://www.vision.org/visionmedia/article. aspx?id=791>.

[311] Wikipedia contributors. "Priesthood of all believers." *Wiki-pedia, The Free Encyclopedia.* 15 Feb. 2011. Web. 13 Mar. 2011. <http://en.wikipedia.org/w/index.php?title=Priesthood_ of_all_believers&oldid=414099620>.

[312] MacCulloch, Diarmaid. (175-176)

[313] McGregor, Sue L. T. (2005) "Consumer Entitlement, Nar-cissism, and Immoral Consumption." <http://www.kon. org/hswp/archive/mcgregor_1.do>.

[314] North, Douglass C. 1992, (2)

[315] North, Douglass C. 1992. (3)

[316] Krugman, Paul. (149-152, 168-169)

[317] Rosen, Christine. (2005) "The Overpraised American." <http://www.hoover.org/publications/policy-review/arti-cle/8093>.

[318] Sennett, Richard. (335-339)

316 Alphern, Henry (140)

320 Hoppe, Hans-Hermann. "F. A. Hayek on Government and Social Evolution: A Critique." <http: //mises.org/journals/rae/pdf/R71_3.PDF>.

321 McGregor, Sue L. T. (2005) "Consumer Entitlement, Narcissism, and Immoral Consumption." <http://www.kon.org/hswp/archive/mcgregor_1.do>.

322 United Nations Paper. "What is Good Governance?" (1) <http://www.unescap.org/pdd/prs/ProjectActivities/Ongoing/gg/governance.asp>.

323 United Nations Paper. "What is Good Governance?" (3) <http://www.unescap.org/pdd/prs/ProjectActivities/Ongoing/gg/governance.asp>.

324 ibid

325 ibid

326 ibid

327 United Nations Paper. "What is Good Governance?" (2) <http://www.unescap.org/pdd/prs/ProjectActivities/Ongoing/gg/governance.asp>.

328 "Towards Good Governance." <http://www.reform.gov.bb/page/GOOD_GOVERNANCE.pdf>.

329 United Nations Paper. "What is Good Governance?" <http://www.unescap.org/pdd/prs/ProjectActivities/Ongoing/gg/governance.asp>.

330 Evans, Robert G. and Kimberlyn McGrail. "Richard III, Barer-Stoddard and the Daughter of Time." *HealthCare Policy.* 3(3) 2008: 18-22. <http://www.longwoods.com/content/19564>.

331 ibid

332 United Nations Paper. "What is Good Governance?" (2) <http://www.unescap.org/pdd/prs/ProjectActivities/Ongoing/gg/governance.asp>.

333 ibid

334 "Golden Rule." <www.answers.com/topic/do-unto-others-as-you-would-have-them-do-unto-you>.

335 ibid

336 Jefferson, Thomas. "I never did, or countenanced, in public life." <www.quotegarden.com/integrity.html>.

337 Wikipedia contributors. "John Locke." *Wikipedia, The Free Encyclopedia*. 18 Mar. 2011. Web. 19 Mar. 2011. <http://en.wikipedia.org/w/index.php?title=John_Locke&oldid=419511286>.

338 Klein, Naomi. 2000 (195)

339 Klatt, Murphy and Irvine. (7-19)

340 Dreisbach, Christopher. "Constitutionally Illiterate." *Baltimore Sun.* February 5, 2010 <www.thenhf.com/article.php?id=937>.

341 Gizmotude Quotation Archives "John Kenneth Gailbraith." <http://gizmotude.www5.50megs.com/archive_silence.htm>.

342 Newman, Rick. (March 2010) "7 Stressors Sapping the Middle Class." <www.usnews.com/money/blogs/flowchart/2010/03/16/7-stressors-sapping-the-middle-class>.

343 McGregor, Sue L. T. (2005) "Consumer Entitlement, Narcissism, and Immoral Consumption." <www.kon.org/hswp/archive/mcgregor_1.htm>.

344 Coale, Helen W. (20)

345 Orchard, Brian. (2004/11/21) "Self-esteem, Entitlement mentality and Victimhood Diogenes the Cynic." <http://diogenescynic.blogspot.com/2004/11/20041121.html>.

346 Borchers, Tim (1999) "Groupthink." <www.abacon.com/commstudies/groups/groupthink.html>.

347 Stolle, Dietlind, Hooghe, Marc and Michelle Micheletti. "Politics in the Supermarket: Political Consumerism as a Form of Political Participation." *International Political Science Review.* 26.3(2005): 245-269. <http://profs-polisci.mcgill.ca/stolle/Publications_files/FinalIJPS2005.pdf>.

348 Wikipedia contributors. "Tea Party protests." *Wikipedia, The Free Encyclopedia.* 13 Mar. 2011. Web. 19 Mar. 2011. <http://en.wikipedia.org/w/index.php?title=Tea_Party_protests&oldid=418539517>.

349 deGeyter, Stoney. "Social Media Marketing is Branding." *Internet Marketing.* March 24, 2008. <http://isedb.com/20080324-1816.php>.

350 Leonhardt, David. "Heading Off the Next Financial Crisis." March 28, 2010, *The New York Times Magazine.* (36) <http://www.nytimes.com/2010/03/28/magazine/28Reform-t.html>.

351 Kemerling, Garth. (2001) "Locke Social Order." <http://www.philosophypages.com/hy/4n.htm>.

352 Locke, John. *The Second Treatise of Civil Government.* Chapter 2 Of the State of Nature Section 6 <http: //www.constitution.org/jl/2ndtr02.htm>.

353 Kay, Neil M. "Game Theory as Dogma." Department of Economics, University of Strathclyde. <http://www.brocher.com/Academic/Game%20Theory%20as%20Dogma.pdf>.

354 Story, Louise. "A Secret Banking Elite Rules Trading in Derivatives." *New York Times on the Web.* December 11, 2010 <http://www.nytimes.com/2010/12/12/business/12advantage.html?pagewanted=1&_r=4&hp>.

355 Davison, Ron. (Sept 2009) "Modern Corporation: Modeled on the Medieval Church." <http://rwrld.blogspot.com/2009/09/modern-corporation-modeled-on-medieval.html>.

356 Tarnas, Richard. (320)

357 Ferguson, Niall. (122-123)

358 Sennett, Richard. (335)

359 Ruggiero, Vincent Ryan. (2000) "Bad Attitude: Confronting the Views That Hinder Students Learning." <http://www.aft.org/pdfs/americaneducator/summer2000/Bad-Summer2000.pdf>.

360 "The Illusion of Knowledge." (Jan 8, 2007) <http://www.extremeperspective.blogspot.com/2007/01/illusion-of-knowledge.html>.

361 Smilansky, Saul. (295)

362 Wikipedia contributors. "Geocentric model." *Wikipedia, The Free Encyclopedia.* 16 Mar. 2011. Web. 19 Mar. 2011. <http://en.wikipedia.org/w/index.php?title=Geocentric_model&oldid=419181472>.

363 Wikipedia contributors. "On the Origin of Species." *Wikipedia, The Free Encyclopedia.* 18 Mar. 2011. Web. 19 Mar. 2011. <http://en.wikipedia.org/w/index.php?title=On_the_Origin_of_Species&oldid=419531150>.

364 Psychologist World. "Freud: An Introduction." <http://www.psychologistworld.com/freud/neo-freud.php>.

[365] Uchitelle, Louis. "Volcher Pushes for Reform, Regretting Past Silence." *New York Times on the Web.* July 11, 2010 <http://www.nytimes.com/2010/07/11/business/11volcker.html>.

[366] ibid

[367] Skidelsky, Robert. "The Remediest." *New York Times on the Web.* December 14, 2008 <http://www.nytimes.com/2008/12/14/magazine/14wwln-lede-t.html>.

[368] Machiavelli, Niccolò. (21-22)

[369] Story, Louise. "A Secret Banking Elite Rules Trading in Derivatives." *New York Times on the Web.* December 11, 2010 <http://www.nytimes.com/2010/12/12/business/12advantage.html?pagewanted=1&_r=4&hp>.

[370] Philosophos. "Immanuel Kant." <http://hubpages.com/hub/kant>.

[371] DeVille, Jard. "Dangerous Narcissism – Wisdom From the Fulfillment Forum." <http://www.selfgrowth.com/articles/Dangerous_Narcissism_-_Wisdom_From_The_Fulfillment_Forum.html>.

[372] North, Douglas C. 2003 (18)

[373] North, Douglas C. 2003 (19-20)

Index

About the Author

Greg Horsman has a degree in Medicine from the University of Manitoba, and postgraduate training in medical microbiology from the University of Toronto. He has worked over twenty years in the Canadian public health system. During this time he has been a student of history, became concerned with the economic debacle and the pervading attitude of cult of self-esteem. For more information on Greg's next book, *Objectivism Lost and an Age of Disillusionment*, please visit QuestioningandSkepticism.com.